MID WALES COMPANION

D0921341

Moira K Stone

Mid Wales
Companion

ANTHONY NELSON

©1989, CYNEFIN a Welsh Conservation Foundation
First published 1989 by Anthony Nelson Ltd
PO Box 9, Oswestry, Shropshire SY11 1BY, England

All rights reserved. No part of this book may
be reproduced, stored in a retrieval system, or
transmitted in any form or by any means, electronic,
mechanical, photocopying or otherwise, without
the permission of the publisher.

British Library Cataloguing in Publication Data
Stone, Moira K.
Mid Wales companion.
1. Wales. Mid Wales – Visitors guides
I. Title
914.29′504858

ISBN 0 904614 38 7

Designed by Alan Bartram
Photoset by Nene Phototypesetters, Northampton
Printed by The Bath Press, Avon

Contents

Foreword

Mid-Wales is a magic place of small towns and villages, full of enterprise, of farms well-stocked with hedgerows and copses, woods, wet bits, dry bits and wayward wilderness well-watered by clouds borne on pure west winds and drained by meandering streams and rivers full of fish and fishermen, some with coracles and most with feathers. Country lanes and trunk roads alike are edged with flowers and lined by trees. Bird-song at morning and eventide tells you that it is all still in good heart. Sweet red-brown earth, hills peeping through the woods, the sounds and sights of green, green Wales. It's all yours to see and share, thanks to the Festival of the Countryside and CYNEFIN. CYNEFIN is a word which, as far as a visitor from over the border can understand, means 'the place in which I would want to live'. CYNEFIN sings it all and this exciting book is your comprehensive songsheet.

DAVID BELLAMY

CYNEFIN

Pistyll Rhaeadr

Mid Wales northern section

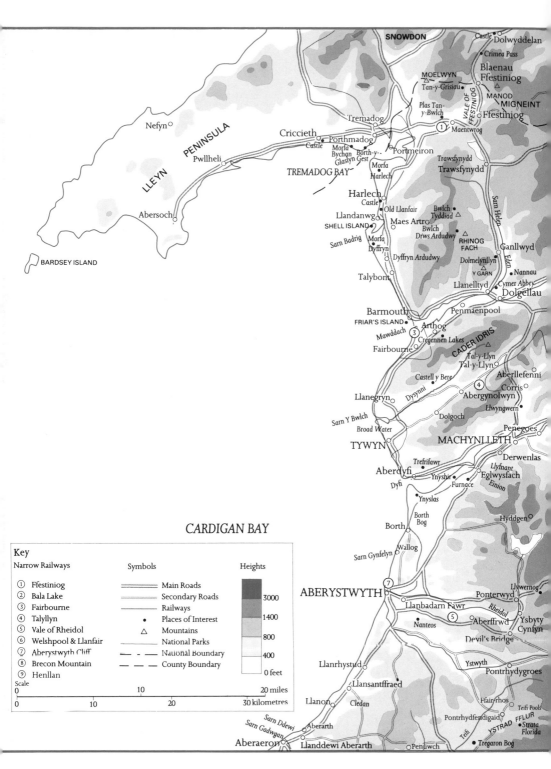

SNOWDON

Castle • Dolwyddelan
• Crimea Pass
Blaenau
Ffestiniog
MOELWYN
Tan-y-Grisiau •
MANOD
MIGNEINT
Plas Tan-
y-Bwlch
Ffestiniog
Tremadog
① Maentwrog
Nefyn ○
LLEYN PENINSULA
Criccieth
Porthmadog
Castle Morfa Bychan Borth-y-
Glaslyn Gest
Portmeirion
Trawsfynydd
Trawsfynydd
Pwllheli
Morfa
Harlech
TREMADOG BAY
Sarn Helen
Abersoch
Harlech
Castle
Old Llanfair
Llandanwg
Maes Artro
Bwlch
Tyddiad △
SHELL ISLAND
Bwlch
Drws Ardudwy
RHINOG
FACH △
Ganllwyd
BARDSEY ISLAND
Sarn Badrig
Morfa
Dyffryn
Dyffryn Ardudwy
Dolmelynllyn
Y GARN △
Eden
Nannau
Talybont
Llanelltyd
Cymer Abbey
Dolgellau
Barmouth
Penmaenpool
FRIAR'S ISLAND
Arthog
Mawddach
③ Cregennen Lakes
CADER IDRIS
Fairbourne
Tal-y-Llyn
Tal-y-Llyn △
Castell y Bere
Aberllefenni
Llanegryn
Dysynni
④ Corris
Abergynolwyn
Sarn Y Bwlch
Llwyngwern
Dolgoch
Penegoes
Broad Water
MACHYNLLETH
TYWYN
Derwenlas
Trefrifawr
Aberdyfi
Ynyshir
Llyfnant
Eglwysfach
Dyfi
Furnace
Einion
Ynyslas
Borth
Bog
Hyddgen
Borth ○
CARDIGAN BAY
Wallog
Sarn Gynfelyn
ABERYSTWYTH
⑦
Llywernog
Ponterwyd
Llanbadarn Fawr
Rheidol
Nanteos
⑤ Aberffrwd
Ysbyty
Cynfyn
Devil's Bridge
Llanrhystud ○
Ystwyth
Pontrhydygroes
Llansantffraed
Llanon ○
Cledan
Hfair-rhos
Teifi Pools
Pontrhydfendigaid
YSTRAD FFLUR
Sarn Ddewi
Sarn Gadwgan
Aberarth
Teifi
Strata
Florida
Aberaeron ○
Llanddewi Aberarth
Penuwch
Tregaron Bog

Key

Narrow Railways

① Ffestiniog
② Bala Lake
③ Fairbourne
④ Talyllyn
⑤ Vale of Rheidol
⑥ Welshpool & Llanfair
⑦ Aberystwyth Cliff
⑧ Brecon Mountain
⑨ Henllan

Symbols

═══ Main Roads
═══ Secondary Roads
─── Railways
• Places of Interest
△ Mountains
─ ─ National Parks
─ · ─ National Boundary
─ ─ ─ County Boundary

Heights

3000
1400
800
400
0 feet

Scale
0   10   20 miles
0   10   20   30 kilometres

WREXHAM

Valle Crucis Abbey

Corwen
Glyndyfrdwy
Llangollen
Dee
Chirk
Dee
Ellesmere

Llyn Celyn
ite Water Centre
ARENNIG
FAWR
Bala

Welsh Frankton

Glanllyn
Caer Gai
wchllyn
Llyn Tegid
BERWYN
Rhaeadr
Pistyll Rhaeadr
Cynllaith
OSWESTRY

Offa's Dyke

Canal

Welsh Frankton

ARAN
BENLLYN
Pennant
Melangell
Llanrhaeadr-ym-
Mochnant
Sycharth
Carreghofa

Bwlch-y-Groes Pass
ARAN
FAWDDWY
Aber Hirnant
Llangynog
Tanat
Llangedwyn
Llanymynech

Llyn Vyrnwy
Llanfyllin
Cain

Dinas Mallwyd
Llanwddyn
Vyrnwy
Vyrnwy
Severn
Dolobran
Meifod
VALE OF MEIFOD
BREIDDEN
HILLS
Alberbury
SHREWSBURY

Llangadfan
Pontrobert
Mathrafal Castle
Guilsfield
Pool Quay
Canal
Strata Marcella
LONG MOUNTAIN

Llanfair Caereinion
Banwy
Buttington
WELSHPOOL
Powis Castle

Castle Caereinion
Belan

Llanbrynmair
Dinnant
Rhiw
Berriew
Garthmyl
Hope
STIPERSTONES
LONG MYND

arowen
Talerddig
Gregynog
Montgomery
Carno
Berws Cedewain
Old Churchstoke

NR
Staylittle
Maesmawr Hall
ROUNDTON
HILL

ife
Trefeglwys
Caersws
Penstrowed
Kerry
Llyn
Clywedog
Van
Mochdre
Newtown
Bryntail
Llandinam
Severn

Llanidloes
Offa's Dyke
Clun
Craven Arms

Llangurig
Beguildy
Ludlow

Wye
Teme
BEACON HILL
Knucklas
Bucknell
Craig Goch
Pen y Garreg
Llananno
Heyop
Llangynllo
Knighton

St Harmon
Llanbister

vyth
ELAN VALLEY
Abbey Cwmhir
Llanddewi
Ystradenni
Dolau
Bleddfa
Pilleth
Whitton
Lugg

Garreg
Ddu
Elan
Nantmel
Llanfihangel
Rhydithon
Casgob

Claerwen
Caban
Coch Resr.
Rhayader
Llanfihangel
Helygen
Crossgates
Penybont
Castell
Collen
Cefnllys
Llandegley
RADNOR FOREST
Kinnerton
Discoed
Presteigne

11

Mid Wales southern section

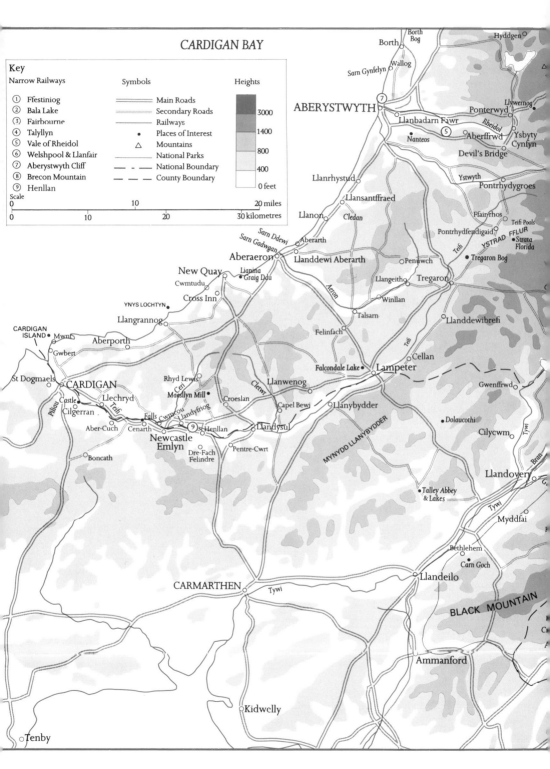

CARDIGAN BAY

Key

Narrow Railways
1. Ffestiniog
2. Bala Lake
3. Fairbourne
4. Talyllyn
5. Vale of Rheidol
6. Welshpool & Llanfair
7. Aberystwyth Cliff
8. Brecon Mountain
9. Henllan

Symbols
━━━ Main Roads
···· Secondary Roads
━━━ Railways
• Places of Interest
△ Mountains
── National Parks
─ · ─ National Boundary
─ ─ ─ County Boundary

Heights
3000
1400
800
400
0 feet

Scale
0 — 10 — 20 miles
0 — 10 — 20 — 30 kilometres

Borth Bog
Hyddgen
Borth
Wallog
Sarn Gynfelyn
Llywernog
Ponterwyd
ABERYSTWYTH ⑦
Llanbadarn Fawr
Rheidol
Aberffrwd
Nanteos
⑤
Ysbyty Cynfyn
Devil's Bridge
Llanrhystud
Ystwyth
Pontrhydygroes
Llansantffraed
Ffair-rhos
Teifi Pools
Llanon
Cledan
Pontrhydfendigaid
YSTRAD FFLUR
Sarn Ddewi
Aberarth
Penuwch
Strata Florida
Sarn Gadwgan
Tregaron Bog
Aberaeron
Llanddewi Aberarth
Aeron
Tregaron
New Quay
Llanina
Llangeitho
Cwmtudu
Graig Ddu
Winllan
Cross Inn
Talsarn
YNYS LOCHTYN
Llanddewibrefi
Llangrannog
Felinfach
CARDIGAN ISLAND
Mwnt
Teifi
Aberporth
Cellan
Gwbert
Falcondale Lake
Lampeter
St Dogmaels
Rhyd Lewis
Llanwenog
Gwenffrwd
CARDIGAN
Ceri
Maesllyn Mill
Llandeilo
Clettwr
Capel Bewi
Llanybydder
Castle
Llechryd
Croeslan
Dolaucothi
Cilgerran
Falls
Cwmcou
Llandyfriog
Pilina
Teifi
⑨ St Henllan
Llandysul
Cilycwm
Aber-Cuch
Cenarth
MYNYDD LLANYBYDDER
Tywi
Newcastle Emlyn
Pentre-Cwrt
Boncath
Dre-Fach Felindre
Bran
Llandovery
Talley Abbey & Lakes
Tywi
Myddfai
Bethlehem
Carn Goch
Llandeilo
CARMARTHEN
Tywi
BLACK MOUNTAIN
Ammanford
Kidwelly
Tenby

12

Cynefin

What is this notion, behind much of Welsh culture, claimed to be untranslatable and unique? Untranslatable by a single word into English perhaps, although other languages certainly have a comparable word. *Heimat*, for example, comes closest to it in German. It may incorporate different local details of language, perhaps or agricultural practice but the feeling is one recognised the world over – a sense of place, a feeling of being at home and a feeling of 'rightness'.

Introduction

Mid-Wales (called *Canolbarth* in Welsh) meets the southern part of Snowdonia, borders on the English Midlands, stretches south to the Welsh Valleys and Pembrokeshire and looks across Cardigan Bay to Ireland. It is remarkable for its breathtaking variety of landscape, wildlife, history, folklore and culture.

The Companion will introduce you to the way these overlap and influence one another, forming mid-Wales's patchwork of life. Whichever area you look into, it will lead to another, making up the sense of place which in Welsh is called CYNEFIN.

CYNEFIN is a cornerstone of the Festival of the Countryside which, since 1985, has presented a summer long programme of rural events. The Companion is a result of the Festival's window on the countryside and answers some of your questions about life in mid-Wales, present, past and future. Part of the joy of discovering mid-Wales is piecing together the jigsaw of the beautiful, the unexpected and the day-to-day.

The book is divided into chapters on the six areas of mid-Wales: Snowdonia, Montgomeryshire, the Heart of Wales, the Brecon Beacons, the Teifi Valley, Cardigan Bay. Inevitably, some subjects considered in one chapter (such as chapels, the Welsh language, mills or quarrying) have relevance to another. At the same time, even within each area there can be great variety.

There is so much going on that this book can't possibly tell you everything but it will give some invaluable insight into mid-Wales. Make full use of the Tourist Information Centres which have up-to-date information on accommodation, travel and opening hours. A number are open all the year round and some are open seasonally at Easter and then from Whitsun through the summer months to September or October.

Croeso i'r Canolbarth!

The Welsh Poppy

The Welsh Poppy (*Mecanopsis cambrica*) was chosen as the logo of the Mid Wales Festival of the Countryside because it is abundant in mid-Wales and can stay in flower from May to September. It is a native perennial found mainly in damp, rocky sites. Look for its distinctive yellow flower on grass verges and walls but, like all wild flowers, please don't pick it.

The Welsh Poppy is illustrated on the front cover.

Snowdonia

Southern Snowdonia, the former county of Merioneth and now the district of Meirionnydd, stretches from high moorland down to the sea at Porthmadog and Harlech and to the eight-mile-long estuary of the Mawddach. There are marvellous and inspiring views as well as secret lanes along which to journey and a different feeling from the more mountainous tracts of Snowdonia further north.

Great geological activity has occurred across the millenia in this area. Four hundred million years ago the area was a Ring of Fire of volcanic activity. No less than any other beautiful place the mountains of Cader Idris, Aran, Arenig, Manod and Moelwyn, the moorland, the estuaries of the Glaslyn, Mawddach and Dyfi and the lakes and reservoirs have inspired artists and uplifted the hearts of others. As Ffynnon Eidda, the spring rebuilt in 1846 high on the peaty moors above Bala, says, 'Yf a bydd ddiolchgar – Drink and be thankful'.

This is also a place where a living, often a hard one, is earned by quarrying, farming and today increasingly by tourism. Over the years people's work and their homes have left their mark – the route of the Roman roads, the castles of the Welsh princes of Gwynedd, the slate tips, the chapels and the fantasy Italianate village of Portmeirion.

The towns of Southern Snowdonia all have their different character – Bala, set on the shores of Llyn Tegid, Blaenau Ffestiniog with its ever-changing colours of slate, Dolgellau, former county town, Harlech with the huge and impressive castle on its rock and Porthmadog, busy and bustling. Look for the buildings hung with slate against the weather and those made of rubble-stone.

The Welsh culture is strong – you may come across the poetry, recitation and music competitions called *eisteddfodau*. This is also the natural habitat of the Welsh poppy whose bright yellow flower you will spot in many places from gardens and walls to roadside verges and wasteland.

Llyn Tegid or Bala Lake

Bala

This very pleasant Welsh town of about 1,850 people is known in Welsh as Y Bala, 'the outlet', describing its position at the point where the River Dee leaves Llyn Tegid (Lake Bala). The tree-lined streets give it a slightly continental air. It is built mainly from grey stone with big lintels but has the occasional red brick or spectacularly painted building.

In the eighteenth and nineteenth centuries Bala was an important centre for the production of knitted goods. In 1805 the enormous amount of between £200 and £500 worth of stockings were being sold every week, some knitted by men, women and children sitting on Tomen y Bala, the site of a mediaeval castle in the town. Many stockings were transported by pack train over the moorland and mountains to the coastal ports and thence to the waiting markets. One satisfied customer was George III who wore Bala woollen stockings to alleviate his rheumatism.

In front of Capel Tegid in Tegid Street stands a statue of the minister Thomas Charles (1755–1814), the 'Wesley of Wales', who aimed to provide Bibles for his congregations during the great eighteenth century Methodist Revival. Mary Jones, a young woman of Llanfihangel-y-Pennant who walked thirty-odd miles to Bala to receive her Bible, inspired the Rev. Charles to found the British and Foreign Bible Society. He also founded the Welsh Sunday School movement, which enabled many people to learn to read and write. Bala became an important centre for Welsh Nonconformism.

In the High Street stands a statue of Thomas Edward Ellis (1859–99), a farmer's son who became Member of Parliament for Merioneth, Liberal Chief Whip and a great campaigner for Welsh Home Rule.

Like all Welsh towns Bala has its fair share of chapels and an imposing Town Hall. Look out also for the former House of Correction at 104–108 High Street and the

Statue of Thomas Edward Ellis,
1859–99, Bala

OPPOSITE
Town Hall, Bala

Gorsedd Circle from the 1967 National Eisteddfod on the Green.

Bala's lake is the largest natural lake in Wales, over four miles / 6.4 km long and in places over 150 ft / 45.7 m deep. It is home to one of the Welsh 'alpine' fish left behind after the Ice Ages, the *gwyniad*, so called because of its white scales. Sailing and fishing are controlled by the Snowdonia National Park Lake Warden who has a hut on the lakeside. For inspiration and the stuff of dreams look at the fish murals in the White Lion Hotel and the fish in cases in the bar.

The reservoir of Llyn Celyn now covers the drowned village of Tryweryn. Its waters supply Liverpool and, as a by-product, provide white water for canoeing. The National White Water Centre is just outside Bala.

Near Llanuwchllyn, the village at the other end of the lake, is the site of the first century Roman fort, Caer Gai, and one of the places where King Arthur and his knights are reputed to lie sleeping. The *Urdd*, the Welsh League of Youth, has a camp at Glanllyn. There are a number of spectacular roads to travel in the area, including the high pass over to Llyn Vyrnwy.

Livestock market day in Bala is Thursday and there are Fair days in May and October.

Nearby places to visit include the Berwyn, Aran and Arennig mountain ranges, the National White Water Centre for white water rafting on Afon Tryweryn, location of the 1981 World Championships. The Bala Lake narrow gauge railway (closed by British Railways in 1965 and opened again in 1972) runs along the lakeside. There is fishing in Llyn Celyn and fishing, sailing and watersports on Llyn Tegid.

For more information about the area, including accommodation, contact the Snowdonia National Park Centre, High Street, Bala, Gwynedd LL23 7AB. Telephone 0678 520367 (seasonal). The Centre is housed in the former British School, founded in 1865.

Blaenau Ffestiniog

Blaenau Ffestiniog is a grey stone and slate town of 4,605 people, the largest in the district of Meirionnydd. It is surrounded by the high mountains of the Moelwyn and Manod ranges (in places over 2,500 feet) and the man-made grey and purple hills of the slate spoil. 'Blaenau' refers to heights or the headwaters of a stream. The town lies near the source of the River Dwyryd which also flows through Ffestiniog, three miles to the south. Ffestiniog means 'defensive position'.

Whether you approach up the Vale of Ffestiniog or over the spectacular Crimea Pass the town makes an impression. It was founded on the slate boom of the early nineteenth century, supplying roofing material and billiard tables all over the world as well as the fence posts so typical of this part of Wales. Slate is still produced here and this is a fascinating town for anyone interested in natural materials or industrial archaeology.

The nine-mile-long Ffestiniog steam railway, converted to steam locomotives in 1863 from a tramway with a continuous gradient, was used to transport slate to the seaport at Porthmadog. Now it has been restored with huge amounts of voluntary labour. Tourists and residents alike can travel to Blaenau to connect with the British Rail service to the North Wales coast at Llandudno Junction, see the hydro-electric power station at Tanygrisiau and Stwlan Dam (1,000 ft / 305 m above sea-level), the impressive Llechwedd slate caverns with an underground train ride into the mountain or alternatively, the Gloddfa Ganol slate mines.

Like many of the quarrying and mining areas of North and South Wales the Ffestiniog area has a tradition of choral singing and male voice choirs. Today there are two famous choirs: Cor Meibion y Brythoniaid (which practises on Mondays and Thursdays in Ysgol Y Moelwyn School) and the Moelwyn Male Voice Choir (at the Salem Choir Centre, Rhiw, on Tuesdays and Fridays).

Nearby places to visit include the Llechwedd Slate Caverns, Gloddfa Ganol Slate Mine, Llyn Stwlan Dam and Tanygrisiau hydro-electric power station. There are many lovely walks in the Vale of Ffestiniog. Take the Ffestiniog steam railway down to Porthmadog or stop off en route and visit Plas Tan-y-Bwlch, the Snowdonia National Park Study Centre and the nearby oakwoods of Maentwrog. Dolwyddelan Castle is just over the Crimea Pass and the lakes of Tanygrisiau and Trawsfynydd offer good trout fishing. The coast of Cardigan Bay presided over by Harlech Castle is within easy reach.

For more information about the area, including accommodation, contact the Wales Tourist Information and Snowdonia National Park Centre, Isallt, High Street, Blaenau Ffestiniog, Gwynedd LL41 3HD. Telephone (0766) 830360 (seasonal),

Dolgellau

Dolgellau (population 2,318) is a typically Welsh market town and the former county town of Merionethshire – a dignified place with much pleasant and bold architecture. It lies at the confluence of the Rivers Aran and Wnion, which drain into the upper reaches of the Mawddach estuary and below the massive north-facing precipices of Cader Idris. The narrow winding streets are made up of houses built of dark grey granite, boulder stone and slate, almost every one of which in the eighteenth century housed its own weaving loom. Early visitors include Owain Glyndŵr who held one of his parliaments in the town. The interesting seven-arched bridge, near the Information Centre, was built in 1638 and is a protected monument. Among other buildings to see are the fellmongers (Y Tanws) and the tollhouse. St Mary's church was built in 1716 in the late Renaissance style and is notable for its unusual timber columns and ceiling as well as a fantastic array of mid-Victorian stained glass.

In the foothills of Cader Idris is the farmhouse of Bryn Mawr where Rowland Ellis, a Quaker, lived in the seventeenth century. In 1686, to avoid severe local persecution, he led a group of his fellow believers to Pennsylvania where he built a replica of Bryn Mawr. It gave its name to a town and later to a well-known college for young ladies, established 'so that they might have an equal opportunity with men'.

In the nearby village of Llanelltyd the twelfth century restored church occupies the circular site of the Celtic religious 'llan'. Another religious building is the Cistercian Abbey of Cymer, founded in 1199 and granted a charter from Llywelyn the Great in 1219. The name Dolgellau probably derives from dôl (a loop or bend in the river and later, water-meadow) and cellau (cells) which probably refer to monastic cells.

The famous Precipice Walk around the mountain tops of Foel Faner and Foel Cynwch over the Nannau estate gives wonderful views of the valley of the River Eden between the Rhinog and Arennig mountain ranges. The house itself is eighteenth century with Adam-style interior decoration. Torrent Walk is the work of Thomas Payne, who designed the Cob embankment across the Glaslyn at Porthmadog. Nearby Brithdir church is an Arts and Crafts church built with North Welsh materials; the architects intended that it should look 'as though it had sprung out of the soil instead of being planted on it.' The choirstalls are carved with animals.

Livestock markets are held every Monday in season and monthly on Fridays. The Women's Institute co-operative market is on Thursday mornings from April to December in Neuadd Idris, Eldon Square in the town centre.

There are many opportunities for easy and more difficult walking around the town and in the foothills of Cader Idris (including the beautiful Cregennen Lakes). Maesgwm Forestry Commission visitor centre has displays on the countryside, forests, history and goldmining – look out for the deer in Coed y Brenin. The RSPB wildlife observatory is at Penmaenpool Visitor Centre overlooking the Mawddach estuary. Harlech Castle and Theatr Ardudwy are not far, nor are the Fairbourne and

Barmouth steam railway and Fairbourne butterfly safari. There is fishing at Llanelltyd and Tal-y-Waen farm has an interesting farm trail. Yet another steam railway can be found at Tal-y-llyn and Corris Craft Centre is within easy reach.

For more information about the area, including accommodation, contact the Snowdonia National Park Centre, The Bridge, Dolgellau, Gwynedd LL40 1LF. Telephone (0341) 422888 (seasonal).

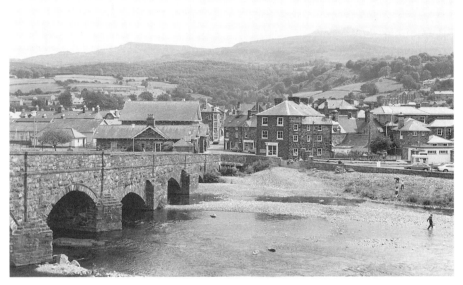

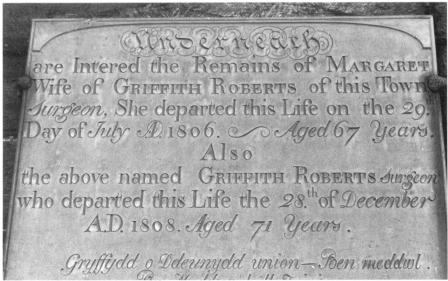

Tombstone, Dolgellau: characteristic lettering on local slate

Harlech

Harlech is a small town today of 2,500 people with spectacular views over
Tremadog Bay, Snowdonia and the Llŷn peninsula. Its name refers to the site of the
castle, deriving from *hardd* (beautiful) and *llech* (slab or smooth rock). In Welsh
mythology Harlech is the legendary home of Brân the Blessed and his sister
Branwen.

The fine castle intimates that the town was once much more important than
today. There may have been an earlier Welsh castle on the site which encouraged
Edward I to develop it as a bastide town, part of the chain of castles and towns built
along the coast from Flint to Aberystwyth to retain control of his newly-won lands
in 1283.

The castle was started in 1283 and is splendidly situated high above the sea on a
steep cliff, with a dry moat cut into the rock on the landward side. When it was built
the sea lapped at its feet – hence the name of the Water Gate – but now the sea has
receded. The castle was of a new and more formidable type than the previous
Norman castles. The massive round towers at the four corners are linked by high
curtain walls and a majestic gate-house, all enclosed by lower walls. Despite its great
strength it was successfully besieged and captured in 1404 by Owain Glyndŵr in his
rebellion against Henry IV and was used until 1409 as one of the chief administrative

Harlech Castle

centres of independent Wales. Its military life ended during the Civil War when the Royalists living here finally surrendered to the Roundhead force in 1647.

The castle's defence by Dafydd ap Ifan ap Einion during the Wars of the Roses is reputed to be recorded in the march *Men of Harlech*.

The other large building in the town is Coleg Harlech, the residential adult education college, built in 1910 and an unusually large Welsh example of an 'Arts and Crafts' inspired building. The college also runs residential Summer Schools. The modern extension is Theatr Ardudwy.

Harlech's sandy beach stretches for miles, backed by dunes. Part of the dune system and marshland forms the National Nature Reserves of Morfa Harlech and Morfa Dyffryn. Behind the beach is the Royal St Davids golf course and an indoor public swimming pool.

Nearby is the Dyffryn Ardudwy megalithic chambered tomb and Old Llanfair Quarry Slate Caverns. Llandanwg beach, a mile to the south, is particularly recommended for disabled people as the car park is adjacent to the fine beach. The ancient church of St Tanwg is hidden amongst the dunes.

For more information about the area, including accommodation, contact the Snowdonia National Park Centre, High Street, Harlech, Gwynedd LL46 2YB. Telephone (0766) 780658 (seasonal).

Porthmadog

Today Porthmadog is a busy town, tourist and yachting centre of almost 3,000 people. It stands in the area known as Eifionnydd at the gateway to the Llŷn peninsula. Without the vision of William Alexander Madocks MP in the nineteenth century, however, Porthmadog, Tremadog and the Cob would not exist.

In 1811 Madocks put up the money to build the almost mile-long Cob holding back the sea across the Glaslyn estuary to enable thousands of acres to be reclaimed and turned into fertile farmland, known in Welsh as the 'morfa'. Crossing the Cob by road today you pay a small toll to the Rebecca Trust, owners of the tollgate since 1978, and the profit is shared amongst local charities at Christmas. A good view of the River Glaslyn, where waterfowl abound, and the Cob, crossed also by the Ffestiniog steam railway, together with a view of the mountains of Snowdonia can be had from Ynys Towyn, a piece of National Trust land.

It is after Madocks that Porthmadog (originally Portmadoc) and Tremadog (originally Tremadoc) were named. Tremadog is an interesting planned village, the birthplace in 1888 of T E Lawrence, Lawrence of Arabia. There is also a legend that Prince Madog ab Owain Gwynedd sailed from an estuary port to discover America. Could this have been in the vicinity of Porthmadog?

In the past Porthmadog was famous for its fast-sailing schooners carrying cargoes of slate. Its ship-building heyday was in the mid-nineteenth century following the rapid development of the slate industry. Brigs, barques and barquentines all sailed out of Porthmadog but especially well-known were the two- and three-masted schooners which carried Welsh slate all over the world. Slate went to home ports, Germany (notably Hamburg following a big fire), other North European ports and South America. As you walk by the harbour you will see Ballast Island in the estuary, made from the stones of ships' ballast carried back from all over the world. The Ffestiniog Railway carried slate and the Welsh Highland Railway brought copper ore from Sygun mines near Beddgelert. With the coming of the Cambrian Railways, however, the shipping trade declined. Today the Maritime Museum, with the old trading ketch Garlandstone outside, tells the story.

Market day is Friday, from Easter to October.

Nearby places to visit include the Ffestiniog steam railway, the Welsh Highland steam railway, the sandy beaches of Borth-y-Gest and Morfa Bychan. The Italianate village of Portmeirion, Harlech Castle, Theatr Ardudwy and Criccieth Castle are all within easy reach.

For more information about the area, including accommodation, contact the Wales Tourist Information Centre, High Street, Porthmadog, Gwynedd, LL49 9LP. Telephone (0766) 512981.

The ring of fire

Rocks of Southern Snowdonia

Southern Snowdonia occupies an important place in the history of geology as a science. It was here that Adam Sedgwick mapped in the early years of the nineteenth century and referred the rocks of the Harlech Dome to the Lower Cambrian system and those overlying them to the Upper Cambrian. At the same time Sir Roderick Murchison working on the rocks of East Wales designated them to an Upper Silurian system and the rocks underlying them to the Lower Silurian. For many years a major controversy raged between these two great geologists over the names and equivalence of the Upper Cambrian and Lower Silurian rocks, and this was eventually resolved by Sir Charles Lapworth who named them Ordovician. Subsequently the names of these three systems became internationally established.

The rocks of southern Snowdonia are of Cambrian and Ordovician age (see map and diagram) which, together with the Silurian rocks exposed over most of central Wales, accumulated in the Lower Palaeozoic era between 600 and 400 million years ago. During this time Wales was the site of a basin in which marine sediments were deposited in both deep water and on shallow shelves. The basin was underlain by older Precambrian strata which are now only exposed on its north-western margin, in Anglesey and Llŷn, and, on its south-eastern margin, in the Welsh Borders. The basin was sited on the edge of a major ancient continent (Gondwanaland) on the south-east side of an ocean (Iapetus). On the north-west side of this ocean lay an ancient North American continent (Laurentia).

This ocean closed gradually throughout Lower Palaeozoic times. The oceanic plates were pushed under the adjacent continental plates and as a result volcanic activity occurred in the vicinity. A similar situation occurs today along the edge of the American continents bordering the Pacific Ocean.

The moving together of the ancient continents caused the rock strata which had accumulated in the ocean and the adjacent basins (like that in Wales) to be folded and uplifted into a great mountain chain known as Caledonides. The eroded remnants of part of this mountain chain form the major part of central and north Wales.

In Wales the Cambrian was a period when great thicknesses of marine sandstones, siltstones and mudstones accumulated in the basin, and in southern Snowdonia these are exposed about the Rhinog Mountains in the core of the Harlech Dome. These rocks were folded and uplifted in late Cambrian times and the first volcano developed in the vicinity of Rhobell Fawr. Subsequently the volcano itself was folded and eroded before being covered by the sea which crossed over the land surface at the beginning of the Ordovician period.

The Ordovician was a period of intense volcanic activity and in Snowdonia it occurred in two distinct phases – the earlier (Lower Ordovician) phase in southern Snowdonia and the later (Mid Ordovician) in central and northern Snowdonia. The deposits of the earlier episode are interbedded with marine sediments in the sequence which overlies and encircles the Cambrian strata of the Harlech Dome. Generally the volcanic rocks are more resistant to erosion than the sedimentary

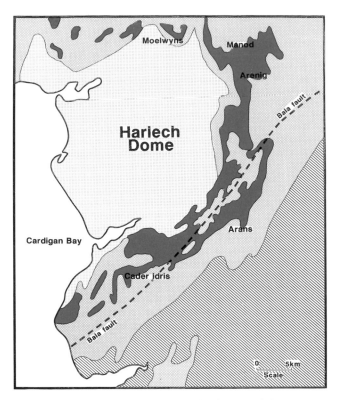

Generalised vertical section of strata & index to symbols on map

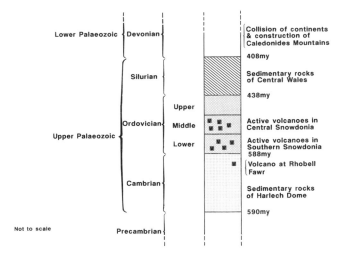

rocks and as a result form the most dramatic topographic expressions – Cader Idris, the Aran, Arennig, Manod and Moelwyn mountains. These have romantically been called the 'ring of fire', although in fact the fire went out over 400 million years ago.

The volcanic rocks are predominantly of acid and basic composition with relatively few of intermediate composition. The acid rocks contain a high percentage (>66%) of silica and the basic rocks comparatively less (<52%). Within the outcrops both extrusive and intrusive rocks can be distinguished. The extrusive rocks were formed by magma (hot molten rock) erupting on to the surface where it cooled and the intrusive rocks formed from magmas which did not reach the surface but cooled in strata beneath the volcano. The extrusive rocks include lava flows as well as fragmented pyroclastic rocks such as tuffs (made of consolidated ash) which resulted from explosive eruption of the ascending magma.

The volcanic activity developed from a number of centres, the largest of which probably lay in the vicinity of Cader Idris and the Manods. No longer do these centres look like present day volcanoes because they developed largely in a marine environment, were eroded and covered with sediments, then folded, faulted and uplifted into the mountain chain and eventually eroded down to the level of the present topography. However, by detailed examination of the rocks it is possible to reconstruct their original distribution.

There's gold in those hills

There are a number of former gold mines (and currently, in 1989, one operational mine) in this area including one on the National Trust's Dolmelynllyn estate in the Mawddach valley on the eastern side of the Harlech Dome. The estate has two main attractions, gold mines and rhododendrons, though you need to be quick to see one through the other. The gold mines are known as the Cefn Coch (the Red Ridge) and lie above the damp oak woods in a barren setting. The multitude of streams which tumble through the woodland were the power source for the mine mills and probably contain much of the gold as extraction was rather inefficient. The local ironmonger in Dolgellau sells prospecting pans, bringing out budding 'forty-niners' during the summer months.

A Gold Mine

The main discovery of gold was made in 1862. It caused controversy in the newspapers of the time as it was almost embarrassing for the 'Royal Metal' to be found in Wales, gold being usually associated with more exotic locations. Gold has, in fact, been known in the area for hundreds of years, and was very popular as decoration for the ancient Britons.

The auriferous (gold-bearing) rocks or lodes of the area are in the Lower Cambrian to Lower Silurian rocks. They are the crystallization of minor igneous intrusions, the metal being found as nuggets or fine strains, differing from mine to mine. The mineralisation took place about 300 million years ago, with the completion of the Western Harlech Dome, now submerged in the semi-mythical kingdom of Cantref Gwaelod.

From 1862 under the management of the Welsh Mining Co, Cefn Coch yielded on average 0.34 oz gold / long ton (2240 lbs). The greatest number of workers employed was 31 in 1894, and only three in 1914 when the mine was abandoned. At one time it was known as 'New California' and was the third-richest mine of the Meirionnydd gold belt, after the now famous Clogau and Gwynfynydd mines.

The Cefn Coch gold was found in a lode of quartz up to 20 ft / 6.1 m thick which also contained amounts of silver, galena (lead), chalcopyrite and sphalerite. The visible workings of the mine show that it was not deep and there is a line of adits (horizontal 'shafts') and shafts which followed the lode up to 1,400 ft / 426.7 m above sea level. Since the adits were used for drainage many have now become stream beds with an abundance of fern and moss at the entrance. None of the mines of the area was operated through shafts but rather drainage, air supply and ore were all taken in through the adit. From the main adit a tramway contours the hillside to the site of the old mill, listed by the Department of the Environment, in a barren area midway up the slopes of Y Garn (2,063 ft / 629 m). The remains of the workers' barracks can also be seen. At every visit a new clue is gleaned – rusted rails in the turf, a wheel pit and reservoir.

Gwynfynydd gold mine

The rock was blasted from the face, then crushed and the metal removed in its native state using a machine such as the noted Cornish Stamp. This was a series or battery of very heavy rods which lifted and fell using a cam mechanism. The rods were driven by steam (with coal from Dolgellau railway station being carried up the steep mountainside at a rate of 12s [60p] per ton). One huge Cornish Stamp ordered for the mill got no further than the Tyn-y-Groes Hotel, having been dragged by horses all the way from Cornwall only to find that the mine was to be abandoned. Any rock too large was crushed with sledge-hammers over an iron grid. After crushing, the 'pulp' was fed over copper plates where the gold amalgamated with a layer of mercury and was then retrieved through a process of distillation. The Britten Pans was a well-known machine for recovering gold.

By 1912, 2,661 tons of ore had been extracted with a yield of 139 oz of gold. The slump years were 1870–80 when the Mawddach Gold Washing Co was set up to work river alluvium near the Tyn-y-Groes Hotel.

Today at the site of the crushing plant the birch scrub has invaded but the iron studs, wheel pit and arrastra (horizontal wheel) can still be seen, as can some waste (known as tailing).

Perhaps of greatest interest is the ruin of a small building below the old mill. Outwardly it resembles a typical old barn but inside a small wheel pit can be seen with a large block with lug holes around its edge and the surface worn by the repeated action of a tilt hammer next to it. This building was in use at least 200–300 years before the larger mill and could be the site that Charles I reputedly visited in 1636.

The paths of the woodland and the old inclines have been opened up to the public at Cefn Coch with information boards at strategic intervals.

Another place of interest for gold diggers in the area is the Forestry Commission's Maesgwm Visitor Centre near Ganllwyd where a restored pan can be seen.

Early visitors
The idea of touring Wales for pleasure did not become popular until the beginning of the Romantic movement at the end of the eighteenth century. These early tourists looked for the 'picturesque' qualities in the landscape – the lofty mountains, the mysterious oakwoods, deep valleys and awe-inspiring waterfalls.

Thomas Pennant undertook well-known tours of Wales in 1773 and 1776. His book *Tours of Wales* gives vivid descriptions of the landscape, rare birds, plants and animals, architectural features, old pictures and furniture as well as interesting insights into trade and mineral resources, local customs and the mansions of his Welsh gentry friends.

He writes of Cwmorthin, a wild and beautiful valley near Blaenau Ffestiniog: 'After the labour of about a mile, reached this strange habitation of two farmers, in a hollow surrounded on three parts by the rudest of environs and containing a pretty lake and two tenements, which yield only grass ...'

William Wordsworth made two trips to Wales in 1791 and in 1793, including a three-week-long 'pedestrian tour'. His diary records his impressions of the Mawddach estuary and Barmouth: 'Took boat and rowed up the sublime estuary, which many compare with the finest in Scotland. With high sea view in front, the mountains behind, the glorious estuary running eight miles inland and Cader Idris in compass of a day's walk, Barmouth can always hold its own against any rival.'

Many of the journals of these early tourists with their remarks about Welsh landscape, history and literature were published. More people were encouraged to venture to Wales instead of to the Continent of the Napoleonic and Revolutionary wars.

By the time George Borrow made his trip in 1854 (recorded in *Wild Wales*) many books had been published about tours in Wales and it had become rather an outmoded literary fashion.

Borrow on the vale of Ffestiniog: 'This valley is fresh and green and the lower parts of the hills on its farthest side are, here and there, adorned with groves. At the eastern end there is a deep gorge, or ravine, down which tumbles a brook in a succession of small cascades.'

On the wild moorland of the Migneint: 'I sped towards it through gorse and heather, occasionally leaping a deep drain. At last I reached it. It was a small lake. Wearied and panting I flung myself on its bank and gazed upon it.

'There lay the lake in the low bottom, surrounded by the heathery hillocks; there it lay quite still, the hot sun reflected upon its surface, which shone like a polished blue shield.'

On Arenig: 'Arenig is certainly barren enough, for there is neither tree nor shrub upon it, but there is something majestic in its huge bulk. Of all the hills which I saw in Wales none made a greater impression upon me.'

Thomas Roscoe, in his 1838 *Wanderings in North Wales*, after spending the night at the Oakeley Arms in Maentwrog, tells us of the oakwoods of Plas Tan-y-Bwlch: 'I entered the grounds of the neighbouring mansion, eager to behold the truly romantic scenery around. Few things can surpass the pleasure of a morning ramble through the woods which clothe the heights above the hall, or the splendour of the prospect from the terrace over the vale, which is delightfully enriched with every feature of landscape and of water, and forms a rich panoramic picture.

'In my walk through the grounds, I observed some magnificent specimens of the rhododendron, of nearly thirty years' growth, and more than forty yards in circumference ...'

Charles Darwin, also writing in the mid-nineteenth century, tells us: 'Old Cader is a grand fellow and shows himself off superbly with ever changing light. Do come and see him.'

And so visitors have continued to do.

Artists' inspiration

'North Wales has everything the landscape painter wants.' Richard Wilson, the first major British artist to concentrate on landscape, is reputed to have said this, and Snowdonia continues to inspire many artists from Wales and elsewhere.

Wilson (1713?–82) was born in Penegoes, near Machynlleth. He spent time in Italy which shows in his serenely lit, rather ideal landscapes such as his *Llyn Cau on Cader Idris* of 1774.

Encouraged by the publication of Paul Sandby's drawings of his 1771 tour with Sir Watkin Williams-Wynn of Ruabon, other artists began to come to Wales. Many of the leading artists of the late-eighteenth and early-nineteenth centuries visited North Wales, including Turner who painted Harlech Castle. David Cox (1783–1859) based himself at Betws-y-Coed to paint Wales's rainy scenery and Samuel Palmer (1805–81) made a trip in 1835. His marriage and resulting two-year honeymoon completely transformed him into an outstanding exponent of the classical pastoral, beginning to be seen in the faery quality of his 1835–36 painting *The Waterfall, Pistyll Mawddach*. William Dyce (1806–64), sometimes regarded as the link between Nazarenes and Pre-Raphaelites, painted in both Wales and Scotland but preferred Wales and its mountains, 'more awful and terrific-looking than anything I know of in Scotland'.

J D Innes (1887–1914), with his great passion for mountains, is often considered to have taken up the mantle of Richard Wilson as the Welsh landscape painter in the twentieth century. He suffered from TB and had spent some time in Spain and France, including Collioure, favoured by the Fauve artists Matisse and Derain. This experience of light and colour together with hints of Japanese composition lends to

Llyn-y-Cau, Cader Idris *by Richard Wilson*

his Welsh work, like Wilson's, a touch of the exotic. Two intensive stays in the area between Bala and Ffestiniog produced powerful and original studies of his favourite mountain, Arennig Fawr.

Innes invited Augustus John to visit North Wales. John, fresh from landscape painting in Provence, produced some of his finest landscapes – quick, bright panels, full of colour and light. Most notable is his treatment of Llyn Tryweryn, at that time a remote lake in the mountains between Bala and Ffestiniog. He wrote to his wife, Dorelia: 'This is the most wonderful place I've seen ... the air is superb and the mountains wonderful'.

Other well-known artists to have spent time in the southern part of Snowdonia are Stanley Spencer (1891–1959), John Piper (b.1903) and Kyffin Williams (b.1918). Williams is best known for landscapes with a feeling of romantic detachment, reminiscent of Innes's paintings of distant mountains. His unvarying, heavy technique with no distinction between contrasting textures or atmospheric effects shows high, menacing mountains, remote farms, dark and empty bleak skies, grey clouds – all suggesting melancholy and a yearning for retreat and escape.

Installation Art has its place. David Nash, who works entirely in wood, planted a circle of ash saplings near Maentwrog in 1977 and is training them to form a 30 ft / 9.1 m living dome. The *Fletched-over Ash Dome* will take about 40 years to be completed as 'a silver structure in winter, a green canopy space in summer, a volcano of growing energy'.

Arenig Mountain *by Augustus John*

Energy

Hydro-electric power

Many people complain about rain, sleet, snow and hail but these form the natural resource for power from hydro-electric schemes – both hydro-electric power-stations and their descendants, pumped storage schemes. It is difficult to store electricity easily and hydro-electric power means it can be made instantly.

The area around Blaenau Ffestiniog has two such power stations: at Maentwrog and at Tanygrisiau, near Ffestiniog.

Maentwrog hydro-electric power-station was built in 1925 to meet the need for electricity of the growing industrial population in England. It uses the power of the water as it rushes downwards to make electricity.

Maentwrog was the scene of a disaster a few years ago when a pipe leading to the power station broke. You can make out the scar on the hillside made by many gallons of water rushing down the wooded slope and across the main A496 road.

Pumped storage is a development of hydro-electric power. Instead of the water flowing away after it has been used once in the generating process, it is retained in a lower reservoir and pumped back up the mountain, using cheap off-peak electricity, to be used again.

Though pumped storage schemes use more electricity than they produce they save millions of pounds each year. Electricity can be supplied quickly so expensive plant is not kept running and at night pumped storage's own demands for power to pump the water back uphill uses the electricity from other power-stations. This helps them to operate efficiently.

Investigation into the feasibility of the Ffestiniog pumped storage scheme bbegan in 1948. Construction of the largest local stone building in the area since the building of Criccieth Castle began in 1957. The scheme was completed in 1963, the first of its kind in this country.

The Yale Electricity Company had constructed a dam in 1898 to enlarge Llyn Stwlan to supply mines in the area with electricity. It was enlarged again to create the upper lake of the pumped storage scheme, and the lower reservoir, Tanygrisiau, was made by damming the Afon Ystradau.

You can travel from Blaenau Ffestiniog up to the Llyn Stwlan dam and reservoir. From there water is released at high pressure through huge pipes to the lower Tanygrisiau Reservoir, operating the turbines to provide electricity at periods of peak demand. In the off-peak period the system reverses and the water is pumped back to the upper reservoir, ready to be called on again. The CEGB have an information centre at Tanygrisiau.

Trawsfynydd nuclear power

In good weather you sometimes get a glimpse of the Trawsfynydd nuclear power-station from the A470 as the road drops down from the Crimea Pass into Blaenau Ffestiniog. For a second, you might think that it's another castle rather than a building of the 1960s, designed by Basil Spence who also designed Coventry Cathedral.

Trawsfynydd: nature trail and power station

It is a Magnox power-station, the first to be built away from the sea in this country and the first to use the waters of a lake for cooling purposes. The lake, Llyn Trawsfynydd, had been created at the end of the 1920s as part of the hydro-electric power scheme at Maentwrog. Trawsfynydd power-station was opened in 1965 and can generate 390,000 kilowatts of energy, enough for a city the size of Cardiff. The ageing Magnox reactors, however, are due to be decommissioned by the end of the century.

The many employees travel to work from miles around. The closure of Trawsfynydd would mean the loss of 1000 jobs, 600 at the power-station (among the best paid in rural Wales) and another 400 it supports indirectly. Without the power-station, will there be other work in the area?

Centre for Alternative Technology

The Centre for Alternative Technology near Machynlleth demonstrates different methods of energy generation, use and conservation. Examples are water-power, wind-power, solar-power, bio-gas, wood gas and insulation techniques. Situated in an old slate quarry, it was set up in 1974 by the Society for Environmental Improvement, a registered charity. Through the Centre's experimentation and development of ideas visitors can gain an insight into the use of alternative (or appropriate) technology which can save resources and cut waste and pollution.

Appropriate technology at the Centre is not only about energy but also food and growing (such as organic vegetables, fish culture, smallholding and forestry), engineering (the blacksmith's forge, electric vehicles and railway) and buildings.

The Centre is a working community not just a place full of working displays. Its philosophy is one of concern for the world, fair and sustainable use, an awareness of everyone's place in the environment. The interests of alternative technology overlap considerably into other areas such as wildlife and habitat conservation, environmental improvement and relationships with the Third World. Entry to the bookshop and wholefood café is free.

Slate and the National Park

Quarries and caverns

The town of Blaenau Ffestiniog could, for many reasons, be described as the 'slateopolis' of North Wales. A number of other towns and large villages in Gwynedd have equally close links with the slate industry – Bethesda, Llanberis and Penygroes are good examples. But at Blaenau Ffestiniog, the close proximity of the quarries to the town, and their effect upon its demography, are both remarkable. Visitors to the town quickly become aware of the links, reinforced by the importance of the slate industry in almost every context: from the development of the Ffestiniog railway to the building of the Nonconformist chapels which were once so popular to the emergence of the quarries as tourist attractions in their own right. But Blaenau Ffestiniog is a living slate town: a number of the quarries are still at work and demand for best quality Welsh slate is encouragingly high.

Slate quarrying in the vicinity of Blaenau Ffestiniog can be traced back to the second half of the eighteenth century. The first quarry to be worked was at Diffwys, where in 1765 Methusalem Jones and William Morris, drawing on experience gained in the Nantlle valley near Caernarfon, established a commercial operation. Many others were to follow their lead, extracting fine-grained slates, grey in colour, from rocks of the Ordovician complex. Among the most famous were William Turner and Samuel Holland, and the profitability of the industry, even in its earliest years, was to attract leading financiers like Nathan Rothschild.

Life could not have been easy for these early entrepreneurs, nor for their workmen. Ffestiniog, at that time the only village of any significance in the vicinity of the quarries, had poor transport links to the coast, and loads of slate were carried down on horseback, later by horse and cart, along indifferent roads as far as the nearest tidal stretch of the Afon Dwyryd near Maentwrog. Here they were loaded into flat-bottomed vessels, tended by crews referred to locally as 'Philistines'. After

A slate quarry

the short journey to Ynys Cyngar, seaward of the present town of Porthmadog, they were transferred into coasters which took them to most parts of Britain and Ireland.

The key to expansion of the quarries around Blaenau Ffestiniog lay in improving its links to the coast. The demand for slate was growing apace; as industrial Britain and Europe grew, so did the clamour of builders requiring slates to roof the new terraces of houses that were appearing around the mines, mills and furnaces which fuelled the Industrial Revolution. Welsh slate was eminently suitable – it was, after all, almost indestructible, cheap to produce and could easily be transported to the industrial zones of Western Europe. If Blaenau Ffestiniog's slate industry was to flourish and compete with its counterparts in the north of Gwynedd, then it too required a railway link to the coast.

This was constructed in 1836 by James and Charles Spooner and became perhaps the best known of all narrow gauge railways in Wales. Initially operated by horses, which rode down on gravity trains and later hauled waggons back up the line, it saw steam traction introduced in 1863 – another first for a most profitable little railway.

These improvements in transport and in the port facilities at Porthmadog, brought a rapid expansion of the slate industry around Blaenau Ffestiniog. The earliest method of extraction had been from ever-deepening open quarries, but soon these proved to be difficult and dangerous to operate, and mining techniques were used instead. The veins of slate locally disappear into the ground at an angle and they are followed down by means of inclined levels, out of which are driven adits. Chambers are opened up from these, and the slate blocks sent to the surface to be split, trimmed and turned into roofing slate. Visitors to the tourist mines at Gloddfa Ganol and Llechwedd can experience for themselves the breath-taking size of the chambers, and attempt to appreciate what was involved in working slate by candle light hundreds of feet underground.

The mines that developed were vast concerns – Oakeley, Llechwedd, Maenof-

Slate quarry, *Corris*

feren, Fotty and Bowydd were probably the best-known – but many others flourished in the area as well, from Parc and Rhosydd in the Croesor valley to Manod and Rhiwbach on the high moorlands between Ffestiniog and Cwm Penmachno. The largest mines were worked by over a thousand men, and by the 1890s the Welsh slate industry employed about 18,000 men to produce over 90% of British slate output.

Where did the quarrymen come from, and where did they live? In 1801, the parish of Ffestiniog had just over 700 inhabitants: by 1881, over 11,000 lived there. Many men commuted daily from neighbouring villages, like Dolwyddelan, Trawsfynydd and Penrhyndeudraeth; others lived in 'barrack blocks' near their places of employment.

The first quarrymen would have been local smallholders or farmers, who had some experience of working the useful rocks that out-cropped on their lands. These were soon supplemented by men who moved in from neighbouring agricultural areas, and who had to be taught the craft of splitting and trimming slates. Others brought with them a set of specialist skills, acquired in the lead mines of mid-Wales or at the copper mines of Parys, near Amlwch. They made Blaenau Ffestiniog a booming, exciting town, where almost all were monoglot Welsh, and many preferred the chapel to the public house. Not that the quarrymen and their families were strait-laced – they enjoyed their *eisteddfodau*, football and brass band competitions, and were renowned as fearsome leg-pullers and practical jokers.

The twentieth century saw a slump in the fortunes of the industry, hit hard by labour conflicts and competition from other roofing materials. War and conscription drew men from the industry and unemployment began to ravage a once-prosperous industry. Quarry managers, accustomed to a sellers' market, could not comprehend the need for aggressive marketing and were consequently driven out of business by those who supplied roofing of all hues to a new suburban Britain and Europe. Welsh slate had no place here and was seen as a working-class, unfashionable material, more associated with industrial terraces.

Blaenau Ffestiniog suffered its share of depression, alleviated to some extent in the 1920s by the effects of the Addison and Wheatley Housing Acts, and again in the 1940s by rebuilding which followed Hitler's blitz of industrial cities. But by the 1960s, all slate mines and quarries appeared doomed to stagnation and eventual closure; the Ffestiniog Railway was a tourist line and, when the Oakeley mine closed, the end seemed in sight for other local concerns.

Thankfully, this was not so. The industrial past of Wales is now a pastime for visitors who come to Blaenau Ffestiniog to marvel at the hard work of those who laboured at the Gloddfa Ganol and Llechwedd mines. This provides employment. More criticially, the mines themselves have discovered new markets, having redeveloped with new techniques and modern machinery. Lorries replace steam locomotives; electricity powers the saws and haulage equipment; and fans extract the dust that once entered men's lungs. Llechwedd and Gloddfa Ganol operate commercially, as does Maenofferen and Cwt y Bugail, and other concerns also flourish. Welsh slate is once again a popular, fashionable roofing material, and an old industry is still proud of its craft skills.

Plas Tan y Bwlch

Plas Tan y Bwlch, which means the *mansion beneath the pass* is situated on the northern slopes of the Vale of Ffestiniog (or Maentwrog as it was named originally) in the heart of the Snowdonia National Park. Since 1975 it has housed the Park's Residential Study Centre and for many years it has played an important role in shaping the regional inheritance.

Maentwrog means the *rock of Twrog*. Twrog was a Celtic saint who ripped out a part of the mountain above the valley to smash a heathen altar erected in the Vale. That rock with the hand-print of Twrog can still be seen by the door of the present church in the village.

The family who occupied the 'Plas' and presided over the material well-being of the Vale were descended from a royal Welsh lineage, but in 1790 Margaret Griffith, the sole heiress, married William Oakeley from Staffordshire and the name Oakeley has been linked to the Plas and the Vale ever since. William Oakeley, *Oakeley Fawr* as he was called, made substantial improvements to the Estate and started to put the Oakeley 'stamp' on the landscape. His son, William Gruffydd Oakeley, took over the inheritance in 1812 and was the first to taste the great wealth to be found in the nearby mountains. This was slate. In 1833 it was W G Oakeley who laid the foundation stone of the Ffestiniog Railway which linked the slate quarry on Oakeley land in Blaenau Ffestiniog with the harbour at Porthmadog. However, it was his nephew, W E Oakeley who reaped the greatest benefits from the blue-grey rock

Plas Tan y Bwlch

when he formed the Oakeley Slate Quarry in 1880. It became 'the largest slate mine in the world', and part of it is now Gloddfa Ganol Mountain Tourist Centre.

W E Oakeley continued the work of his predecessors in the Vale over much of the last century. He nursed the oak woodlands, enlarged the village, improved the gardens of the Plas and extended and embellished the mansion itself. He left his mark on the Vale in no uncertain manner as he even had his initials arranged in planted conifers in the middle of the oaks on the southern side of the Vale, opposite his country house.

Unfortunately, the small revival in the slate industry during the 1980s came too late to save the Oakeley Estate. The last of the family to occupy the Plas, Mary Caroline Inge (a niece of WEO), died in 1961 aged 96. In 1969, the Oakeley Quarry was sold to a local family who still run both the extractive and the tourist businesses on the site.

In 1969 Plas and the estate were bought by the forerunner of Gwynedd County Council. Since 1975 Plas Tan y Bwlch, sponsored by the Countryside Commission as well as by the County Council, has been running short courses for the general public on the physical and cultural heritage of Snowdonia. The woodlands and the formal gardens, once the exclusive joy of the rich and the privileged, are now open to all.

Roads and buildings

Roman roads and 'Roman Steps'

Soldiers occupied defensive sites and traders imported goods from far afield long before the Romans, but it is the Romans who seem to stick in our minds and who give their name to many interesting places. In the part of Snowdonia east of the Rhinog mountains there are two such places where archaeologists and historians are piecing together slowly the stories behind the Roman names.

Roman roads

Life at the Iron Age smelting settlement at Bryn y Castell near Ffestiniog cannot have been easy, but the discovery of beautiful glass bangles and scratched slate gaming boards with black and white stones for pieces, now at Plas Tan y Bwlch, as well as over a ton of iron-working slag, gives some hint of what it might have been like. Just a few miles away in Trawsfynydd Lake was found the only complete tankard of Celtic design, its wooden staves complete in its bronze casing and with an elaborate handle. It was a lifestyle with these sorts of trappings which was disrupted by the Romans.

In AD61 Suetonius Paulinus, the seasoned African campaigner and Governor of Britain, led a swift raid across North Wales into the Druidic stronghold of Anglesey, a centre of anti-Roman feeling. However, the rising of Boudicca and the Iceni in East Anglia immediately called him back to England and protracted fighting in Wales dragged on for 18 years. The powerful and warlike mid-Wales tribe, the Ordovices, used guerrilla tactics in the mountains, harrassing lines of communication and falling savagely on any small force of Romans which became detached from the rest. Though in pitched battle the discipline and armour of the Roman legion was always the decisive factor, guerrilla warfare was a different matter. All the same by AD78 Druidic influence was virtually destroyed and a new political will from Rome encouraged Julius Agricola, the Governor of Britain, to lead a punitive force against the Ordovices in their mountain strongholds in southern Snowdonia. The previous year the tribe had almost annihilated an entire Roman cavalry regiment and Agricola told his troops to give no quarter. Almost the whole tribe was exterminated.

Agricola imposed a typically Roman strategic military communications network. A western route to the south was built from the fort at Caernarfon (Segontium) down eventually to Carmarthen (Moridunum). This long stretch of Roman road is known as Sarn Helen and its route can be made out in some places such as near the A470 through Trawsfynydd down to Dolgellau. The name is probably a corruption of the Welsh *sarn y lleng* (the legion's road). A story in the Mabinogion, a mediaeval collection of Welsh prose tales compiled from centuries of oral storytelling, tells us that a Welsh princess, Elen of the Hosts, married to the Roman deputy emperor, Magnus Maximus, had it built.

'Elen thought to have highways built from one fortress to another across the island; these were built and are now called the highways of Elen of the Hosts, because of her British origin – that is, because the men of the island would not have assembled for anyone but her.'

The Romans built a fort at Tomen y Mur, near Trawsfynydd (now on private land) as a control post with clay and turf ramparts. It was rebuilt in the early part of the second century with a bath-house, parade ground and siege-engine platforms and the 'amphitheatre' (perhaps a demonstration arena or cockpit). Nearby are practice camps, the by-product of field exercises. Much later a Norman castle was built on the ramparts.

'Roman steps'

To the west of Sarn Helen lies the wild and rugged Harlech Dome and Rhinog Mountains. There are few routes through, and it would have been ideal country for the Ordovices' guerrilla activity. The two main routes are the pass of Bwlch Drws Ardudwy (leading up from Cwm Nantcol between Rhinog Fawr and Rhinog Fach) and Bwlch Tyddiad (leading up from Cwm Bychan below the slope of Rhinog Fawr).

These routes have probably been in use for thousands of years. Metal-traders in the Bronze Age (about 2,000BC), for example, marked their route (from Llanbedr to Carreg to Moel Goedog) with tall stones in order to avoid the hazards of mountainous and boggy country. These are the *maenhir* we can still see today.

The most famous route is the so-called 'Roman steps' through Bwlch Tyddiad where hundreds of slabs of gritstone have been laid to make a well-defined path leading to the summit of the col. The Romans probably improved and consolidated an already ancient pathway which was improved further in mediaeval times, perhaps towards the end of the thirteenth century when Edward I built Harlech Castle. It would have offered him a good supply route through the Rhinog mountains and then across moorland to Bala when normal sea access was threatened. In more peaceful times the paved way was used as part of a packhorse trail.

Castell y Bere – a Welsh Castle

Castell y Bere lies in a spectacular location on an isolated rocky outcrop in the upper part of the Dysynni valley. It is seven miles / 11.3 km north-east of Tywyn and 12 miles / 19.3 km from Dolgellau, below the southern slopes of Cader Idris. A little down the road is Bird Rock (Craig yr Aderyn), nearly 800 feet high with a precipitous front rising straight up from the flat valley floor. Thirty to forty cormorants nest here during April and May on the only cliffs to be found between Aberdyfi and Barmouth, a reminder of the hundreds of birds which used to breed here when Cardigan Bay was full of shoals of herring and mackerel.

This is one of the largest and most ornate of the native Welsh castles and was begun by Prince Llywelyn the Great (Llywelyn ap Iorwerth) around 1220 with later building by Edward I in the 1280s. Today the remains of a rectangular keep, three towers and a large triangular barbican make it a place full of mystery and romance.

The story behind its building is complicated, reflecting different alliances and often bloody power struggles in the Wales of the early thirteenth century. An important part in the story is played by the House of Gwynedd and in particular by Llywelyn ap Iorwerth and his grandsons Dafydd and Llywelyn ap Gruffudd. In brief, Gwynedd saw itself as a kingdom rather than a princedom. Other Welsh rulers did

Castell y Bere – reconstruction by Alan Sorrell

not see it that way: they felt Gwynedd could never be more than a 'keystone in an arch of kings'. Llywelyn ap Iorwerth realised that owing fealty to the English king helped his attempts to win superiority within Wales.

Llywelyn built three stone castles in naturally strong positions away from the older centres of cantref or commote after a settlement with other Welsh rulers in 1216. The castles may have been to secure his southern boundary with his new allies and his eastern boundary with the English.

In 1221 the Chronicle of Princes (the main Welsh historical source for this period) tells us: 'Llywelyn took from Gruffud (his son) the cantref of Meirionnydd and the commot of Ardudwy. And he began to build a castle there for himself.'

This was probably Castell y Bere.

Castell y Bere continued to play a part in the complicated relationships between England and the House of Gwynedd after Llywelyn the Great's death in 1240.

After the end of the First War of Independence (Edward I's campaign 1276–77) Dafydd ap Gruffudd established himself in Castell y Bere. Like many other Welsh leaders he grew restive under Edward I's harsh settlement terms.

In 1283 the castle was the last point of Welsh resistance to Edward in the Second War of Independence (1282–83) and was besieged by forces which had advanced up the Dysynni valley. It was captured on 25 April 1283 and Dafydd escaped into the mountain fastnesses of Snowdonia only to be betrayed and executed as a traitor in 1283 after he was captured at Caergwrle, near Wrexham.

Edward put five masons and five carpenters to work at the castle to carry out 'various works', among them probably the building of the massive curtain walls which enclose the formerly open area and rock-cut ditch in front of the southern apsidal tower. Standing in this massive enclosure, imagining the tower in its previously isolated and commanding position, it can easily be seen as the sanctum of the Welsh princes, Llywelyn the Great and Dafydd.

The castle was designed and built originally to be defended by the men of Gwynedd who fought mainly with the long spear (although arrowloops in the south tower suggest that some crossbowmen were deployed). The English, on the other hand, used mainly the crossbow. They built their castles with a continuous curtain wall and circular and semi-circular flanking towers so that the archers could cover practically all of the wall against attack. A curtain wall was added when the English took Castell y Bere. Unlike nearby Harlech, however, it is not an integral part of the design and defence system and is merely a means to link towers to one another and to enclose the courtyard with its various buildings.

Perhaps because Castell y Bere on its triangular rocky outcrop could not be moulded successfully into Edward's idea of a castle it did not last as long as some of the others. In 1294 during Madoc ap Llywelyn's rising it was besieged and the English were victorious. They then appear to have deserted and destroyed the castle so that it could not be used by the Welsh again.

Chapels

Wherever you go in Wales you see chapels in various states of repair, in use as places of worship or sometimes as garages or DIY stores. It has been estimated that between 4,000 and 5,000 chapels were built throughout Wales and their presence can raise a host of questions – why so many, why such different styles, why so many different denominations, how important were they?

The word 'chapel' can, however, mean much more than just the building, evoking the essence of so much of the cultural, political, educational and religious life of Wales. In the past the chapel was a central part of very many people's daily life. The mention of Sunday School, communion, the charabanc outing, *te-parti mawr* (large tea party), Big Meetings, *y gymanfa ganu* (singing festival), recitations, baptism, *eisteddfodau*, Band of Hope, *seiat* (fellowship meeting) and *cyfarfodydd gweddi* (prayer meetings) still raises a mixture of memories and emotions for many Welsh people.

In the seventeenth century Dissenters had to meet secretly to worship. Persecution continued even after the 1689 Toleration Act which condoned worship only in a licensed place. Non-conformists began to register and adapt existing buildings into simple preaching places to hear the Word.

When chapels began to be specially built they were still simple meeting places and they echoed at first the vernacular tradition of barns, farms and other large buildings. As in the long-house of rural mid-Wales the long side wall was the facade. Soar y Mynydd, near Tregaron was built with a house and stable under one roof.

In 1811 the (Calvinistic) Methodists broke away from the established Church and there followed a rapid growth and swelling of numbers through religious revivals.

Chapels were purpose built in substantial numbers in almost every village or town and given biblical names like Salem, Moriah, Zion or Tabernacl.

By the mid-nineteenth century there were many non-conformist sects in Wales but, though varying in detail, the chapels showed a common distinctive character. They were the product of local builders and perhaps designed by the local minister.

The form was a rectangular box with a pitched roof and gable ends. Inside there was no need for an elaborate layout for ceremonial ritual. It was laid out as an auditorium chapel, a People's Theatre to hear *y Gair* (the Word), the fundamental message of Christianity, in the sermon which was the most important part of the service. The original chapel was often not large enough and was extended with an oriel (galleries or balconies) on three sides. Jerusalem, Blaenau Ffestiniog seated 900 people. Deep pen pews countered the cold of winter and draughts during long hours of sermons.

TOP LEFT
Independent Church, Bala

LEFT
Statue of Thomas Charles in front of Capel Tegid, Bala

ABOVE
English Presbyterian Church, Bala

Portmeirion – Home for Fallen Buildings

Portmeirion may mean pottery to many people. But just off the A487 at Minffordd, near Porthmadog, the fairytale village of the same name is set on the rugged cliffs of the Aber Iâ peninsula above the shores of Cardigan Bay. Miles of sandy beaches and the wilds of Y Gwyllt's hanging woods and subtropical gardens (now fighting free of the invasive Rhododendron ponticum and laurel) enclose the village with its shops, restaurants and pastel-washed cottages. Visitors can enjoy the village on day visits or stay at the hotel or in self-catering accommodation.

Portmeirion was created by the architect Sir Clough Williams-Ellis from 1925–75. The income from his practice and the discovery of the beautiful peninsula close to his home, after many years of searching for the right site, enabled him to fulfil a childhood dream of building his ideal village. He wanted to show 'that one could develop even a very beautiful site without defiling it and indeed, given sufficient loving care, that one might even enhance what nature had provided as your background'.

Sir Clough also wanted to awaken in people an interest in architecture, landscaping and design generally. And although 'architectural good manners can also mean good business', Portmeirion was meant to be fun for the creator and visitor alike.

The village was originally inspired by Portofino and is often described as Italianate. The style developed, however, into one more eclectic and personal, Sir Clough's 'light opera approach' to architecture. Buildings that were in danger of perishing elsewhere were taken down, moved and re-erected at Portmeirion. The vaulted plaster ceiling showing the life and labours of Hercules and the panelling of the Town Hall comes from the late 16th century Banqueting Hall from Emral in Flintshire; the Sandstone Colonnade was originally built in 1707 at Arnois Court near Bristol; the Dome Facade is a Norman Shaw fireplace from Hooton Hall. He once called the village his 'home for fallen buildings'. Other bits and pieces were used if they fitted in – a giant Buddha left over from a film set, gilded Burmese dancers on Ionic columns, a carved head to embellish a petrol pump.

To make the village look old, faded and stained, colour washes were used on the exteriors of the buildings. Some are newly painted, some faded, and some obviously in need of attention, giving the impression of a living village.

A recent addition to the village is the restoration of the Hotel Portmeirion, originally opened in 1926 but gutted by a fire in 1981. Non-residents can dine in the hotel overlooking the bay where at high tide one almost seems to be on a liner afloat at sea.

The bright domes, turrets and spires of the village rising up between two rocky headlands and surrounded by woodland make it a fascinating place to visit. It is a remarkable monument both to its creator and to the teams of craftsmen who dismantled and rebuilt the complex pieces of old architecture.

Portmeirion

Hill farming

Hill farming in Wales is best suited to rearing strong cattle and sheep as there are not the fertile soils and dry sunny climate for growing and ripening good quality arable crops.

In the past Snowdonia's farmers practised a farming system called transhumance. This was common to mountain pastoral activity the world over and entailed moving up with the flocks to the sweeter high pastures (the 'ffridd') in the summer. It may ring bells from Joanna Spryi's book *Heidi*, set in Switzerland. Throughout Snowdonia you will see the names 'hafod' (summer house) or 'hendre' (the old winter home) on farm or other buildings.

The traditional Welsh farmed landscape is one of small fields, divided by standing stone banks and natural woodlands of oak, ash and alder which provide a network of habitats.

Nowadays high livestock to land ratios demand the best possible grass yields for summer grazing and winter silage fodder. Many farmers have put tremendous effort into reseeding their land. Large boulders, originally deposited by the glaciers, are dynamited away and the stones are used for the repair of dry stone walls, a valuable shelter for stock which reduces the cost of fencing. Over the years many stones have been cleared from fields and used in building farmhouses, barns and walls. The land is then ploughed and reseeded with ryegrass, timothy and clover.

Today sheep are kept for their crop of quick-fleshing lambs and the weight and value of the wool clip.

Tan-faced sheep resulting from interbreeding between the white-faced Roman sheep and the native Soay have been on the hills of Wales for 2,000 years. You will see the Welsh Mountain sheep, the smallest of the commercially important breeds, whose extreme hardiness enables it to thrive in the hostile mountain environment with high rainfall and poor or scarce grazing. It has a tanned face and bright, prominent eyes and small ears. The ewes have a very gentle look and the rams have well-curved horns.

Sheep pastures and Cader Idris

The Welsh Mountain cannot usually be successfully enclosed on lowland pastures and is 'hefted' (*cynefino* in Welsh, from the word *cynefin*) to its part of the mountain above the ffridd wall.

You may also see the Speckled Face breed, bigger than the true mountain sheep, with, not surprisingly, a distinctly speckled face.

Lambs are born in March and April, after the end of winter. Most male lambs are castrated to help fattening and all are ear-marked. Care is taken to select the best ram and ewe lambs for breeding as quality, size and healthy looks attract the attention of other farmers when selling. The best ewe lambs are kept for flock replacement and are put to the ram in their first year but not until the end of October so that their lambs are born to miss the winter. Fat hill lambs go to the butcher between mid-July and November as they reach a suitable weight – fed on ewe's milk and upland grass, without agro-chemicals, feed additives or antibiotics. Shearing takes place in mid-June. The four-year-old ewes are sold every September to lowland farms where better conditions mean that more lambs can be produced.

The Welsh Black are the native cattle of Wales and there are references to them in the earliest Welsh literature. Their outstanding characteristic is their hardiness, enabling them to thrive in environments too harsh for other breeds. This quality is now recognised far beyond Wales and they are becoming increasingly popular. They were traditionally a dual-purpose breed providing both milk and meat but today are thought of as beef cattle producing high quality meat.

They calve in May and June after being turned out after winter. Calves are weaned in January and fed on silage and barley until they are turned out to grass in spring. They are sold in the following September as strong store cattle to lowland farmers who fatten them to slaughter weight. The best heifer calves are retained every year for breeding or replacing old and unproductive cows.

You can find out more about working hill farms by visiting one of the farms in Snowdonia and other parts of Wales which have open days or farm trails. Watching sheepdog trials at one of the many events during the summer gives some idea of the skill involved in working a hill farm successfully.

Moorland and woodland, birds and flowers

Moorlands and black grouse

The extensive open landscapes of southern Snowdonia may appear wild and natural, but in fact reflect centuries of human usage. The rolling moorlands of Berwyn and Migneint may, around the Neolithic period, have comprised extensive patches of woodland separated by marshes in the valleys and perhaps open mountain or low scrub on the higher tops. Following extensive clearances for creating pasture, for fuel, charcoal, ship-building and so on, came the remarkable period when wealthy landowners maintained vast tracts of heather moorland through selective burning and widespread grazing.

To what end? Mainly for producing, then shooting enormous numbers of those birds which spend practically the whole of their lives on those open heather moorlands: red grouse. Estates vied with each other over the numbers of grouse shot, and over the quality of management for their quarry. The heather was burnt in patches to provide fresh growth as food for the birds, alternating with areas of older heather where they could hide from predators, nest and rear their young.

Another species of grouse also lived in a slightly different part of the moorland: black grouse, which preferred the edges of the moor, where the heather grades into scrubby woodland or rushy pasture. This bird of the moorland edge has had a varied history in Wales. It may well have been fairly common in the early eighteenth century (though we have no detailed knowledge from that period), but it certainly declined right up until about 1940. Several estates had tried to encourage this bird for sport – even though it was 'wilder' and less amenable to being driven over waiting gunners – and went so far as to introduce it into localities like Vyrnwy and the Berwyn.

The fortunes of the black grouse revived considerably when the Forestry Commission began establishing their Welsh forests. The exclusion of sheep, prior to planting young trees, permitted a rapid growth of heather and bilberry (the black grouse's two main food sources here), while the growth of young conifers provided cover and nesting sites. But by 1975 numbers were again declining, which prompted the Royal Society for the Protection of Birds to seek grant aid from the Forestry Commission to research the black grouse's habitat and food preferences. Most of this work was carried out in south-eastern Snowdonia in 1985–88.

The fringes of the Berwyn massif nowadays seem to provide the main stronghold for Wales's remaining black grouse. In central and southern England it has disappeared entirely from haunts known at the turn of the century, though it is still secure in Scotland and parts of northern England. Reasons for its demise are thought to be linked with change in habitat, and perhaps increasing disturbance and predation.

Research showed that black grouse favoured areas where the two shrubby species, heather and bilberry, grew in association with conifer plantations. It seemed likely that the recent decline in numbers was linked to a combination of two circumstances. Firstly, the growth of conifers eventually excluded light from the forest floor and so gradually killed off the birds' food species. Secondly, since

Black grouse, Lyrusus tetrix

1980 relatively little planting had been carried out on newly-enclosed land, so that conditions especially favourable to black grouse were fewer than in the heyday of forest establishment in the 1950s and 1960s.

With the co-operation of the Forestry Commission, RSPB researchers advised on ways of managing the forest edge for the benefit of black grouse – without high management costs and with little loss of land for timber production. The essence of this plan was to maintain areas of heather, bilberry and cotton-grass, especially where young trees were being grown near the moorland edge. The Commission's shooting tenants agreed not to shoot black grouse in the forests for a trial period. Efforts were to be made to control the birds' presumed predators. Crows are likely to take eggs and perhaps small chicks, and foxes can capture female black grouse on nests, eat eggs and chicks, and perhaps kill some roosting on the ground.

In 1986 there were almost certainly fewer than 1,000 black grouse in Wales. A positive response to these management measures would put them out of the danger zone, and make the interface between Wales's forests and moorlands that much richer.

'Traditional' woodland

Many people feel a deep affection for woodland and for trees, especially native broad-leaved species. After all, they have been around a long time. Trees began to colonise Britain after the Great Ice Age and by 5,000BC all those we are familiar with today had arrived.

Today, however, native broad-leaved woodland covers only 3% of Wales. More than half of Wales's woodlands have been lost through afforestation or urban and agricultural development in the last 50 years. Equally serious is their failure to regenerate – 80% in Snowdonia. There is no lack of tree seed or seedlings (in fact, the sessile oak may produce several hundred small acorns to the square metre), but not enough are surviving to replace earlier generations of trees. This is the result of grazing, especially by sheep which will eat the buds and leaves of young trees and even strip off the bark. In Snowdonia more than two-thirds of the total wooded area is open to stock and often there is no shrub layer left; in oak woodlands this is made up of birch, rowan, alder and holly.

Loss of woodland is not new. Throughout the centuries (starting in the Neolithic period around 2,000BC) people's demands for timber and the need to clear the land for agriculture have reduced the amount of native oakwoods.

With good management, however, woodland can make a real contribution to the landscape, wildlife, farm incomes and employment. The type of management regime will depend on the purpose to which the wood is to be put – timber production, landscape and wildlife conservation, sport or recreation.

Managing woodlands for nature conservation will ensure the protection of a variety of species. It may mean fencing completely around an enclosure to keep out stock, or creating a variety of habitats within the wood. Making clearings or meadows encourages violets, celandines and primroses in the spring, as well as bracken, wild raspberry and bramble. Leaving rotting branches and trunks encourages the plants and animals which live on them, such as toadstools and woodlice. Holes in rotting trunks are nesting sites for certain birds, and nesting boxes also encourage them.

In Snowdonia there are a number of woodland reserves managed by the Nature Conservancy Council as National Nature Reserves to ensure their survival and to maintain the diversity of wildlife which they support. In Coedydd Maentwrog – relict sessile oakwoods which are typical of the uplands – there is a nature trail around Coed Llyn Mair.

Oakwoods provide a very rich environment in which a large number of plants, animals, insects and birds live, some of which only exist on oak trees. More than 300 insects, for example, are associated with the oak tree, more than with any other native British tree and many more than with introduced species.

Green woodland mosses, which like the generally high rainfall and the shade provided by the trees, cover the ground and the bark of many trees. There may be grey lichens on the bark of some trees which are only present where the air is unpolluted. Several types of fern can be seen including the common polypody fern on the branches of some of the trees, a moist surface on which to grow.

Ivy-clad trees provide nesting sites and essential shelter for birds to roost in during the long and cold winter nights. Birds you may see or hear include jays, pied flycatchers in summer, robins, little owls, tawny owls, chaffinches and willow warblers.

Jays, squirrels, mice and voles help oaks spread acorns into clearings by collecting them and burying those surplus to their needs. Many are recovered in the winter but some are overlooked.

You may see the common green-veined white butterfly in clearings and meadows in the wood. Plants typical of woodlands are wood sorrel, bluebell, red campion, moschatel, primrose, dog's mercury, pignut, wood anemone and sweet vernal grass.

Rhododendron – scourge of the Park

The plant we love to hate in Snowdonia is Rhododendron ponticum, and despite years of publicity, it is still difficult to convince many people why it is so undesirable.

R.ponticum was introduced into Britain from the Mediterranean in 1763 and planted as an exotic in its own right, as a root stock for other less hardy ornamental rhododendrons and as pheasant cover. In the large estates and gardens where it mainly grew, there were plenty of gardeners to keep the beast in check. And beast it proved to be.

Each bush produces over a million fertile seeds, which allows the plants to spread quickly in areas of poor acid soils and high rainfall – conditions prevalent on the western seaboard of Britain. (It is the only rhododendron genus in this country to

Intrusive rhododendron

produce fertile seed.) As fortunes declined, gardeners became luxuries, were made redundant, and over the garden wall leaped R.*ponticum*. In its native habitat, R.*ponticum* probably has its own enemies to keep it in check. These were left behind when it was introduced here. It is very poisonous to livestock, and is now considered to be one of the most invasive and undesirable plants in Britain. Why?

A recent survey of the Snowdonia National Park showed that it had colonised huge areas. Where it grows, its dense shadow, together with chemicals produced by its roots, prevents the growth of all other plants. While it produces a dazzling display of colour during its late-spring flowering season, it remains a monotonous ever-green during the rest of the year. Where R.*ponticum* becomes dominant, gone are the glorious deciduous colour changes which grace our countryside.

Once all the other plants have been suppressed, the insects that depend on them for food disappear. So too do all their insect predators and, in turn, their bird predators, and so on up the food chain. Where R.*ponticum* takes a hold, virtually nothing is left. And the stuff is spreading very rapidly in some areas. Farmers are losing hill grazing, foresters are losing timber-growing land, conservationists are losing wildlife and country-lovers are losing landscape diversity and beauty.

Despite a well-attended national conference in Snowdonia in 1987, which showed irrefutably that the spread of R.*ponticum* is not confined to the west coast, almost nothing is being done about it. Though it is a very difficult plant to destroy, herbicides have now been developed which can do the job. A few organisations like the RSPB, the National Trust and the Forestry Commission are doing what they can, but unless a great deal of money is made available, huge areas of Snowdonia and, indeed, the rest of Britain will be inundated. Effective control is labour-intensive and very expensive. But if we truly value our wildlife and landscape, we must tackle this bizarre problem very soon.

Montgomeryshire

The district of Montgomeryshire broadly encompasses the old county of that name with a few additions, stretching from the English border across the Cambrian Mountains to Machynlleth at the head of the Dyfi estuary. It corresponds to the area of the Princes of Powys which was given the title *Powys, paradwys Cymru* (Powys, the paradise of Wales) by the sixth-century poet Llywarch Hen. Approaching Montgomeryshire from the rest of Wales is always spectacular – whether over the Berwyn Mountains from Bala along the B4391 with its scree slopes or along the winding valley of the Ithon from the Heart of Wales or east along the A44 from Aberystwyth, past Plynlimon where both the Rivers Wye and Severn rise. From England changes appear more gradually (except, of course for the Breidden Hills, jutting up like alps on the approach from Shrewsbury on the A458), reflecting the to-and-fro of border fighting and warfare of which this area has seen so much. Roundton Hill, a local nature reserve near Montgomery, is a good vantage point over the Marches.

Montgomeryshire differs from north to south and from east to west in its variety of countryside, wildlife and buildings. The east where the Severn Valley brings the lowlands right up to the Cambrian Mountains was an area famous for its strong oak timber (and its poor building stone) which produced so many timber-framed buildings and characteristic timber belfries. In the west the stone buildings resemble more those of Southern Snowdonia. The east of the area has little villages and the small grassy fields of lowland pastoralism while to the west across the sparsely populated mountains are large expanses of moorland and forestry.

Montgomeryshire has seen its share of industrial change. Canals opened up the countryside to goods from outside. Despite mechanisation the weaving industry saw itself overtaken by the North of England. Railway schemes planned for mid-Wales never came to fruition since they failed to take into account the enormity of the mountains in their path. Newtown has been a 'new town' at least twice in its life.

Some of those who have made their mark in history have lived here: Robert Owen, the Utopian Socialist, David Davies, the engineer, Bishop William Morgan, translator of the Bible, Owain Glyndŵr, fifteenth century Prince of Wales, Ann Griffiths, hymn writer and St Monacella, patron saint of hares. Some of them had a lasting impression and influence on Wales, others made their mark further afield.

Montgomeryshire has many interesting and beautiful places to visit beyond those mentioned here: Berriew with its timber-framed buildings next to the canal, Montgomery which gave its name to the county, Llanbrynmair in the mountains, Llanfyllin on the River Cain, Llanidloes with its market hall and close to Llyn Clywedog, Welshpool, known for Powis Castle, the Monday market and the Welshpool and Llanfair Light Railway.

And its rivers are lovely, among them the Vyrnwy, the Tanat, the Cain, the Rhaeadr and the Severn, in whose valley badgers live.

Llanfyllin

Llanfyllin is a small, compact town of 1,000 people. In the upper reaches of the River Cain, (the 'sparkling' or 'elegant' river), it acts as a natural centre for the beautiful and fairly remote countryside of North Powys.

The town developed from the original llan, established in the sixth century by the Irish St Moling of Ferns on the banks of the river. He is thought to be the first cleric in Britain who baptised by total immersion and apparently spent so much time in the water that he was known as the sant mewn llyn ('the saint in the lake or the water') which nickname in time changed into St Myllin. The recently restored holy well is in a local beauty spot with panoramic views over the town.

Towards the end of the thirteenth century the newly-planned settlement of Llanfyllin was grafted on to the existing church hamlet and in 1293 through Llywelyn ap Gruffydd ap Gwenwynwyn, Lord of Mechain, the town was granted a charter as a borough.

Llanfyllin today has considerable architectural variety and there are many half-timbered farmhouses, especially to the east and south. The High Street dates mostly from the eighteenth and nineteenth centuries. The area has seen much industry and in Rhiwlas Terrace poor timber-framed industrial housing built before 1830 can be seen, originally with two rooms and a ladder by the open fireplace to get to the top room. Maltings thrived and contributed to the town's reputation for making excellent (if rather too strong) ale and thus the saying 'Old ale fills Llanfyllin with young widows.' There were shoemakers, tanneries and also brickworks. Llanfyllin today is noteworthy for the number of buildings made in the local brick, the earliest of which is the battlemented church of St Myllin from about 1706. It is a rare Welsh ecclesiastical example of the eighteenth century classical style and well worth a visit to see the gallery, parish benefaction boards, stained glass and numbered pews.

The Manor House is a beautiful early Georgian house built in 1737 and the Council House (1740), has murals painted by Captain Augerau, one of the Napoleonic prisoners of war billeted in the town from 1812–14. He later returned and married the Rector's daughter. Pendref Congregational Chapel, one of the oldest nonconformist places of worship in Wales, saw the conversion in 1796 of Ann Griffiths (1776–1805), the writer of some of the most moving hymns in the Welsh language. The first chapel built in 1708 was destroyed in 1715 by a Jacobite mob and the second was raised in 1717 with a government grant. The present chapel was built in 1829 with a classical side elevation to the road.

The striking complex of Y Dolydd, outside the town on the Welshpool road, is now an adventure centre. It was built in 1838 as a workhouse for 250 people to serve the Llanfyllin Poor Law Union of 19 parishes. To avoid the cost of reburying vagrants in their native parishes a small cemetery was built nearby in 1842.

Local attractions around Llanfyllin include the fine show of azaleas and rho-dodendrons during May and early June at Bodfach Hall, a mansion since the Middle Ages, the Festival of Music in July and the local Agricultural Show in August.

Pennant Melangell's twelfth- to fifteenth-century church stands on the banks of the upper stretches of the Tanat and houses the shrine of St Monacella, the patron and protector of hares.

Pistyll Rhaeadr waterfall near the border village of Llanrhaeadr-ym-Mochnant is the highest in Wales and one of the Seven Wonders of Wales. The river drops 240 ft / 73 m from the high moors of the Berwyn mountains into a rock basin, then under a natural arch of stone to fall again. George Borrow remarked, 'I never saw water falling so gracefully, so much like thin beautiful threads as here.' Near the base of the falls is a small farm guest house and café and an information board about the falls.

Llangedwyn Mill on the banks of the River Tanat close to the English border, has been restored to form a craft centre of six workshops with café and picnic area.

A railway was built along the Tanat Valley in the nineteenth century carrying farm materials, livestock, passengers, lead and slate from the Llangynog quarries. The aim was eventually to reach the sea at Porthmadog, so giving a through route to Ireland. With the realisation that a long tunnel would be necessary through the Berwyn Mountains in order to reach Bala it faded.

Llyn Vyrnwy, which now covers the old village of Llanwddyn, is a reservoir for Liverpool with a striking late nineteenth century Gothic tower. There is a nature reserve and RSPB Visitor Centre. Another nature reserve is Coed Pendugwm, near Pontrobert, eight acres of mature beech and sessile oak woodland.

After the Vyrnwy has received the waters of the Banwy it flows down the Vale of Meifod meeting its tributaries the Cain and the Tanat before reaching the Severn. Mathrafal Castle, once the seat of the Princes of Powys and now merely earthworks, is set beside the River Banwy with a good view down the valley to beyond Meifod.

The general market in Llanfyllin is held on Thursdays and the livestock market seasonally on Fridays. The Women's Institute co-operative market is held on Saturday mornings in the Institute.

For more information, including accommodation, contact the Wales Tourist Information Centre, High Street, Llanfyllin, Powys SY18 6EF. Telephone (0691-84) 8868 (seasonal).

Llanidloes

Llanidloes, with a population of 2,500 people, lies at the confluence of the Clywedog and Severn rivers, today crossed by the Long Bridge. The original town, including the site of the church, developed near a ford used by ancient trackways. Most of the remainder dates from the 1290s, following the granting of a market charter by Edward I to the client Lord Owain de la Pole of Arwystli. The noteworthy Congregational chapel of Zion occupies one burgage plot of this thirteenth century plan.

The tree-lined streets have a mixture of old and new architecture with Georgian and Victorian terrace houses and some older shop-fronts such as Perllan Dŷ (Orchard House) on the Llangurig road, a half-timbered merchant's house built in the early seventeenth century. In the centre of the town is the half-timbered Market Hall, built around 1600 and the only such building to have survived in Wales. The arcaded lower floor, open to the street, was used for market stalls, and the floor above, now occupied by a local museum, has housed the Assize Court, a Quaker Meeting House, Wesleyan and Baptist chapels, a public libary and a Working Men's Institute.

Llanidloes was famous for its weaving and Welsh flannel but low wages and poor harvests during the early nineteenth century depression encouraged interest in the Chartists' six point plan to improve the state of the workers through electoral reform. When Hetherington, one of the founder members of the Chartist movement toured the mid-Wales flannel towns in 1839 there were riots in Llanidloes, houses were raided and arms stolen. Two hundred special local constables were sworn in and the Home Secretary sent three London policemen. As a consequence the Trewythen Arms was attacked to release prisoners, and in the process the cellars were emptied. Three men were transported to New South Wales. Nowadays Llanidloes is known all over the world for its Laura Ashley clothes shop. The company's first factory is in nearby Carno.

St Idloes' Church, with a typical Montgomeryshire two-stage timber belfry, has a beautiful five-bay Early English nave arcade, removed in 1542 after the Dissolution of the Monasteries from Abbey Cwmhir, 12 miles / 19 km to the south-east. The magnificent hammerbeam roof may have also come from the Abbey, when perhaps the carved gilded angels were added. The original lead flashing on the roof would have been local, perhaps from the Dylife lead-mines, the Bryntail lead-mines (near Clywedog) or the Van lead-mines (in the 1870s one of the most productive mines in Europe). The Van's output was so rich that in 1871 a standard-gauge railway, six miles / 9.6 km long, was built to join the Cambrian main line at Caersws. The manager of this new railway was John Hughes, who under his bardic name of Ceiriog is well-known for the poem 'Myfanwy', now set to music.

Llandinam, a pretty village downstream which has won several Best Kept Village and Wales in Bloom awards, had the mother church (or *clas*) for the area before the building of St Idloes' Church. It was also the home of David Davies, who was greatly involved in the building of railways in mid-Wales and later the highly successful Ocean Collieries, Barry Dock and Railway in South Wales. There is a memorial statue by Alfred Gilbert (also known for the statue of Eros in Piccadilly) to Davies in the village by the A470 roadside.

The massive dam and reservoir of Clywedog, in the foothills of Plynlimon, was begun in 1964 primarily to control the floodwaters of the Severn for the sake of the many large towns on its lower reaches. Some water is provided locally, there is a small amount of electricity generation, and fishing and sailing are available on the beautifully-situated reservoir. At the base of the dam are the remains of the Bryn Tail lead mines and an industrial archaeology trail. To the west is the almost 20 miles^2 / 52 km^2 of the Hafren Forest conifers. Beyond is the isolated settlement of Staylittle, where drovers stayed the night and where there is an early Quaker graveyard.

A few miles west is Llangurig, a good centre for fishing the upper reaches of the River Wye, with a craft centre and a fifteenth century church on the site of a *clas*, rebuilt by Sir George Gilbert Scott and Arthur Baker.

The present-day market hall of Llanidloes is on the ground floor of the Town Hall. Market-day is Saturday.

For more information, including accommodation, contact the Wales Tourist Information Centre, Longbridge Street, Llanidloes, Powys SY18 6EF. Telephone (055-12) 2605 (seasonal).

Machynlleth

Machynlleth is the main town of the Dyfi valley with a population of 2,000 people. It lies at the lowest bridging point of the River Dyfi, surrounded by the mountains of Cader Idris in the north, Aran Fawddwy in the north-east and Plynlimon in the south. The Dyfi Bridge, built in 1805, crosses the salmon river which marks the border between Meirionnydd and Montgomeryshire. Two miles downstream is Derwenlas, Montgomeryshire's only port, from which Corris and Aberllefenni slate and Dylife lead were shipped.

The distinctive hill of Penrallt on the north side of Machynlleth has been used, like many similar up and down the country, for bonfires to celebrate major events.

The town has a T-shaped plan where the east-west road from Newtown meets the north-south Barmouth-Aberystwyth coast road. The site is an old one marked by at least one Bronze Age standing stone, that of Maenllwyd, over five ft / 1.7 m high, which has given its name to a housing estate. The white fragments of stone, which gave the main street of Maengwyn Street its name, can be seen against its wall.

In 1291 a market and fair charter was granted by Edward I to Owain de la Pole, Lord of Powys, and the Wednesday market in Maengwyn Street has taken place ever since. The market now has only street stalls, livestock being sold in the Smithfield.

Most buildings in Machynlleth are Victorian although there are notable exceptions. Plas Machynlleth, formerly the home of the Marquis of Londonderry, was presented to the town in 1948 by the seventh Marquis and now houses offices of Montgomeryshire District Council. The original building dates from 1653 although the present frontage was built in 1853. The decorated Castlereagh Memorial Clock Tower was built by the townspeople in 1873 to celebrate the coming of age of Viscount Castlereagh, the eldest son of the Marquis of Londonderry. In Pentrehedyn Street a terracotta doorway in the shape of a horsehoe was built to show off the smithy for a royal visit by the Prince of Wales in 1896.

The town is the site of Owain Glyndŵr's 1404 Parliament, although it is generally agreed that the Owain Glyndŵr Parliament House was built more recently. This building, made out of small split stones, is a Grade 1 scheduled building, a rare example of a late mediaeval Welsh town house. It adjoins the slate-hung Owain Glyndŵr Institute built in 1911. These buildings form the Owain Glyndŵr Centre which houses the Mid Wales Regional Office of the Wales Tourist Board and its permanent interpretative display of aspects of past and present life in the Dyfi Valley. There is also a range of replica memorial brasses for rubbing.

At the eastern end of Maengwyn Street can be seen the seventeenth century half-timbered Court House of Lordship of Cyfeiliog, built in 1628. The Chest Hospital on the opposite side of the crossroads was originally the Poor Law Union, the workhouse built in 1834. The Graig Congregational Chapel which was founded in 1789 – though this building dates from 1824 – is interesting for its small burial ground, an early example of the establishment of separate burial facilities for non-conformists.

The railway (which arrived in 1863) and its depot became the largest employer in Machynlleth. Now the station buildings are to become the Wales centre for modern art.

Along the A487 to the south is the beautiful Llyfnant Valley which leads the walker to the Gelli cascades and the Cwmrhaeadr waterfalls. Further south are the roadside waterfalls at Furnace, the restored waterwheel and furnace and Artists' Valley, the valley of yet another stream, the Einion. On the coast is the Ynyshir RSPB reserve.

Within easy reach is the Centre for Alternative Technology and its café, three miles to the north at Llwyngwern Quarry. Beyond is the Corris Craft Centre which houses a number of local craft workers and their wares. Further north is Tal-y-llyn with its narrow-gauge railway to Tywyn on the Cardigan Bay coast.

To the east at Penegoes is Felin Crewi water mill, a completely-restored seventeenth century water mill producing wholewheat flour. There are demonstrations of milling and the dressing of mill-stones and a riverside walk, nature trail and cafe. It was here that Richard Wilson, the landscape painter was born in 1714. Beyond, along the mountain road to Dylife lead-mines, is Glaslyn Nature Reserve, 395 acres / 160 ha of unspoilt heather moorland on the Plynlimon uplands, including part of Glaslyn Lake (the bottomless 'blue lake' of legend) and a large spectacular scree-sloped gorge at the bottom of which flows the Afon Dulas.

Market day in Machynlleth is Wednesday. On Thursday there is another market for livestock in Cemmaes Road, further up the Dyfi Valley.

For more information, including accommodation, contact the Wales Tourist Information Centre, Canolfan Owain Glyndŵr, Machynlleth, Powys SY20 8EE. Telephone (0654) 2401.

Newtown

Newtown has become a 'new town' at least twice in its history. In 1279 a market charter for Llanfair Cedewain was granted to the Marcher Lord, Roger de Mortimer, after his successful siege of Llywelyn the Last's Dolforwyn Castle. The name Newtown was used alongside that of Llanfair Cedewain from 1321 until 1832. More recently the town has acquired a new Welsh name, Y Drenewydd, a translation of Newtown.

Newtown's rapid expansion in the early nineteenth century and the development of the flannel industry gave it the nickname the 'Leeds of Wales'. In the industrial quarter of the north bank of the Severn is the Newtown Textile Museum in Commercial Street. It is housed in a building typical of those in which handloom weavers lived and worked.

The tallest building in Newtown is the 1861 Royal Welsh Warehouse of Sir Pryce Pryce-Jones, the first mail-order company in the world, patronised by Queen Victoria and still open to the public.

Robert Owen, the great social reformer and father of trade unionism, was born in Newtown and returned there to die in 1858. His body is buried in the churchyard of the now-ruined St Mary's Church by the river; he is remembered with a statue, bas-relief and Memorial Museum.

The flooding of the Severn is now controlled by the immense Clywedog Dam upstream and by the embankments along the river where there is a pleasant three mile / 4.8 km promenade. A new suspension footbridge leads to the 32 acre / 13 ha public park of Dolerw.

Since 1965 Newtown has been one of the designated towns of Mid Wales Development (a regional aid agency based in the town and funded by central government) and in 1967 was declared a 'New Town' once again. New housing,

civic offices, two new bridges and Theatr Hafren followed, and in twenty years the population doubled to 9,000. The site of Newtown Hall was used for the building of the Town Hall in the mid-60s in the modern Georgian style and also the Davies Memorial Gallery which shows travelling exhibitions. The W H Smith shop has been restored to its 1927 style with one of the few original facades in the country and a museum upstairs.

There are many interesting half-timbered and other buildings such as Maesmawr Hall Hotel, near Caersws, and Gregynog Hall, four miles / 6.4 km to the north, given to the University of Wales by the Davies family of Llandinam and an early example of the use of concrete moulded to imitate timbering. The grounds are occasionally open to the public.

Newtown's street market is held on Tuesday and Saturday, with the livestock market every other Thursday. The Women's Institute co-operative market is on Fridays, Saturdays mornings and, once a month, on Tuesdays at the Market Hall.

Montgomery to the north-east of Newtown is the former county town. It became a chartered borough in 1227, the oldest in Montgomeryshire, and has a long and varied history. The thirteenth century castle was built as a front-line fortress by Henry III and the centre of the town, where the Town Hall and Georgian houses are grouped around a central square with cobbled pavements, has an appearance largely unchanged since the eighteenth century. The market is held on Thursday. The Roundton Hill nature reserve, near Old Churchstoke, gives splendid views across the countryside.

For more information, including accommodation, contact the Wales Tourist Information Centre, Central Car Park, Newtown, Powys SY16 2PW. Telephone (0686) 25580 (seasonal).

Welshpool

Welshpool, with a present-day population of 5,400, occupies a position on the Severn between the Long Mountain and Breidden Hill, rising suddenly in the east from the Shropshire Plain, and the Berwyn foothills to the west. This border area has seen much dispute and warfare. The ridge along the top of the Long Mountain was the main drovers' road to Shrewsbury until the opening of tollgate roads, and was used even then to avoid the tolls. Rodney's Pillar stands on top of Breidden Hill commemorating the victory of Lord Admiral Rodney over the French in 1782. Outside the door of St Mary's Church is the Maen Llog megalith, part of the abbot's throne from the nearby monastery of Strata Marcella; it could originally have been part of a Druidic altar slab.

Welshpool, originally known as Pool, stood at the limits of navigation on the Severn, kept navigable by a massive 44 ft / 13.4 m weir built by the monks of Strata Marcella and finally broken by floodwater in 1881. In 1835 it was renamed Welshpool to distinguish it from Poole in Dorset. Its Welsh name is Y Trallwng, which may describe the boggy, marshy nature of the ground or Llyn Du, a lake in the parkland near the castle.

The town received a market charter in 1263 from Gwenwynwyn, Prince of Powys and has been protected since the thirteenth century by the Princes' Powis Castle (sometimes known as Castell Coch, the Red Castle), the finest and best preserved mediaeval castle in Wales and now in the care of the National Trust.

The origins of the castle are confused. The present building was begun about 1275 by Gwenwynwyn's grandson, Owain, who adopted the Norman surname of de la Pole, and despite many additions and alterations has been continuously occupied for more than 700 years. Most of the castle seen today was built in the early

fourteenth century. During the times of the Princes of Powys it changed hands several times and in 1587 was bought by Sir Edward Herbert. It fell to Parliamentary forces in the Civil War but escaped damage.

The castle contains the finest country collection in Wales with many paintings, tapestries and pieces of period furniture and the Clive Museum. This family cabinet of 'Indian Jewels, Curiosities, Arms, etc' was begun by Robert Clive, 1725–74, the great general and administrator 'Clive of India' and continued by his son Edward, 1754–1839, Governor of Madras. Over 300 objects represent a broad spectrum of the arts of India between 1680 and 1800.

The gardens were laid out formally in four seventeenth century terraces and the parklands were landscaped by Capability Brown in the early nineteenth century. In the grounds there is a Douglas Fir over 160 ft / 48 m high, claimed to be the tallest tree in Britain.

Welshpool has a range of architecture, the oldest of which, half-timbered to Georgian and Regency, is in Mount Street and High Street. One house has a mid-seventeenth century door studded with a pattern of nails reading 'God Damn Old Oliver', referring to Oliver Cromwell and reflecting the owner's support for the Royalist cause during the Civil War. On another a notice says, 'This house was erected by Gilbert and Ann Jones 1692 whose ancestor Roger Jones is said to have been the first Jones.' The same house was lived in during the eighteenth century by the grandfather and father of Robert Owen. There is a restored eighteenth century cockpit, one of few such brick buildings in Wales. The Powysland Museum in the town holds collections of local historical and archaeological interest.

In 1794 the Montgomeryshire branch of the Ellesmere Canal was authorised and today its towpath offers pleasant level walking with much interesting plant and

St Mary's Church, Welshpool

wildlife to observe. The long-distance footpaths of Glyndŵr's Way and the Offa's Dyke Path meet at Hope, below the Long Mountain.

Welshpool has two railways. The Welshpool and Llanfair Light Railway runs for eight miles along the valley of the Banwy to Llanfair Caereinion. It was opened in 1903 and after its closure was eventually bought outright by the Preservation Society in 1973. The Cambrian Railways reached Welshpool in 1862; their headquarters were in the station, once a very impressive building.

Nearby is Severn Farm Pool, a three acre / one ha Montgomeryshire Wildlife Trust nature reserve. It includes a pond, wetland, scrub and mature trees, with bird and bat boxes and a bird observation hide with wheelchair access. The reserve is situated between the Severn Farm industrial estate and the railway line, just off the road to Montgomery.

Cwm y Wydden is another nature reserve, near Dinnant, off the B4390 west of Berriew, itself a village interesting for its half-timbered buildings and topiary. The reserve is a nine acre / 3.6 ha woodland dominated by sessile oak with hazel, hawthorn and occasional holly trees.

One mile north of Welshpool is the Moors Farm Collection of rare breeds of animals and over a hundred varieties of poultry, pheasants and wildfowl. Beyond is the village of Guilsfield whose church has one of the richest mediaeval church interiors in the country.

Welshpool's large livestock and general market is on Mondays and the Women's Institute co-operative market on Saturday mornings in the Market Hall. There is a seasonal livestock market at nearby Llanfair Caereinion on Tuesdays.

For more information, including accommodation, contact the Wales Tourist Information Centre, Vicarage Garden Car Park, Welshpool, Powys SY21 7DD, located in a purpose-built building. Telephone (0938) 2043 / 4038.

Powis Castle

Habitats of plants and animals

The Upper Severn

The Upper Severn is a major feature of Montgomeryshire, the river rising on the flanks of the Plynlimon uplands just inside the border with Dyfed, close to the source of that other great Anglo-Welsh river, the Wye.

By the time it leaves the county at the English border, the Severn is already a large river, having crossed eastern Montgomeryshire and been joined by numerous tributaries, among them the Clywedog, the Rhiw and the beautiful River Vyrnwy.

The wildlife of the Severn valley has adapted to a man-made landscape that ranges from the large conifer plantation of Hafren Forest near the river source, to the intensively-farmed floodplain nearer to the English border. In places a great deal of work has been and is being undertaken to prevent flooding and improve drainage. The variety and quantity of wildlife in a landscape that is attractive but greatly modified by human activity is much reduced.

For all this, the Severn is a beautiful river, with reaches of fast broken water and deep sluggish pools, here shingle banks standing above the river surface and elsewhere soft, undercut sides, all creating distinct habitats for wildlife.

Where the banks are lined by broadleaved trees and woodland the quality of the river is enhanced. Trees such as willow and alder help to stabilise the banks and prevent erosion. They also provide areas for feeding and cover for wildlife, as well as breeding sites. In winter look for parties of tits, particularly long-tailed tits, and finches foraging through the branches.

Where the fields are cultivated right up to the river's edge, accelerated erosion and collapse is a natural consequence. But such places can provide nesting sites for sand martins, which breed in large colonies on several stretches and make a dramatic sight as they search out airborne insects over the river during the summer.

Wildlife along the Severn ranges from the rare to the common, the spectacular to the homely. The source of the river lies in red kite country, mid-Wales being the stronghold of these rare birds of prey. You have a very good chance of seeing them in the Plynlimon area, particularly at the Glaslyn nature reserve owned by the Montgomeryshire Wildlife Trust. Then there are dippers and kingfishers to be seen, even where the river flows through towns. Near Newtown in autumn and winter whooper swans (regular visitors to Montgomeryshire) can be seen in the fields by the river at Penstrowed. And you may see otters throughout the Upper Severn catchment area if you are very lucky.

Roundton Hill

Roundton Hill, near Montgomery, is one of the finest viewpoints in Montgomery-shire, with wide-ranging views over the border country of Wales and Shropshire, where a great sea of fields, hedgerows and woodlands laps to the feet of bare hills. In England, to the east, are the Long Mynd and the Stiperstones and to the west are the town of Montgomery and the Severn valley with the Welsh uplands rising beyond.

Roundton is of volcanic origin and its 1,200 ft / 366 m summit is occupied by an

River Severn at Llandinam

Montgomery

Iron Age hillfort. A range of wildlife is supported here, the habitats including ancient grassland with a wealth of wildflowers. There are also open woodland, scrub, screes and a stream, pond and wet areas.

Roundton Hill is a nature reserve with free public access all year. There is a car park, an information board and leaflets about the reseve.

Whether to see wildlife, enjoy the views or just walk in some fine countryside, Roundton Hill is well worth a visit. Montgomeryshire Wildlife Trust which owns the reserve, is pleased to supply further information on request.

Badgers

The badger (*Meles meles*) is a mainly nocturnal animal which lives in underground setts on hillsides and open woodland. It is heavily built, a male weighing about 22 lbs / 10 kg with a greyish coat and short but very strong legs for burrowing. However, it is the black-and-white striped head which is its most familiar and easily recognisable feature.

Badgers are clean animals and indulge in social activities such as bed-making (replacing used bedding with fresh grass) and grooming. They have very poor eyesight but counter that with excellent senses of smell and hearing.

Gareth Morgan who has spent some interesting summer hours observing one particular sett in Montgomeryshire, says that he was able to recognize the badgers individually: 'Naturally you could pick out the parents first as they were much bigger than the newly-born cubs. But soon they all grew to about the same size, and then you could only recognize them by their behaviour.

They eat a variety of foods: 'Worms are top of the list, but they also eat beetles, grubs and small mammals like moles, hedgehogs and young rabbits. They are not really hunters and will eat carrion. What they also enjoy are wasp grubs; their hair stands on end to stop the wasps stinging them as they dig down into the nest.'

Gareth Morgan also believes that the official campaign against badgers was misguided: 'For a start cyanide gas was not a humane way of killing them and many thousands died agonizing deaths. Secondly, the new method of cage-trapping sometimes traps sows which means cubs starve to death. And thirdly, there is no need for badger control. Between 1974 and 1986 7,000 badgers were killed in the south-west of England to stop the spread of TB from badgers to cattle. Ministry reports now confirm that TB has actually *increased* amongst cattle there, so I think this pointless killing and massive expenditure should stop.'

Canals and railways

The Montgomeryshire Canal

At the end of the eighteenth century the country was gripped by 'canal fever'. Local landowners were as keen to become involved in building canals as building turnpikes. One horse could pull less than a ton by cart on the roads but with a canal boat, 72 ft / 22 m long and 7 ft / 2.1 m wide, could pull 35 tons / 35.6 tonnes. Later competition from the railways and road transport caused a decline in trade and lower profits for the canal companies. One lorry could transport the loads of seven boats.

Today most of the 30 miles / 50 km of the Montgomery Canal towpath can be walked along. It is a corridor for wildlife travelling between fields, woodlands and marshes, and sections of it have been designated as Sites of Special Scientific Interest (SSSI). It is regularly re-stocked with fish for match fishing.

In the 1790s the Ellesmere Canal Company planned a grand scheme of waterways to link the Mersey, Dee and Severn, the key junction of which was to be at Welsh Frankton, near Ellesmere. The Montgomeryshire Canal Company was formed following a meeting at the Royal Oak Hotel in Welshpool in October 1792. Over half the shares were bought by local landowners who were looking for increased returns from the agricultural improvements made possible by the lime brought by canal, as well as any profit on the shares.

The Montgomeryshire Canal Act was passed in 1794 and the canal built between then and 1821. The work was carried out manually by navigators ('navvies') using picks, shovels and wheelbarrows. After the channel was dug it was lined with a bed of puddled clay up to two ft / 0.7 m thick, trampled in by the navvies or sometimes by livestock, to make a watertight lining.

The first section from Welsh Frankton to Llanymynech was built as an extension of the Ellesmere Canal. It was opened in 1796, reaching the valuable limestone at Llanymynech, much in demand as a road material as well as a fertiliser. Tramroads led down from the quarries to the canal. The limestone was carried by canal in its raw state as close as possible to its destination and then burnt, stacked with alternate layers of coal, in canalside kilns as the lime tended to burn the timber of the barges.

Further along the canal there were lime kilns every mile or so serving the large estates of Powis, Glansevern and Vaynor Park. Iron from the Tanat valley and oak timber were also exported from the Llanymynech wharves.

The Eastern Branch was opened in 1797, extending the canal another 16 miles / 25.7 km from Llanymynech through Welshpool to Garthmyl. The Carreghofa Locks were the original junction between the Montgomery Canal and the Ellesmere Canal where tolls were levied. Here a water supply for the locks, which can use 30,000 gallons / 136,400 litres every time a boat goes through, was obtained from the River Tanat.

At Buttington Wharf, to the north of Welshpool, there is a picnic area, a small car park and a bank of three well-preserved lime kilns. The canal's offices were in Canal Yard, Welshpool, near the Severn Street Bridge, and the canalside was lined with wharves for shipping coal, timber, stone and general merchandise. The Limekiln Houses at Belan Locks, south of Welshpool, were built soon after 1800 by the canal company which saw them as a capital asset. They were built to last and lived in by the workers at the limekilns, the busiest on the canal.

The building of the last section from Garthmyl to Newtown was held up by the Napoleonic Wars and so Garthmyl was the terminus for nearly twenty years, developing a number of wharves and lime kilns.

In 1815 a separate company, the Montgomeryshire Canal Company, Western Branch was formed, backed with £50,000 of the money of William Pugh of Brynllywarch, Kerry. (This was one of the first of his investments, which included the building of Newtown Flannel Exchange, power looms and the introduction of gas to the town – and resulted in him dying a poor man in France where he had taken refuge from his creditors.) This seven mile / 11.2 km stretch of the Newtown Extension was completed by 1821 which gave a boost to the expanding Newtown woollen industry.

Newtown became the terminus of the canal and a large canal port developed with wharves, warehouses and canal cottages. In Canal Road, Newtown there is a terrace of double-decker houses built around 1840 for canal workers against a steep hillside above the canal bank. Two-storey cottages face the canal and on top of them is another layer of two-storey cottages which open onto the road. This economical way of housing industrial workers is echoed in the handloom weavers' accommodation shown in the Textile Museum in Commercial Street, not far from the canal basin.

In 1852 the Wolverhampton Swift Packet Boat Co began to operate a service of swift passenger boats from Newtown to the railway at Rednal to connect with the rail service to Liverpool, Chester and Shrewsbury, but this did not last long.

The Montgomeryshire Canal survived until 1936 when a breach in the bank near Welsh Frankton led to its closure and the canal was officially closed to navigation by Act of Parliament in 1944.

Although it is now only partly navigable the canal serves as drainage and as a water supply for commercial and domestic use. Since its closure many road bridges have been flattened, parts have become overgrown and the last few miles into Newtown filled in. However, canal enthusiasts have restored to navigation the 1.5 mile /

2.4 km length through Welshpool and the six mile / 9.7 km Prince of Wales length nearby as well as the Carreghofa and Welsh Frankton locks. Along this the Heulwen / Sunshine boat provides holidays for disabled people. Other trips on the canal are available from Welshpool.

Railways

Like the share-holders in the canal companies, some of those involved in the railways believed that these would eventually connect up across mid-Wales. Their construction, however, did not go smoothly, and there were frequent delays and bankruptcies.

The name of David Davies, Llandinam is connected with the construction of many of the railways in mid-Wales. He liked to be known as 'Top Sawyer', as his Llandinam statue is called. (The man below in the saw-pit would have the sawdust falling on him.) He is famous for building Barry docks which opened in 1889 and could take the largest trading ships to export iron and coal from South Wales. Davies's first contract was to build the railway from Shrewsbury via Newtown and Llanidloes to Llangurig and Aberystwyth. In 1859 the Llanidloes – Newtown railway was the first to be finished in Montgomeryshire and included the railway station at Llandinam, his home village, built about 1856.

The next length to be built was Oswestry – Pool Quay, opened in 1860. This was continued through Llanymynech to Llanfyllin by 1863. By 1881 this station was full of activity associated with the building of the Vyrnwy dam.

The ambitious Manchester and Milford Railway was authorised in 1860 to construct a line from north of Carmarthen to Llanidloes as part of a grand trunk route, between Manchester and the deep-water port of Milford Haven. At the northern end only three miles / 4.8 km were completed from the junction with the Mid-Wales railway, just south of Llanidloes, before money ran out near Llangurig. The southern section made better progress to Strata Florida and then the impossibility of joining the two sections across the Plynlimon massif was realised, despite grandiose plans for extensive tunnels, colossal earthworks and a bridge 240 ft / 73 m high and 170 ft / 52 m in span across the Ystwyth river. (The Berwyn Mountains presented a similar problem to the railway in the Tanat Valley.) The northern section of railway was abandoned and, to salvage something of the scheme, the remaining 27 miles / 43 km were extended westwards to Aberystwyth. Llanidloes Station, an imposing Grade II Georgian-style listed building, was built in 1864 by the Llanidloes and Newtown Railway with the unfulfilled intention of sharing it with the Mid-Wales and Manchester and Milford Haven companies.

In 1863 came the opening of the Newtown – Machynlleth railway via the impressive Talerddig cutting. This is 693 ft / 211 m above sea-level, the highest point on the line, and still in use today. When the 120 ft / 36.6 m cutting was made, sheer through the rock, it was the deepest in the world and led to the discovery of the geological features now known as the Talerddig grits.

The Van railway was opened in 1871, built privately by Earl Vane and David Davies to link the Van lead mines with the main line at Caersws.

The Montgomeryshire Canal Act in 1794 had authorised a mineral railway up to a distance of three miles / 4.8 km away from the canal and such a line had run, pulled by horses, from 1818. The proposal by David Davies for a steam railway in 1864 was opposed by the Earl of Powis and it was not until 1903 that the Welshpool and Llanfair Railway opened carrying passengers, sheep, cattle and goods. In 1931 it closed for passenger traffic and closed altogether in 1956. The Welshpool and Llanfair Light Railway Preservation Company Ltd, however, re-opened its first section in 1963 and the whole line in 1981. Its lovely route along the Banwy valley continues to be very popular.

Despite high hopes the railways did not bring prosperity to Montgomeryshire and mid-Wales: they served to help in the steady depopulation of the countryside after bad harvests and the decline of the local weaving industry. Today, however, it is narrow-gauge trains such as the Welshpool and Llanfair Light Railway which attract many people to the area.

ABOVE
Statue of David Davies, Llandinam

RIGHT
St Mary's Church, Llanfair Caereinion

Wool and the weavers
Remnants of the textile industry

Until the very end of the eighteenth century most carding, spinning and weaving was carried out at home, often by women in the isolated upland cottages and farmhouses of Montgomeryshire. The turnpike roads helped the export of the cloth to England, and Llanbrynmair, for example, was an important centre for its distribution. With the invention of mechanical carding and spinning machinery many small factories were set up, generally family concerns using local wool and powered by water. The first carding factory in this area opened in an old iron forge at Dolobran, near Meifod in 1794, run by the Lloyd family, who founded the bank. Handloom weavers began to move into the towns to be near the source of raw materials and fell under the control of master weavers.

By 1820 most Powys woollen mills were situated beside a river with water-powered carders, spinning mules, and fulling stocks. Most of the small villages had a mill or two but the towns and larger villages became important centres, especially Llanidloes and later Newtown. Between 1801 and 1831 Newtown's population increased rapidly from 990 people to 4,550 with 1,000 more living in the surrounding countryside. There were 1,200 hand-looms in the town and machinery for the flannel industry was made there.

The coming of the canal encouraged the woollen industry's development and by 1825 there was a regular service from Newtown to Manchester which took six days and cost 35p per cwt / 50.8 kg. In the same year the Newtown–Builth road made it possible to send flannel by cart and wagon to South Wales.

The building which now houses the Textile Museum at 5–7 Commercial Street, Newtown was built about 1830 and portrays the type of life lived by handloom weavers. The arrangement is typical of many: the top two floors of the three- to four-storeyed brick warehouses with many windows where the hand-loom weavers worked were usually entered by the outside staircase from below, where they lived. The museum building is six very small back-to-back houses, the top two floors are open from end to end and the looms stand between the casement windows. The collection includes old hand-looms and ancillary equipment, clothing and fabrics, an exhibition telling the story of wool, a fellmonger's, a clogmaker's shop and a collection of old documents and photographs of Newtown.

This kind of accommodation (now often demolished) was built all around the town and was laid out in a regular fashion in the Penygloddfa area of Newtown about 1790. When power looms were eventually introduced in 1850, factories were built near the canal basin, now filled in, on the north bank of the Severn. The canal had been brought to the town by the entrepreneur William Pugh of Brynllywarch (later debt-ridden and exiled) who also built in 1830–32 the Newtown Flannel Exchange (now a cinema and night club). This replaced Welshpool as the chief flannel market in Wales.

Despite the expansion of the industry there were frequent periods of depression, and gardening was an important supplementary source of income. Weavers undercut one another's wages, children undercut adults, and many migrated to Yorkshire, Lancashire, Flintshire and America. Chartism took hold and there was much violence during 1839 in Newtown and Llanidloes, emanating from Mochdre, a fulling and weaving centre a mile from Newtown. Such confrontations between weaver and master did not encourage investment in the Montgomeryshire industry.

The Newtown industry was reluctant to adopt power looms in the 1840s and 1850s. There were four in Newtown, owned by William Pugh, but over 1,000 in Lancashire. Unlike Newtown these were close enough to the coalfields to be run without prohibitive cost. The industry in the north of England prospered using finer wool from Australia and with better communications to the markets, saturated them with cheap flannel, virtually indistinguishable from that of Powys. In the early part of the nineteenth century the threat of competition, especially from Rochdale, was real. Eventually, in the 1850s and 1860s new large mills were built in Newtown but the owners over-committed themselves and the modernisation came too late to save the industry.

In 1859 Sir Pryce Pryce-Jones began the first mail-order business in the world, based entirely on Welsh flannel at Newtown, but the business came too late to help the Montgomeryshire industry and he eventually had to buy Rochdale flannel to redistribute.

From 1861–71 the weaving population halved as people migrated to England and by the end of the century little was left of what had been the centre of the Welsh flannel industry.

Today the Laura Ashley company produces clothing and textiles at Carno, near Newtown, and has started a mail-order service, thus continuing two great Montgomeryshire traditions.

Robert Owen

Robert Owen, the great social planner and factory reformer, was born in Newtown in 1771. His father was an ironmonger and saddler and his mother the daughter of a local farmer. After a short education in the school room in Newtown Hall (owned by the Pryce family) he was apprenticed as a draper and left Newtown at the age of 10 to seek his fortune. Before he was 20 he had become the manager of a huge Manchester cotton mill and at 23 the manager and part-owner of the immense New Lanark Mills, near Glasgow. His pioneering development work here became famous as he established a model industrial village with pleasant working conditions and without sweated child-labour. Good homes were provided cheaply for the workers as well as free medical service, a sick-club, a savings bank and infant education. If the mill had to close down for a few months, full wages were paid and Owen still managed to make a profit.

In 1825 he set up a co-operative settlement at New Harmony in the USA and in 1834 became the leader of the first mass trade union in Britain, the Grand National Consolidated Trades Union. In 1841 be began the development of a new colony at Queenswood in Hampshire. Although the two attempts at social planning were short-lived, in Wales two 'Owenite' communities were set up at Pant Glas, near Dolgellau in 1840 and at Garnllwyd, near Carmarthen in 1847.

Robert Owen was a successful capitalist but he urged comprehensive provision for the poor. He was a Utopian Socialist, the founder of the distributive co-operative movement, a pioneer of factory reform and is sometimes called the 'father of British socialism'. At the end of his life he returned to Newtown where he died on 17 November 1858. He is buried in the churchyard of the old church, St Mary's, in a grave surrounded by Art Nouveau iron railings. The town has honoured him with a statue on the Green, opposite the Post Office in the town centre, and an informative Memorial Museum.

Statue of Robert Owen, Newtown

Did they change Wales forever?

Owain Glyndŵr (c1359–c1415)

Owain Glyndŵr (or Owen Glendower), Shakespeare suggested, was the 'begetter of more ballads and tales perhaps than any other Welshman'. In his day he had a reputation as a wizard and his near-achievement of a united and independent Wales has put him down in the history books as the warrior-statesman of the fifteenth century.

Glyndŵr was a member of the mixed Welsh-English society of the Marches, a direct descendant of the Princes of both Powys and Deheubarth and related to the Tudors. He was sent away to study at the Westminster Inns of Court, he knew the poet Chaucer and probably served with Richard II as a squire. He was one of the few Welsh landowners who held estates from the Crown, two of which were Glyndyfrdwy and Sycharth, to the north-west of Llanfyllin and close to the English border, where the Cynllaith brook meets the Tanat river. It was here that he retired, at about the age of 40, with his wife and maybe nine children, after his military career with the English crown seemed to be over in 1398. This fortified manor house was described by Iolo Goch in a poem of about 1390. It was set on top of the old Norman motte and surrounded by a fine circle of water within an embankment with numerous halls and guest chambers, a chapel, orchards and well-stocked fishponds, a dovecote, peacocks and a herd of fallow deer. There was marvellous entertainment and no-one was turned away, but it was burnt to the ground in 1403 by English forces under Prince Henry, the Royal Deputy in Wales who was to become Henry V.

The end of the fourteenth century was a time of unrest, poverty and hunger for English and Welsh peasants alike. The Black Death in the middle of the century had devastated much of Wales, and landowners had begun to enclose common lands for profitable sheep-farming and to turn out tenant farmers by increasing their rents. In addition the pro-Welsh Richard II was forced to abdicate in 1399 in favour of Henry Bolingbroke (Henry IV) and was never seen again.

In September 1399 Glyndŵr's neighbour, Sir Reginald Grey of Ruthin, stole some of the land of the Glyndyfrdwy estate. Glyndŵr, trained at the Inns of Court, chose to pursue this matter legally but for a number of reasons – including Grey's close friendship with the new king and Glyndŵr's association with the former – his pleas for justice were turned down. Such injury was compounded by the insulting remark which accompanied it, 'What care we for barefoot Welsh dogs?'

The beginning of the new century saw the new king, Henry IV, increasing the taxes on the already over-burdened peasantry, and Grey continued his treacherous behaviour towards Glyndŵr. On 21 September 1400 Glyndŵr attacked Grey to reclaim his territory and attacks on English-held property spread. From the beginning he and his supporters (including his Anglesey cousins, Gwilym and Rhys ap Tudor) harried the English towns and strongholds in guerrilla fashion. Believing most of the English monks to be spies, they even attacked Abbey Cwmhir, despite the fact that the headless body of Llywelyn the Last lay under the altar. High on the slopes of Plynlimon the twin quartz boulders of the Covenant Stones commemorate Glyndŵr's rout of the Flemings in 1401 at Hyddgen. In addition to this destruction, he assumed the title Prince of Wales.

The rebellions were quelled by Prince Henry and the newly-appointed Chief Justice of North Wales, Sir Henry Percy (made known through Shakespeare as Harry Hotspur), an experienced and respected soldier. Pardons were offered to the Tudors but not to Glyndŵr, and his confiscated lands were given to the Earl of Somerset.

At the same time Henry IV passed vicious anti-Welsh legislation through Parliament: no Welsh person was permitted to hold office, to marry an English man or woman, or to live in England. And the damage done to English property in the 1400 rebellion had to be paid for. These measures angered and encouraged the Welsh to even more rebellion and the following two years saw further guerrilla activity and increasingly strong support.

Glyndŵr's growing confidence is shown in a letter: 'We hope to be able to deliver the Welsh People from the captivity of our English enemies who . . . have oppressed us and our ancestors.'

In 1402 Glyndŵr's reputation as a wizard summoned by higher powers grew. The bards believed that the appearance of a brilliant comet told of the liberation of Wales, and English strongholds fell to the rebels in every part of Wales. Henry IV's attempted invasion in September to subdue Glyndŵr was prevented by violent and stormy weather, which confirmed his reputation as 'that great magician, damned Glendower'.

In the spring Glyndŵr captured Lord Grey of Ruthin and held him to ransom for £10,000 (which Parliament eventually chose to pay), and in June 1,000 English were slaughtered at the great battle near Pilleth, Knighton. The Welsh archers in Mortimer's English army appear to have changed sides, as did the captured Mortimer, who had a claim to the throne of England through the Earl of March and no affection for Henry IV. Mortimer was soon married to Jane, one of Glyndŵr's daughters, and his brother-in-law, Hotspur and his father, the Earl of Northumberland, were also prompted to change sides. Even the defeat and death of Hotspur in 1403 at Shrewsbury, as he marched south with his forces from the turbulent Scottish border, did not slow the impetus of the revolt.

In 1403 the conflict spread into south-west Wales and settlers were forced to take shelter within walled towns or castles which were besieged by the Welsh. The administration in the lordships broke down and it became impossible to collect rents. An alliance between the French and the Welsh meant that the south coast and the Channel were under threat.

In 1404 the rebels tried to take the castles of Beaumaris, Caernarfon (held by just 28 men) and Harlech. The 16 men holding Harlech mutinied, and Glyndŵr made it his capital and lodged his family there. After the fall of Aberystwyth and Criccieth Castles, Glyndŵr was able to rule from Caernarfon to Cardigan virtually unchallenged. Representatives were called to a parliament at Machynlleth and in front of envoys from Scotland, France and Castile, Owain Glyndŵr was crowned Prince of Wales at a spot somewhere near the present Parliament Building. Another parliament was later held at Dolgellau.

In 1406 Glyndŵr, Mortimer and the Earl of Northumberland signed the Tripartite Indenture, a pact to defeat the King and divide up England and Wales between them, with Glyndŵr to receive Wales and a large part of England. It was in this year that he sent the famous letter from Pennal to Charles VI, King of France, expressing his wishes for a Welsh church under the leadership of the Archbishop of St David's, free from Canterbury and 'to have two universities or places of general study, namely one in North Wales and the other in South Wales, in cities, towns or places to be hereafter decided and determined by our nuncios or ambassadors for that purpose.'

By the end of 1406 Welsh confidence was declining, and many of the border castles were surrendering through lack of food and perhaps conviction.

The rebellion carried on, but Glyndŵr's allies, Louis of Orleans and Northumberland were killed in 1407 and 1408 respectively, and Aberystwyth was captured. In 1409 Mortimer died, Harlech was taken, and Glyndŵr's wife, two daughters and three grand-daughters were captured and moved to London. Glyndŵr, and his remaining son, Maredudd, were forced into the life of guerrillas on the run, yet England continued to keep troops in North Wales.

From 1412 nothing at all was heard from or of Glyndŵr.

Henry V ascended the throne in 1413 and in July 1415 offered Glyndŵr and the rebels a pardon if they would submit to him. There was no reply.

There are many stories of Glyndŵr, by this time an old man by mediaeval standards, wandering the country alone or with just a few men. Did he take refuge with his daughter Alice and her husband Hugh Scudamore in the secluded manor of Monnington Stradell in the Golden Valley in Herefordshire, or live at Pwlliwrch, Darowen, near Machynlleth? Was he last seen near Valle Crucis Abbey? Here he is said to have met the Abbot, on a morning walk and remarked, 'You are up too early, Abbot.' The Abbot replied, 'No, sire, it is you who are about too soon . . .'

The revolt of Glyndŵr against the English failed, leaving the countryside in ruins, trade badly affected and towns, manors and castles plundered and burnt. Although the dream of an independent Wales was not realized in the fifteenth century, the work of both English and Welsh bards and word of mouth has ensured that the name of Owain Glyndŵr remains part of Welsh culture today. The rebellion of Glyndŵr encouraged self-confidence and a renewed spirit of Welsh nationalism was awakened.

William Morgan and the Welsh Bible

The name of Bishop William Morgan (1545–1604) is known to many throughout Wales as the translator of the Bible into Welsh, yet there is no contemporary portrait of him.

He was born at Tŷ Mawr in the Wybrnant Valley in Gwynedd, the second son of John ap Morgan and his wife, Lowri who were fairly wealthy tenants on the estate of the Wynns of Gwydir, near Llanrwst. His early schooling was probably provided by the Wynn family chaplain at Gwydir and his own family had enough money to afford to pay for a university education. At the age of 20 he went to study at St John's, Cambridge where an uncle was a Fellow.

Soon after graduating in 1568 William Morgan was ordained a priest at Ely and in 1572 was granted a living at Llanbadarn Fawr, near Aberystwyth. He became Vicar of Welshpool in 1575. While studying for further degrees he probably spent most of his time at Cambridge until in 1578 he became Vicar of Llanrhaeadr-ym-Mochnant in the old country of Denbighshire, the parish with which he is usually associated.

Llanrhaeadr-ym-Mochnant is a beautiful village whose name refers to the River Rhaeadr which, at nearby Pistyll Rhaeadr, drops down the highest waterfall in Wales before entering the River Tanat. The church and old vicarage are at the centre of the village with gardens running down to the river. Tradition has it that the Reverend Morgan would walk across the river into Montgomeryshire, climbing through the steep woods from where he could see the church and village. On summer days he would study in a little arbour amongst the woods at Pen-y-Walk. Another activity, with the high level of concern about a possible Spanish invasion, was drilling a 'Home Guard', with the assistance of a veteran soldier who had fought against the Spanish in the Netherlands. About 1578 he married Catherine ferch George from nearby Oswestry, who had already been married and widowed twice. Reverend Morgan suffered many difficulties with his parishioners and in-laws and several law-suits ensued, which makes it all the more surprising that he met the challenge of translating the Bible during his time in Llanrhaeadr-ym-Mochnant.

From 1549 the Book of Common Prayer had been introduced into every church, with instructions from Archbishop Cranmer that it should be read regularly. For the first time in many parts of Wales, English was heard every Sunday. This instruction followed hard on the heels of the 1536 and 1542–43 Acts of Union which forbade the use of Welsh in public life, relegating it to the status of a mere dialect. In 1563, however, after the reign of the Catholic Queen Mary, an Act was passed which, perhaps surprisingly, allowed the translation of the Scriptures and the Book of Common Prayer into Welsh. It also directed that, when complete, these should be used in place of the English versions in areas where Welsh was the everyday language. This Act was probably helped through by Richard Davies, Bishop of St David's and a friend of William Salesbury who had already published an anthology of lessons in the Welsh language.

With the political threat from Spain, a Welsh Bible must have seemed a small price to pay as insurance against the Welsh turning Catholic. In 1567 the Book of Common Prayer and the New Testament translated by Davies and Salesbury were published – unfortunately in a translation which did not flow and which was extremely difficult to read aloud. Davies and Salesbury struggled on with the Old Testament translation but finally gave up.

William Morgan took up the challenge soon after arriving at Llanrhaeadr-ym-Mochnant. He believed, with scholars like Salesbury, that the Welsh people were starved without a knowledge of the Scriptures and that the word of God should be freely available in Welsh. As well as philosophy and divinity his university education had given him a knowledge of Hebrew and Greek, the original languages of the Bible, along with Latin, French, and English. From his Wybrnant days he also had a good command of Welsh and the literary language and metres of the Welsh poets, the form in which he chose to translate.

In 1587 Reverend Morgan had to spend the whole year in London seeing the translation through the press of English printers. Printing was a fairly new art at this time and without such dedication such a major work in Welsh might not have been printed. Luckily Gabriel Goodman of Ruthin, the Dean of Westminster and one of his Cambridge friends, offered him encouragement and hospitality and he stayed at the Deanery beside Westminster Abbey.

The 1588 Bible was welcomed warmly upon publication for its clarity, natural style and consistency. Ieuan Tew from Kidwelly wrote,

'The Great Bible in our tongue
Gives great light like unto the Sun.'

The Morgan translation was in good, poetic Welsh, not too archaic and without colloquial English borrowings. He chose some words from the North (*agoriadau* – keys; *nain* – grandmother) and some from the South (*llaeth* – milk; *gyda* – with), and kept to them consistently. The style was sensitive and flexible and had great dignity.

It drew upon the best traditions of Welsh writing and, in the absence of other literature, came to play a central role as the basis for modern Welsh. Its publication, just as Welsh was beginning to decline in official status and to diverge into different dialects, meant that the reading of the Bible and Book of Common Prayer every Sunday was almost the only link between the different parts of Wales. It was also an encouragement for priests to learn to read and speak good Welsh.

Reverend Morgan re-edited the Book of Common Prayer for re-publication in 1599 and also worked on his New Testament version with which he was not content. Although this was completed for publication in 1603 it was lost when Thomas Salesbury, who was taking it to London, had to escape the plague. In 1620 there was a new edition which took out some colloquial Welsh forms and made the text more consistent with the Authorised Version of the English Bible of 1611. This became the basis for all subsequent Bibles up to the late twentieth century, the first popular edition coming out in 1630.

William Morgan's fame as a translator and preacher spread and he soon became a bishop. Although he was Bishop of Llandaff (1595–1601) and Bishop of St Asaph (1601–04) he died a poor man, with only £110 to his name.

Montgomeryshire villages

Timber-framed houses

Timber-framed buildings are typical of the borderlands of Montgomeryshire and can be found around the Severn Valley as far west as Llanidloes. There are even some unusually westerly examples in the stone-building area of Machynlleth.

Montgomeryshire stone tends to split easily and so, in an area where climate and altitude encouraged good oak, timber was used for construction. It was even used in church belfries as vibration from the bells might have cracked the local stone. Montgomeryshire two-stage timber belfries can be seen at Betws Cedewain, Llanidloes, Kerry, Newtown and Pennant Melangell. A lack of suitable timber towards the end of the eighteenth century led to an increased local use of brick and its more widespread use from about 1825.

Early timber-framed houses were built using crucks, a piece of timber which curved from the ground to the ridge of the house. These were arranged in pairs (cut from the same piece of timber) and crossed at the apex to form forks supporting the ridge-piece. There were usually three or four pairs in a house and they carried the whole weight of the roof. Sometimes the central cruck was carved to form a showpiece. The walls were filled in against the weather with stone, clay or lightweight wattle-and-daub panels. Early houses of this type usually had one large room open all the way to the roof.

Through time these houses, originally owned by the upper classes, were handed down and often ended up as barns. In Montgomeryshire over 53 cruck-built buildings have been discovered, dating from the 1400s to as late as the 1660s. The only aisled-hall house in Montgomeryshire, at Tŷ Mawr, Castle Caereinion, dates from about 1400 and has been recently used as a barn. It has a decorated central arch and an aisle down each side like a church.

A period of affluence, which began around 1550 in England, saw much rebuilding of houses. This stage, which came much later in Wales, took place in Montgomery-shire from 1650 to 1750 with the building of houses rectangular in plan with a box-frame, the form common over much of northern Europe and southern Britain. The earlier examples were usually built at right angles to the contour of the slope.

The Montgomeryshire form of box-frame construction is the generally western type with vertical and horizontal timbers bordering square infill panels with straight-angle diagonal braces to keep the building's corners at right angles. Sometimes there are curved embellishments at the corners of the panels (for example, cusped quatrefoils, forming stars when grouped together, as at Maesmawr Hall, now a hotel, near Caersws) or lozenges (as at Rhyd-y-Carw, Trefeglwys). Sometimes those struts which are secondary to the framework are decorative (for example, the close-studding of closely spaced upright timbers as at Talgarth near Trefeglwys, or carved as at Maesmawr Hall). It became fashionable to blacken the timbers which were originally natural in colour.

Montgomeryshire developed its own regional style of box-frame house with a central chimney stack for two back-to-back fireplaces heating a hall (on the left, the main living room) and a parlour (on the right). Entering the house you find a lobby and the side of the chimney stack ahead. Beyond the hall are the dairy and the larder. On the far side of the chimney are the stairs leading to a similar arrangement of rooms above. In smaller houses these partly occupy the roof space and have dormer windows. Some houses have a jettied first floor overhanging the floor below, probably for visual effect. Examples of this can be found at Rhyd-y-Carw near Trefeglwys, Plasau Duon near Carno, The Vicarage at Berriew and particularly large jetties at Maesmawr Hall. Other improvements include a porch which sometimes has a jettied room above.

There are many interesting examples of timber-framed houses in Montgomery-shire, especially in the Severn Valley. Most are in private ownership but can be viewed from the outside. Examples are in and around Churchstoke, Guilsfield, Welshpool, Castle Caereinion, Berriew, Newtown, Caersws and Trefeglwys in the Severn Valley.

Those at Berriew on both sides of the river were largely restored by the Vaynor Estate around 1880. The Vicarage is the best example, dated 1616 with the initials of the rector, Thomas Kyffin.

However, not all houses are timber-framed as they appear at first glance. Gregynog, now in the ownership of the University of Wales, is made out of concrete, moulded so that strips stand proud and painted black and white. It was built around 1860–70, perhaps by Henry Hanbury Tracy, to show the potential of concrete, the new building material on which he was very keen. After the First World War it was bought from their brother by the Misses Gwendoline and Margaret Davies, the grandchildren of David Davies, who made it an artistic centre for Wales. From 1923 to 1940 the Gregynog Press produced 42 books in limited editions and in 1975 was restarted by the University of Wales. The Davies sisters' remarkable collection of paintings, especially French Impressionists and Post-

Berriew

Impressionists, was left to the National Museum of Wales. Festivals and special services were held in the music room. The house and its traditions were left to the University of Wales in 1960. The Gŵyl Gregynog Festival of Music continues the musical tradition and residential courses are held, surrounded by the lovely wooded park and well-kept gardens.

Llyn Llanwddyn (Lake Vyrnwy)

Whichever route you have travelled, whether you have tested your driving and your nerves by climbing Bwlch-y-Groes or felt the exhilaration of coming over the Aber Hirnant Pass or even negotiated the hairpin bend on the Llanfyllin road, the arrival at Lake Vyrnwy is a complete contrast.

The tranquillity of the scene, especially on a clear, sunny day when the surrounding hills and forests and the imposing tower are reflected perfectly in the calm water, is very soothing. You could be forgiven for believing it had always been so; it seems so natural. Even the stone-masonry dam with its characteristic turrets has mellowed.

Had you arrived a hundred years ago, however, it would have been a very different spectacle. Then, before the reservoir was complete you would have seen the old village of Llanwddyn, two miles up the valley. It was a typical Welsh village of that period with a school, church, two chapels and about 40 houses and cottages. The inhabitants were all Welsh-speaking and were mostly shepherds although there was also a blacksmith, cobbler, miller, seamstress, vicar and schoolteacher. There was a tavern kept by Elen (Tafarn Elen) who used to imitate the whistles of the shepherds, a signal to meet, and get them to come to her tavern and drink her beer. Edward Crydd would play his violin at such gatherings to accompany the dancing

Montgomery: brick buildings with, in the distance, a timber-framed house

and singing, but the chapelgoers of the Methodist Revival frowned on these activities and his violin was bought for 15 shillings (75p) and then destroyed.

Football was a popular sport, not the modern version but the kicking-about of a blown-up pig's bladder. The 'ball' was kicked up and down the valley, usually at night, with anyone joining in. Throwing the 'Maen Gamp', a round stone weighing 75.5 lbs / 34.3 kg was another challenge to strong young men. The stone can be seen in the church today and picking it up is a feat in itself. Tradition says that a local strongman, Llywelyn Fawr o Fawddwy, held the record for the throw at 15 yds / 13.7 m.

Llanwddyn people, it seems, were very superstitious and believed in ghosts. There are many stories of strange experiences. One very troublesome spirit, known as Dic Spot, had been coaxed by a conjuror into a quill feather and laid under a boulder at Pont Cynon. When the dam was built this stone was moved and finally blasted. No local workman would go near it, and it is said that when the dust settled a large frog or toad climbed out and rubbed its eyes sleepily.

This way of life changed with the creation of the reservoir for Liverpool Corporation in the 1880s. All the buildings in the old village were demolished; the cemetery was sealed and the remains removed to a new graveyard by the church, rebuilt and dedicated to St Wddyn. This church has lately been re-roofed and repaired. A new village was built below the dam with masonry to match it. The Methodist Chapel was rebuilt and is now used as the RSPB Visitor Centre. A new school building in Glanrafon served until 1950 when the present school and Community Centre in Abertridwr, lower down the valley, were constructed.

The coming of the reservoir caused a great upheaval in this remote area. The population doubled with the arrival of the workforce: labourers, stonemasons, waggoners, gaffers and engineers. Temporary accommodation had to be found and workers lived in huts which had only the basic amenities and could not have been

Lake Vyrnwy

very comfortable. There is an obelisk overlooking the lake, near the hotel, with the names of those who were killed or died during the building of the dam. One wonders what stories lie untold there.

There were highlights during this time. There was a great meeting when the first foundation stone was laid by the third Earl of Powys on 14 July 1881 and a commemorative slab can be seen at the end of the dam. More great ceremonies followed including a royal visit in 1910 when the Prince of Wales came to inaugurate the completion of the scheme to divert the Marchnant and Cownwy rivers. He planted an oak tree which can be seen near Pont Cynon, at the turning to Tynygarreg Farm. A silver tray which was used to serve the royal breakfast is still in the possession of a local family.

In the ensuing years the community settled down to a fairly regular routine. The men were employed by the Liverpool Corporation in farming, forestry or general work on the estate. There was very little work for the women except at the hotel. After the Second World War when employment was high in Llanwddyn more houses were built at Abertridwr to house the employees and their families. The school and Community Centre were also built at this time. The latter has excellent facilities for recreation and has been a great asset socially with its attractive hall, library, billiard room and use of the school canteen.

With the re-organisation of the water industry in 1974 the Lake Vyrnwy estate fell into the area of the Severn-Trent Water Authority and most of the Llanwddyn undertaking passed to them. In the 1980s there has been a great fall in local employment and as a result the community is ageing with fewer schoolchildren and young people to lead in village life. The development of tourism is a possible employment alternative and the Lake Vyrnwy Hotel has been refurbished attractively and has many sporting facilities. The RSPB reserve brings many hundreds of people to the area and the bird hides, organised walks and exhibitions at the Visitor Centre are very popular. There are two very pleasant caravan parks close by and farm walks and visits are arranged.

Meifod

The River Vyrnwy bends sharply north-east after it leaves the charming village of Pontrobert to flow between the wooded slopes of Broniarth Hill, Gallt yr Ancr and Allt-y-Main and through the wide pastures of the Vale of Meifod. The Vale has been renowned for centuries as a beautiful and holy place, the 'Meifod Vale most fair' of Sion Ysgrifen.

St Gwyddfarch lived as a hermit (or anchorite) on Gallt yr Ancr during the sixth century and the first church built at Meifod was dedicated to him. A second church in the huge churchyard was dedicated to St Tysilio, son of Brochfael the Fanged, Prince of Powys and the third to St Mary. Meifod became the site of a pre-eminent Celtic clas, from which the churches at Llanfair Caereinion, Guilsfield, Pool and Alberbury were founded. It was an especially holy place where the church entertained many bards and travellers. It subsequently belonged to the Cistercian Abbey of Strata Marcella.

The meaning of 'Meifod' is unclear and may be of pre-Christian importance.

There are suggestions that the name means 'lowland pasture dwelling' or 'summer residence'. A story is also told that when the early Christians came to build the church the walls were repeatedly pulled down by an invisible power, accompanied by a voice which cried 'yma y mae i fod' ('it should be here') indicating where the churchyard is today. The voice was believed to be that of St Gwyddfarch and the name Meifod derived from his words.

Mathrafal, close to Meifod, was the seat of the Princes of Powys from the end of the eighth century when they moved from Pengwern (probably Shrewsbury) perhaps because of attacks by Offa, King of Mercia. It remained their seat until Gwenwynwyn moved it to the defended Red Castle, Powis Castle, in the twelfth century. The bard Cynddelw described Meifod and Mathrafal about this time,

'Stately is the holy place by candleshine,
Gracious its men with their long drinking horns of flashing blue.'

The Princes of Powys are buried in the huge nine acre / 3.6 ha churchyard. It is suggested that the intricately-carved cross slab in the church, with Celtic plaits, Norse knots and animals including a running hare, might be the tombstone of

Madog ap Maredudd, Prince of Powys, who died in 1164, although it could date from an earlier time.

Meifod has an interesting lay-out along a wide street which, with its large churchyard, gives it a different feel from other Montgomeryshire villages and dispersed settlements. There are many interesting buildings and delightful footpaths around the area which is rich in religious associations.

Dolobran, hidden away near Pontrobert, has a small Quaker meeting house, built in 1700 but a meeting place for the Friends even before this. William Penn, the founder of Pennsylvania, worshipped and may have preached here and it is still a place of pilgrimage for Quakers.

Pennant Melangell
In the secluded upper reaches of the Tanat Valley beyond Llangynog is to be found the church of Pennant Melangell, dedicated to St Monacella.

St Monacella was a young Irish woman in the early part of the seventh century who had withdrawn to this isolated spot in the manner of mystics of the time. She had been there for perhaps 14 years when one day, as she was praying, Brochfael

Reconstructed shrine of St Monacella, Pennant Melangell

Pennant Melangell Church with BELOW *the fifteenth-century frieze*

Ysgithrog (Brochfael the Fanged), Prince of Powys, went past, hunting hares with his pack of hounds. One of the hares ran to shelter under her skirts and his dogs were mesmerised. When asked who she was the woman replied that she was Monacella, daughter of the King of Ireland from whom she had fled rather than marry the man he had chosen. Brochfael was impressed by the woman's religious devotion and gave her land next to her cell for a sanctuary which became eventually a nunnery.

St Monacella was given power over hares and they accompanied her everywhere, as tame as lambs. In the area they became known as St Monacella's lambs.

The church, with a Montgomeryshire timber belfry, is set in an almost circular churchyard with the high hills of the Berwyn Mountains rising up on both sides of the valley. It is interesting architecturally but its outstanding feature is the shrine of St Monacella, incorporating fragments of the original. In the second half of the twelfth century a Romanesque shrine of red sandstone with a reliquary supported on columns was made for the saint's remains. In the fifteenth century an effigy of the saint was substituted for the shrine as an object of reverence. The fourteenth century effigy of a woman has two hares peeping around the waist of her gown. The shrine was reconstructed in 1958 and is being remounted in 1989. It is the only one of its kind in Britain and is visited by many for prayer, especially on St Monacella's festival day of 27 May.

The fifteenth century rood loft unusually portrayed a frieze of the figures of Brochfael with a horn to his lips, St Monacella with a crozier, the hare and some hounds. It now forms part of the eighteenth century vestry partition. There are also eighteenth century Royal Arms and a benefaction board.

Heart of Wales

Water may seem the unifying factor in the Heart of Wales, occasionally referred to as Wales's best-kept secret. The River Wye, from its source on Plynlimon in the Cambrian Mountains, close to that of the Severn, makes its way through some grand scenery. In these mountains you may see the rare red kite – once common in the big cities of Britain but now confined to Wales – and the buzzard circling and mewing or perching on a fence-post. The mighty reservoirs of the Elan Valley, built by the Victorians to supply Birmingham with water, dam the rivers of the Elan and Claerwen.

The spa towns of Llandrindod, Builth, Llangammarch and Llanwrtyd Wells and other smaller springs were popular for 'taking the waters' in the eighteenth and nineteenth centuries, and Llandrindod's annual Victorian Festival gives an impression of what daily life must have been like then.

The area's rolling hills were crossed by drovers taking their livestock 'on the hoof' from West Wales to sell in English markets. Today these hills and rivers are used by those pursuing a variety of outdoor activities. And the local people's long interest in horses finds expression in the trotting races held in beautiful surroundings.

The turnpike road to Aberystwyth used to make its precipitous way across the Cambrian Mountains from the old county town of Presteigne via Rhayader and Devil's Bridge until a safer way was found from Kington via Rhayader and Ponterwyd. Another track crossing the area belongs to one of Britain's most beautiful railways, the Heart of Wales line, on its way from Shrewsbury to Swansea with many halts and stations en route for the walker and cyclist. One station is at Knighton, the only town on the eighth century Offa's Dyke, which still forms the basis for the boundary with England and now a long-distance footpath from the Severn Estuary to the North Wales coast.

In previous centuries the conjurors (or wizards) of Radnorshire were well-known. Country churches are built on the circular site (or *llan*) of the old Celtic churches which may in turn have occupied earlier sacred sites. Today they may well be surrounded by yew trees many hundreds, if not thousands, of years old. The Heart of Wales also serves as a meeting ground for the people of North and South Wales, especially during the Royal Welsh Show at Llanelwedd, near Builth Wells.

Eighth century coin of Offa, King of Mercia

Builth Wells

Builth Wells, a town of 2,200 people, stands at the meeting-point of half a dozen valley and mountain routes and at the confluence of the River Wye and River Irfon. Builth is an English rendering of *buellt* ('cow-pasture') from its Welsh name of Llanfair ym Muallt, 'St Mary's in the cow-pasture'. The suffix 'Wells' was added when the chalybeate springs began to attract visitors in the eighteenth and nineteenth centuries. In 1691 the town, then consisting of about 80 houses, was destroyed by fire which necessitated much rebuilding, though the architecture today is mostly nineteenth century. The six-arched bridge over the River Wye was originally built in 1779. The former Assembly Rooms and Market House in Castle Street, now the Wyeside Arts Centre, were built in 1875, based roughly on thirteenth and fourteenth century Italian town halls and using stone, terracotta and red tiles.

Only extensive earthworks remain of the castle. It was originally built as a motte and bailey at the end of the eleventh century to command the Lordship of Buallt, and eventually rebuilt by Edward I in 1277 as one of his eight castles to enforce control over the Welsh. It suffered early in the fifteenth century at hands of the supporters of Owain Glyndŵr and was probably destroyed during the reign of Elizabeth I to provide material for new mansions being built in the neighbourhood.

The rivers have good salmon and trout fishing and from Builth to Glasbury the Wye offers sport for canoeists.

The Royal Welsh Show is usually held in the third week of July at the Royal Welsh permanent showground at Llanelwedd.

Wyeside Arts Centre

Four miles / six km west at Cefn-y-Bedd, Cilmeri is a jagged monolith of Caernarfonshire granite, erected in 1956 to mark the place where Llywelyn ap Gruffudd, the grandson of Llywelyn ap Iorwerth, Llywelyn the Great, was killed in 1282. He is also known as *Llywelyn ein Llyw Olaf*, Llywelyn our Last Leader, the last native Prince of Wales. During the Second War of Independence (1282–83) English forces were sent to surprise and capture Llywelyn at his hunting lodge at Aberedw but he hid in a cave amongst the dramatic rock formations near the village. He then tried unsuccessfully to raise support from the townspeople and garrison at Builth.

Leaving to rejoin his followers, tradition tells that he had his horse's shoes reversed, knowing the English were close at hand. Unfortunately the blacksmith was a traitor and Llywelyn, with one companion and almost unarmed, rode into a band of English soldiers on 11 December and was killed by Adam Francton, a common soldier. His head was cut off and sent to Edward at Rhuddlan and thence to London to be exhibited on a stake outside the Tower, following the custom of the time. His body may have been buried at Abbey Cwmhir. Caer Beris Manor at Cilmeri is a large neo-Jacobean timber-framed house, built between 1896 and 1911 on a twelfth century motte, with a replica of the courtyard of an English border counties manor house.

The stock market at Builth Wells is held on Mondays. The Women's Institute co-operative market is from February to December on Friday mornings in the Strand Hall, Council Offices.

For more information, including accommodation, contact the Wales Tourist Information Centre, Groe Car Park, Builth Wells, Powys LD2 3BL. Telephone (0982) 553307 (seasonal).

Groe Park

Knighton

This interesting and charming Welsh border town, at the confluence of the Teme and the Wilcome Brook, has a population of 2,600 people. It is built on the side of a hill (700 ft / 213 m above sea level), commanding the western part of the Teme Valley. In the past it was the scene of much military contention and bloodshed as the gateway between Wales and the fertile lands of Hereford and Worcester to the east. Caer Caradoc, probably named after Caractacus, a British leader who fought against the invading Romans, is three miles / five km to the north-east and the eighth century Offa's Dyke runs through the town, the headquarters for the Offa's Dyke Association.

As the only town on the dyke, Knighton's Welsh name is Trefyclo (or Tref y Clawdd, 'the town on the Dyke'). The derivation of the name Knighton is unclear, perhaps from the Welsh Cnwc-din, 'fort on the hill spur' (there are the remains of two castles in the town) or from the Norman knight, Sir Roger Mortimer or even from 'knights' as used in the mediaeval sense of servants or personal followers of a baron or lord. Knighton is halfway along the Offa's Dyke long-distance footpath and is also at the beginning of another, Glyndŵr's Way. Pilleth, a few miles to the south-west of Knighton, is the site of Owain Glyndŵr's greatest military success against the English, his defeat of Edmund Mortimer in 1402. The trees at Bryn Glas are said to cover the burial place of the fallen.

The town grew rapidly after the building of a Norman motte and bailey castle, and following the granting of the market and fair charters in 1230 soon became one of the borders' major trading centres.

Knighton's sloping, winding streets have historical and architectural interest

including half-timbered houses. In the steep Narrows most buildings date from the seventeenth century but Old House, set back where the Narrows join Broad Street, although disguised by a seventeenth century facade, was originally a cruck-built open hall. The Horse and Jockey in Wylcwm Street is basically a mediaeval stone house. The clock tower dates from 1872. Knighton Church has a timbered belfry, similar to those of Herefordshire, and is the only church in Wales dedicated to St Edward, probably associated with the presentation of Edward's relics to Leominster Priory on its refounding by Henry I. Jacket's Well, less than half a mile from the centre of the town, and the site of a Bronze Age burial ground, is a holy well formerly known as St Edward's Well. 'Jacket' derives from the Welsh word for healing, iachâd, the waters being thought helpful when applied externally to sprains and rheumatism.

There is good fishing on the River Teme. The ridge of Kinsley Wood, in England but clearly visible, has different species of trees to depict E.R. in gold on both sides of the hill, commemorating the coronation of Elizabeth II.

One of the castles destroyed by Owain Glyndŵr was Knucklas, a place where Arthur and Guinevere were reputed to have lived. Some stones from the ruins were used to build the thirteen-arched nineteenth-century castellated viaduct which carries the Heart of Wales railway line (formerly the London and North Western Railway) across the valley. Knighton railway station is in the Victorian Gothic style.

Beguildy in the upper stretches of the Teme Valley was one of the family estates of Dr John Dee (Ieuan Ddu) the famous mathematician, astrologer and magician, tutor to Elizabeth I. He was much respected at court, and Shakespeare probably based Prospero in The Tempest upon him. This part of Radnorshire was famous for wizards (or conjurers) who cured animals and people by spell-casting.

To the south are the small and interesting towns of Presteigne (the former county town of Radnorshire on the River Lugg, once on the main London-west coast coaching route, and with many attractive buildings dating from the fourteenth century) and Kington, and the Hergest Ridge. Stanner Rocks National Nature Reserve is the best example in Britain of a base-rich igneous outcrop with its associated specialised flora. New Radnor is still bounded by the ditch of its mediaeval defences and overshadowed by the earthworks of its vanished castle. Stretching north towards Bleddfa is Radnor Forest, in mediaeval times an area of unenclosed heath and bog country reserved for hunting, now planted with conifers. The waterfall of Water-Break-Its-Neck, spectacular in winter, is to be found here. Casgob Church in its round churchyard is in the Forest, approached by a minor road. In the Old School Gallery at Bleddfa is The Bleddfa Trust, a centre for 'caring' and the arts. Bleddfa means 'the place of the wolf' and is reputed to be where the last wolf in Wales was killed.

Knighton's livestock market is held on Thursday and the May Fair and the Autumn Fair are still held. The Women's Institute co-operative market is held on Saturday mornings in the Cattle Market Canteen.

For more information, including accommodation, contact Offa's Dyke Heritage Centre, West Street, Knighton, Powys LD7 1EW. Telephone (0547) 528753.

Llandrindod Wells

Although there are many older settlements in this area, Llandrindod Wells itself is little more than a century old. At one time it was known as Ffynnon-llwyn y Gog, 'the well in the cuckoo's grove', after one of the springs which was to bring it fame as a spa town. Llandrindod means 'Church of the Trinity', the old parish church on the hill above the town's lake. In the nineteenth century the Archdeacon ordered that this church and that of nearby Cefnllys should be unroofed in order to force people to attend the new town church, a ploy which failed. It was at the old parish church in 1920 that the Welsh bishops elected the first Archbishop of the Church in Wales.

Today Llandrindod's population is 4,200 people. The area's history can be seen in the museum which illustrates life from the time of the Roman settlement at Castell Collen in AD78 (now grassed-over mounds following the last excavation in 1954–55) to the present day, including the town's development as a spa town. There is a reconstruction of a chemist's shop, a Victorian kitchen and a blacksmith's shop, a doll collection, artefacts from the Roman excavation and an impressive (probably mediaeval) dug-out boat found in the River Ithon.

The rediscovery of mineral waters in the mid-eighteenth century and the coming of the railway in 1865 meant that by the 1880s Llandrindod had become a fashionable watering place. Within two decades the town's planners built broad tree-lined streets and spacious squares on the mountain site 700 ft / 213 m above sea level above the River Ithon. The outflow from a marshy hollow was dammed and a fine 14 acre / 5.7 ha boating lake created, a tranquil place with wooded hills on one side and a broad common on the other, where people fish, stroll and feed the ducks.

Llandrindod's Victorian air can be felt today, especially during the festival at the end of summer when the whole town dresses up in Victorian costume and even business continues in Victorian style. The Grand Pavilion and the Grade II listed Albert Hall, a Victorian theatre, hold concerts and other nostalgic entertainments.

In Rock Park, known for its bowling greens, the Pump Room and Pavilion have been restored and the waters can still be taken. The chalybeate spring set in the wall by the Arlais Brook is free. The Automobile Palace, an unusual building with a tiled facade, holds the Tom Norton collection of old bicycles and tricycles. There is also fishing in the Ithon.

Bailey Einon Wood, now a nature reserve, is one of the best examples of the rich lowland Ithon valley forests, situated in the borough of Cefnllys. This has been a local beauty spot since the last century when visitors came to see the original 'shaky bridge'.

Other annual events in Llandrindod include the National Drama competition in late spring, the Welsh Two-Day Motor Cycle Trials in June, the Bowling Tournaments in June and August, the Open Golf Week in June, Trotting Races in August and the local Eisteddfod in October.

There is plenty to visit and explore in the winding country lanes and hills around Llandrindod. To the east, below Llandegley Rocks is the Pales Meeting House, built by the Quakers in 1716. There are other places of religious significance to the north: St Michael's Church at Llanfihangel Helygen with its charming interior of stone-flagged floor, box pews, a three-decker pulpit and whitewashed walls; the ruins of Abbey Cwmhir, founded in 1143 and Llananno Church, beside the River Ithon, with a wonderfully intricate rood screen and loft. To the south, Disserth Church, also in an idyllic situation beside the River Ithon, retains the atmosphere of the seventeenth and eighteenth centuries with a three-decker pulpit and box pews dated from 1666 to 1722, carved or lettered with their owners' names and dates. To the west where four valleys converge at the bridge and ford is Newbridge-on-Wye, formerly part of the drovers' route and once famous for its horse-fair.

Market day in Llandrindod is Friday. The Women's Institute co-operative market is held on Friday mornings at the Railway Station.

For more information, including accommodation, contact the Wales Tourist and Radnor District Council Information Centre, Rock Park Spa, Llandrindod Wells, Powys LD1 6AA. Telephone (0597) 2600.

Llanwrtyd Wells

Llanwrtyd Wells, in the Irfon valley between the Cambrian Mountains and Mynydd Epynt and with a population of 500 people, is officially recorded as the smallest town in Britain.

Its sulphur and chalybeate springs from the surrounding igneous rocks were rediscovered by the Reverend Theophilus Evans in the eighteenth century. When the railway opened in 1868 the town became very popular as a spa, especially for the nonconformist middle classes from South Wales. The Dol-y-Coed Wells in the garden of the hotel can still be visited and the Victoria Wells are being reopened.

Nowadays Llanwrtyd Wells is an outdoor activity resort for pony trekking, riding, walking, fishing, shooting and bird watching. It was a founder centre of the Pony Trekking Society of Wales. A number of major events are held here, including the Man versus Horse competition when athletes compete against horses and riders (and mountain bikers) over a 22 mile / 35 km course, ascending in total 4,000 ft / 1,200 m, over farm tracks, forestry roads and open moorland. There are also the Drovers' Walks (for which drovers' inns en route re-open specially for the day), the Welsh International Four Day Walks and the International Red Dragon Hundred (100 miles / 160 km for horses and riders over difficult terrain). In August the Llanwrtyd Wells and District Show is held and in September the annual Eisteddfod. The 20th November used to see the Hiring Fair (*Ffairbont*) when farmers would hire staff for the following year, settle their accounts and people had a day out. This no longer takes place but the annual Beer Festival continues the tradition.

The parish church has a fine oak statue of St David and a Celtic pillar stone from the seventh to ninth centuries incised with a circled cross divided horizontally. There is also a picture of William Williams, Pantycelyn, writer of many hymns and curate here in the early eighteenth century.

The Cambrian Factory, established in 1918 to give employment to ex-service men and women disabled in the First World War, now employs both ex-service personnel and other disabled people producing Welsh tweed. A tour is available to see each stage of its production: wool sorting, dyeing, carding, spinning, weaving and winding, and there is a shop and café.

There are many places to visit in this area of wild and awe-inspiring scenery. To the north there is no 'A' class road for 30 miles / 48 km and several valleys have been flooded for reservoirs like Llyn Brianne. The road to Abergwesyn follows the narrow valley of the River Irfon between afforested hills. The National Trust-owned Abergwesyn Common is a 12 mile / 19 km stretch of high and beautiful common land, accessible by public footpaths. From Abergwesyn another road runs through the wild valley of Wolf's Leap to climb Devil's Staircase, a 1:4 gradient with sharp bends. This old drovers' road to Tregaron (and on to Cardigan Bay) passes through many miles of unspoilt mountain scenery where red kites and other birds may be seen. To the south is Mynydd Epynt and the Upper Tywi valley.

Market day in Llanwrtyd Wells is on Thursdays (fortnightly and seasonal).

For more information, including accommodation, contact The Bookshop, Llanwrtyd Wells, Powys LD5 4SS. Telephone (0591) 3391.

Rhayader

The market town of Rhayader, with a population of 1,700 people, is noted for its livestock markets and its central position on the A470, midway between North and South Wales. In the past it was an important point on the coach and droving road over the Cambrian Mountains from Aberystwyth via Devil's Bridge, Cwmystwyth and the Elan Valley to England. Today the crossroads is at the clock-tower. The many turnpike gates erected around the crossroads were torn down during the Second Rebecca Rising in 1843. This protest against high toll charges was made by men who dressed in women's clothing and, in a Biblical reference, called themselves 'Rebecca's Daughters'.

The name Rhayader means 'waterfall'. The Welsh name is Rhaeadr Gwy, 'the waterfall on the Wye', which distinguishes it from other waterfalls on other rivers. The small falls in question were largely destroyed when the bridge over the Wye was built in 1780. On the banks of the river is Waun Capel Park, one of the most beautifully situated parks and recreation grounds in Wales. There is trout and salmon fishing on the Wye and its tributary, the Marteg.

From 1893 to 1904 the chain of three large reservoirs was built at Elan and then followed by a fourth on the adjacent Afon Claerwen. Before the reservoirs were built the scenery was considered marvellous by the poet Shelley and his wife Harriet who stayed in a mansion now beneath the waters. The Elan Valley has a visitor centre with exhibitions and other information.

Typical of Cistercian foundations, the ruins of Abbey Cwmhir, built in 1143, are situated in the narrow remote valley of Clywedog, enclosed by magnificent hills and were difficult to reach before the winding road was built. The body of Prince Llywelyn ap Gruffudd is said to have been buried beneath the altar stone in 1282. The Abbey was destroyed in 1401 by Owain Glyndŵr and the damage never fully repaired before the Dissolution of the Monasteries in 1536. The beautifully proportioned arches, windows and pillars were removed to Llanidloes Church.

Rhayader is well-known as a walking and pony-trekking centre. Gigrin Farm, just outside the town along South Street, has a two-mile-long self-guided trail.

The livestock market is on alternate Fridays and the general market on Wednesdays. The Women's Institute co-operative market is held on Wednesday mornings in the foyer of the Community Centre.

For more information, including accommodation, contact Wales Tourist Information Centre, The Old Swan, West Street, Rhayader, Powys LD6 5AB. Telephone (0597) 810591 (seasonal).

Taking the waters

Mineral-rich waters and spas

The mineral-rich waters of this area and their healing powers have been known at least since Roman times. As rainwater penetrates the earth it dissolves the many minerals in the rocks and by a local geological freak brings the water back to the surface in a series of mineral springs. The iron (chalybeate) and sulphur springs (with their characteristic smell of hydrogen sulphide) probably come from water breaking down pyrites (fool's gold). The saline (mainly sodium chloride) springs are perhaps due to salt deposits in the nearby Downtownian rocks, as in the West Midlands.

Spa treatments using the waters were developed during the eighteenth and nineteenth centuries and people in their thousands flocked to the towns. Some claims, such as the ability to cure plague, were exaggerated but others were based on fact.

Sulphur was said to be good for some skin complaints such as eczma, and also for bronchial ailments, gastritus, heartburn and diseases of bladder and kidneys. Taken in conjunction with the saline water, sulphur water was also thought to be beneficial to those complaining of gout and rheumatism. Cook's Typography of Wales warned in 1830, however, that sulphur was a strong purgative and 'should on no account be taken in the afternoon'.

Magnesium was recommended for similar complaints and also for 'diseases of tubercular nature'. Barium chloride was believed to help heart conditions. Chalybeate was prescribed for anaemia and general debility.

There are a number of spa towns in mid-Wales today and in the past there were also several springs of local interest, for example at Garth (magnesium) and Llanbister (sulphur).

It was strongly recommended that taking the waters should be supervised. In 1897 the Llandrindod Wells Guide Book advised,
'From two to six glasses should be taken before breakfast, and perhaps another or more in the forenoon, but not later in the day. Each dose should be followed by active exercise ... It is important that those who come secure experienced advice. Better stay at home than subject one's organisation to the careless use of these waters.'

Llandrindod has a number of different springs, some of which were used by the Romans who knew them as *Balnea Siluria*. In more recent times Mrs Jenkins's saline cure for her daughter's ulcerated head in 1736 became famous and she treated many local people with various ailments. The popularity grew, especially after the *Gentlemen's Magazine* in 1748 published these verses written by a visitor

'Let England boast Bath's crowded springs,
Llandrindod happier, Cambria sings'.

A hotel was built near the parish church and was crowded during the season until it was closed in 1787 by the authorities. This may have been due to local disapproval which saw it as 'a rendezvous chiefly for fashionable gamesters and libertines'. In the 1820s several large boarding-houses were built and Llandrindod's popularity returned.

The second half of the nineteenth century saw the discovery of more springs and wells, coinciding with the arrival of the railway. Pump rooms and bath houses were built, including the Rock Park Hotel and Pump House Hotel (now the offices of the Powys County Council) which supplied magnesium, saline, sulphur and chalybeate water 'with every form of spa treatment, high class accommodation, concerts, entertainments and dramatic attractions.' The waters are available today from the free chalybeate spring and in the Pump Room, restored to its former glory and refurbished in the Edwardian style.

Builth's saline spring was said to have been discovered by a party of mowers in 1830. The Nant yr Halen ('Salt Brook') was soon exploited commercially and two wells were set up at Park Wells and one at Glannau. The saline spring was very strong and had barium and lithium traces. Chalybeate and sulphur waters were also present.

The barium chloride spring at Llangammarch is said to have been discovered one dry summer by a cotter who was out looking for a pig. He saw it welling up from the dry bed of the River Irfon. A well and bath house were constructed; the barium well has been recently rebored to provide a better supply of spa water to the Lake Hotel.

The Reverend Theophilus Evans who suffered from chronic scurvy, a disease almost as bad as leprosy, discovered the sulphurated hydrogen spring at Llanwrtyd in 1732. He had heard of the spring by recommendation and discovered the waters by their strong smell and by 'following his nose'. Until he saw a frog he did not like to try them but then concluded that they 'could not have any poisonous quality'. After two months of treatment his skin disease was completely cured. The spring was originally called Ffynnon Drewllyd ('Stinking Well') but was renamed Dol-y-Coed Well after the spring had been diverted into a well and bath houses built. Another sulphur well was built at Victoria Wells and chalybeate water was also available. It

Hotel Metropole, Llandrindod Wells

was claimed that Llanwrtyd water had the highest sulphur content in Britain and had been famous even in the fourteenth century.

Llangammarch's rare barium chloride spring was renowned for its success in curing heart conditions and rheumatism.

Llandegley's very strong sulphurous spring and its chalybeate spring made it a spa almost as well known as Llandrindod during the second half of the eighteenth century and first half of the nineteenth.

Reservoirs of the Elan Valley

The beautiful valley of Cwm Elan and the splendid surrounding scenery of wooded hills and vast open moorland were popular with tourists long before it was flooded to provide Birmingham with water. When the waters of Caban Coch Reservoir are low, the garden walls of the house of Nantgwyllt can be seen about a mile beyond Garreg Ddu Viaduct. The poet Percy Bysshe Shelley (of whom there is a sculpture, between the river and the Visitor Centre) and his wife Harriet lived there for a short time, and this inspired the novel 'The House Under the Water' by Francis Brett Young. But Birmingham required more clean water for its growing population and new industry, and for improving hygiene to prevent the fatal slum diseases of typhoid and cholera. The existing local supply from nearby rivers was insufficient and of dubious quality.

The catchment area of the Elan and Claerwen rivers had a high rainfall (70 in / 1780 mm a year). Their narrow valleys made the building of dams easier and the impermeable bedrock would retain the stored water well. The area's altitude meant that there was no need to pump the water to far-off Birmingham; it could travel by gravity.

Birmingham Corporation needed a parliamentary Enabling Act before building the dams, as the construction work would destroy the homes and livelihoods of over 400 people, as well as affecting the rights of the people downstream and along the line of the aqueduct. Landowners received compensation but there was none for tenant farmers, smallholders, servants and miners, many of whom emigrated to the colonies. Ironically Rhayader itself was having difficulties with its own water supply and had been given £27 to solve the problem – a small sum beside the £6 million being spent on the Elan reservoirs.

The Act was passed in 1892 and so a whole valley was drowned, complete with 18 farmhouses, a school and a church, and replaced by the chain of lakes nine miles / 14.5 km long which provides Birmingham with its daily water requirement of 75 million gallons / 341 million litres.

Large numbers of workers were employed to build the dams. Itinerant workers were allocated to the huts of the Doss House. If they proved themselves to be healthy and well-behaved they moved into village accommodation. This was of several types, and included housing for married people and a school. Such provision of housing for 1,500 men (and over 50,000 passed through the site) was considered very advanced.

The railway was constructed (33 miles / 118 km of single-gauge track) linking the Mid-Wales line at Rhayader to the work-sites at Elan. From Doss House Junction additional branches zig-zagged down the hills to the base of each dam. The railway took three years to build.

Foundations for the dams were blasted out of the river bed and the massive blocks of the embankments built. Although powerful new machinery was used (such as steam-powered cranes, drills and crushers) much of the work was done manually by skilled and unskilled workers among whom there were many accidents. The Cyclopean masonry was faced by hand with blocks of dressed stone. In 1904 the scheme was officially opened.

After the dams were constructed, Elan Village was built near Caban Coch dam to house people employed to maintain the dams and filter system. As a model village in the fashion of the period no two houses are the same. There are differences in the shape and position of the windows, gables and doorways and Victorian attention to detail and decoration in the finely-finished window-surrounds and stonework.

In 1946 Claerwen reservoir (holding 10,000 million gallons / 45 million litres of water, equal to the combined storage capacity of all three original reservoirs) was built. It was constructed of mass concrete, but faced with gritstone from South Wales and Derbyshire to harmonise with the older dams. Completed in 1952, it is the highest gravity dam in Britain.

The water from the Elan and Claerwen rivers is stored in the four main reservoirs of Claerwen, Craig Goch, Pen y Garreg and Caban Coch which act as storage tanks to top up the supply in Garreg Ddu in times of shortage. This stored water is abstracted at the copper-domed Foel Valve Tower on the Garreg Ddu reservoir, cleaned of peat, bracken and bacteria at the filter beds, and then with chlorine and fluoride added, flows 73 miles / 118 km by gravity to Frankley Reservoir in Birmingham. In order to give the required fall of 169 ft / 52 m for the water to reach Birmingham by

Craig Goch dam, Elan Valley

gravity the outlet for the supply is at the Foel Tower rather than at the lake's outlet which is lower. The Garreg Ddu Reservoir is separated from the Caban Coch reservoir by a unique submerged dam which supports the Garreg Ddu Viaduct on piers. When Caban Coch is full after periods of heavy rain the water flows over the top of the 122 ft / 37 m high dam in a most spectacular fashion. The highest overflow rate yet recorded was in September 1946 when the depth of water on the crest of the dam reached 35.9 in / 91.1 cm, a flow of 196 million gallons / 891 million litres an hour.

Water is released to maintain and regulate the flow in the River Elan. This 'compensation water' (29 million gallons / 132 million litres a day) is also used to power turbines which provide electricity for the water treatment works and the village, any surplus being fed into the National Grid.

The area has been connected with military activity since at least the beginning of the century. In 1904 the area was used for target practice, as it has been more recently. During the First World War large amounts of sphagnum moss were used to treat the wounds of the injured in France. During the Second World War a small coffer dam on Nant y Gro, built originally to provide electricity and water to the Elan Village, proved to be of the same design as the enemy target of the Ruhr Dams. Barnes Wallis used this to calculate the size of the bouncing bomb needed for the 'Dambusters' raid in 1943. Today the area is still used for training marches and for low-flying air exercises.

The ecology of the Elan Valley with its many plants and wildlife draws visitors to this remote area. At one time there was a proposal to extend Craig Goch Reservoir. This would have formed the largest artificial lake in Europe with significant consequences for the ecology but as there seemed no need for so much additional water, the plan was shelved. The Wye Abstraction scheme, however, which takes water from the River Wye at Monmouth for use in South Wales, is supported at times of low water levels by releases from the Elan Reservoirs which make their way via the River Elan to the Wye at Rhayader. The effects of the Elan reservoirs have been felt downstream at Hay-on-Wye where there is no longer such disastrous flooding.

Today the Elan Valley Visitor Centre has been converted from workshops into an exhibition centre, audio-visual theatre, information centre, shop and café to help visitors enjoy their visit to the area. A range of leaflets is available on the wildlife of the area and walking. The lakes can be fished for trout by permit holders.

The Welsh Water Authority runs the management of the estate, reservoirs and dams and the Severn-Trent Water Authority runs the filter beds and the aqueduct.

Toads

Toads (Bufo bufo) can be distinguished from frogs by their rough, warty and rather dry skin and the way in which they walk, with occasional short leaps, rather than leaping long distances like frogs. Their colour is variable and they usually blend in well with their surroundings. Male toads are about 2.5 in / 60 mm long, usually smaller than females which are about 3 in / 75 mm long. They take at least two years to reach sexual maturity, males generally maturing a year before females. They spend most of their time on land but in early spring the Llandrindod toad population converges on Llandrindod Lake to breed from up to half a mile / one kilometre away. On warm spring evenings 6,000 males and 2,000 females make this journey across from the woodlands to the water of the lake.

This 3:1 sex ratio is caused by the earlier sexual maturity of the males together with annual mortality rates. Males compete fiercely to obtain mates, frequently sitting in the middle of the road to get a clear view of approaching females. About 70% of females arriving at the lake are already in the nuptial embrace called amplexus.

Each female lays about 1,500 eggs in long strings of spawn attached to underwater vegetation. About 2.5 million eggs are laid every year in Llandrindod Lake which within two or three weeks develop into tadpoles. After eight to thirteen weeks the tadpoles have lost their tails and have developed limbs. In June and July about 100,000 of these 'hoppers' leave the lake for their home range where they will feed on worms, beetles and spiders. Only about 40% of the eggs originally laid leave as hoppers, for reasons such as fungal attack and predation by water beetles, dragonflies, larvae and ducks.

When road works caused traffic from the A483 to be re-routed around Llandrindod Lake at the time the toads were crossing, toad patrols were set up to stop them being crushed and in this way Llandrindod became known as 'Toad Town' to CB enthusiasts. The several hundred killed on the road prompted a study by the Hereford and Radnor Nature Trust and University of Wales Institute of Science and Technology to find out whether these road casualties would make the toad population extinct. The study found that only 4% of toads die by being run over whereas total casualties from all causes are 50–60%. Nevertheless, warning signs saying 'Migrating Toads Crossing' are erected in the spring to slow down any traffic as the toads cross the road to their spawning sites in the lake.

Wildlife of the River Wye

Plynlimon, the source not only of the Severn, Great Britain's longest river, but also of the Wye, one of its cleanest and most beautiful, is one of the few mountains whose height is easy to remember – 2468 ft (metricate that to 752 m and it's just as easy to forget). But from Plynlimon follow the Wye – which Borrow described as 'the most lovely river, probably, the world can boast of' – to its mouth in the Severn Estuary and none of its 150 miles will be forgettable.

Near its source the infant river runs through such wet ground that it is difficult to distinguish where the river ends and 'dry' land begins. Here the wet conditions have allowed dark oozy peat to form over the last few thousand years, producing an environment as acid as vinegar to which the wildlife has adapted. The sundew seeks its sustenance by attracting insects to the adhesive tentacles on its sticky leaves. Cushions and carpets of spongy bog moss, or sphagnum, scavenge rainwater for every last nutrient and in the process acidify its habitat, keeping less well-adapted plants at bay. The young river is mossy both on its banks and in the water, where the rocks are stable enough to guarantee a future for the plants. Elsewhere clean gravels, pebbles and sand are evidence of the erosive force of this fledgling river which over the last 8,000 years has carried away, as sediment, a thousand million tonnes of Welsh and Border landscape down to the Bristol Channel.

If we leave the open uplands to the meadow pipit, the white-rumped wheatear of the old stone walls, the raven which shares the crags with the peregrine falcon, we reach the river valley. If the valley slopes and the hills above them were covered in heather as they were half a century ago, then certainly grouse, and probably the diminutive, pipit-hunting merlin would both be commoner than they are now.

In the search for fuel, centuries of lead mining have denuded the hill sides of their scrubby sessile oak cover, and much has also fallen to the tanners' barking tools. However, within the Wye catchment such woodlands as remain still act as nesting grounds for that scarce mid-Wales speciality, the red kite. In summer they are alive with insects which in turn attract the best array of birds of any terrestrial habitat in Wales. Nowhere will you see and hear more of the migrant pied flycatcher, redstart and woodwarbler than here in mid-Wales. On the fast-flowing waters of the Upper Wye Valley the high pitched calls of the common sandpiper and dipper carry over the sounds of the stream.

Over the last twenty years whooper and more particularly Bewick swans have taken to wintering in the Wye Valley where it turns east towards Herefordshire. Previously these swans with yellow topped bills had scarcely been seen here for a century.

Less sentiment is often expressed about the fish-eating sawbilled duck, the goosander which in a decade, has taken the mid-Wales rivers, and some say their fish, by storm. But the decline in the fishery cannot be blamed just on the goosander. Commercial exploitation at sea of salmon stocks, disease, and not least the acidification of the rivers by the wastes of civilization, have all been greater influences. In the first half of this century the average weight of a rod-caught salmon in the Wye was over 15 lbs / 6.8 kg. By the mid-1980s it was down to 11.5 lbs / 5.2 kg in this, the finest salmon river in England and Wales. Trout also have declined but there is still a rich variety of river fish to be found including minnow, bullhead, pike, stoneloach, eel, chub, grayling and three species of those most ancient of fishes, the parasitic sea and river lamprey and harmless brook lamprey.

The Wye also has another two species of fish which, like the salmon, enter the river from the sea to spawn. These are the alis and twaite shad which generally reach only as far as Builth where shoals of spawning shad can sometimes be seen from the bridge in early summer. But look as you will, you are unlikely to see the monster sturgeon which occasionally entered the river a century ago. A 7 ft 6 in / 2.3 m long, 131 lb / 59 kg specimen was caught at Boughrood in 1832.

Otters you will be lucky to see because they are scarce, nocturnal fishers; but mink, though smaller and blacker, are far less shy, and are spreading.

Until you reach the vast water-crowfoot beds of Herefordshire no great quantity of plant-life other than moss and algae grow in the river. Downstream from Builth, banks and emergent rocks are decked with wild chives, thought by some to be the original Welsh leek, here at its most abundant. On one car-sized lump of rock grow a few plants of rock cinquefoil, known elsewhere only in the Breiddens in eastern Powys and at one site in Sutherland.

Dykes, roads and tracks

Offa's Dyke

The Dyke was built, it is believed, in the late eighth century on the orders of Offa, the powerful King of Mercia (AD757–796). Mercia lay broadly in the area of the present-day Midlands and had a long border with the lands of the Welsh princes. It is generally agreed that the Dyke was thrown up to mark this border but it may have been either a defensive frontier or just an impressive and undisputed 'boundary fence'. The original length of the Dyke is also unknown. Present-day archaeologists compare their findings and interpretations with the great survey work of Sir Cyril Fox carried out between 1926 and 1931.

Eighty miles / 129 km of the Dyke are clearly visible today. Its line generally follows high and / or west-facing slopes, which may indicate that it was designed as a defence against marauders from what is now Wales. In the eighth century it must have been a very large obstacle. Even today parts of the Dyke, particularly in the Knighton area, are up to 20 ft / 6 m high and difficult to climb, even when undefended. Other stretches have been badly eroded over the last 1,200 years and appear as no more than a hedge bank.

The border between England and Wales roughly follows the line of Offa's Dyke with some sections of the earthwork lying in England and others in Wales. It passes through beautiful countryside and in 1955 was chosen by the National Parks Commission, forerunner of the Countryside Commission, as the basis for one of the new Long-Distance Footpaths. After much planning and negotiation with landowners and others, the Offa's Dyke Path was opened in 1971. It is 168 miles / 270 km long, stretching from Chepstow on the Severn Estuary to Prestatyn on the North Wales coast and walked every year by people from all over the world. Good

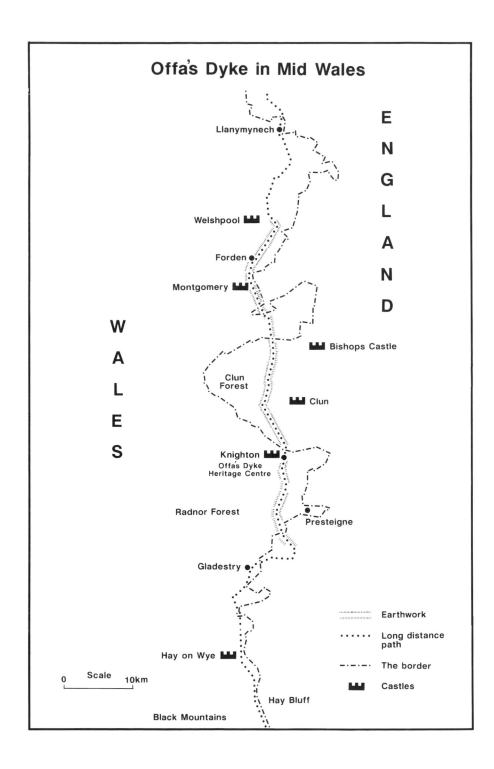

Offa's Dyke in Mid Wales

Llanymynech

E
N
G
L
A
N
D

Welshpool

Forden

Montgomery

Bishops Castle

W
A
L
E
S

Clun
Forest

Clun

Knighton
Offa's Dyke
Heritage Centre

Radnor Forest

Presteigne

Gladestry

Earthwork

Long distance
path

The border

Castles

Scale
0   10km

Hay on Wye

Hay Bluff

Black Mountains

maps are recommended although the path is waymarked with arrows, the Country-side Commission's white acorns and bi-lingual fingerposts stating 'Llwybr Clawdd Offa – Offa's Dyke Path'.

Between Kington in Herefordshire and Llangollen in Clwyd the path follows the earthwork, crossing many hills with fine views into Wales and England. The path passes the door of the Offa's Dyke Association at the Offa's Dyke Heritage Centre in Knighton where there is an exhibition and a section of the earthwork in the adjacent park.

Drovers' roads

In the past animals were reared on the upland pastures of Wales and then transported 'on the hoof' to be fattened on the lowlands in England, close to the markets and slaughterhouses.

Large numbers of cattle and sheep, with some pigs and geese, were purchased at the Welsh spring and autumn fairs, and then assembled at a central point. Cattle had their hooves shod by smiths who moved from fair to fair, and geese were herded through a mixture of sand and tar to harden their feet for the long distances. Pigs were kitted out with leather-soled socks. The drove then moved off and within several days had settled down to a steady two miles / three km an hour. This speed allowed time for grazing along the way but still managed to cover between 15 and 20 miles / 24 and 32 km a day. Welsh Black cattle could be driven for up to 12 hours without losing too much condition, which would have to be recovered in the English pastures.

When the drovers returned they brought back such goods as salt and cloth but also news of the outside world. Before newspapers became readily available this was a valuable service to rural communities.

It takes skill to drive large numbers of animals. The drovers (or porthmyn in Welsh) rode ponies and were helped by dogs (often corgis) to encourage those animals which wanted to dally. The drovers also had to have courage and stamina as the job could be dangerous. There were wolves in the early years (the last in Wales is reputed to have been killed at Bleddfa) as well as cattle rustlers and robbers looking for the cash carried on the way home. Some people travelling to England for employment or education accompanied the drovers for safety. After the Bank of England suspended the redemption of its notes in cash in 1797, during the French Wars, many local banking houses were established, some by drovers. Many crashed during the financial crisis of the 1820s but the Bank of the Black Ox in Llandovery (established in 1799 by David Jones and later taken over by Lloyds) and the Bank of the Black Sheep, Aberystwyth were two which survived.

Drovers also had to be articulate in order to drive a bargain at market and honest enough to bring the proceeds of the sale back to the farmer whose livelihood depended on the drove's success. In Tudor and Stuart times drovers needed to hold a licence, annually renewable at the Quarter Sessions, and be married householders over 30 years of age. There were severe penalties for cattle-stealing and driving livestock on Sundays.

In the eighteenth century a few well-publicised cases of drovers who defaulted on credit notes, gave rise to rumours that they were dishonest rogues. The vast majority were scrupulously honest.

Over the years centuries-old routes along ridgeways and through valleys evolved into a few recognised long-distance droving routes. These can be made out today, perhaps as sunken grass lanes where driven animals were confined to a fairly restricted area or as wide turf tracks where the livestock was less confined. The animals' constant treading has left the tracks still free of bracken today. Characteristic extra-wide grass verges may be noticed where the drovers' roads have developed into modern roads. These routes were also used by the hosiers of Tregaron on their way to the markets in South Wales.

Parts of some routes across mid-Wales can be followed today by car. They are narrow, often single-track with passing places, but have splendid views. From Pontrhydfendigaid, near the ruins of the Cistercian abbey of Strata Florida whose monks were famous for their agricultural success, a road leads north to Devil's Bridge and across the mountains to Rhayader. Also from Strata Florida, and from Tregaron further south, roads lead over the Cambrian Mountains to Abergwesyn and points east. More southerly routes come from Llandovery across Mynydd Epynt, heading for the ford over the Wye at Erwood.

After turnpike roads were set up in the eighteenth century some drovers did use them although the tolls were high. The turnpikes meant they could get their stock to markets more quickly than their competitors and sell it for higher prices.

Drovers needed places to stay overnight and pasture for the droves along the way. Farms supplemented their income by catering for the drovers and there is a legend that food, accommodation and pasture were advertised by planting three Scots pine trees near the farm. Another legend has it that Scots pines were planted by Welsh Jacobites identifying safe houses to those on the run from the authorities.

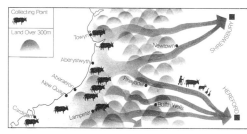

ABOVE
Drovers' roads

RIGHT
Dai Jones of Abergwesyn, drover

The Welsh drovers were known in Midland and Home Counties villages long before the coming of the railways. Their influence can be seen in English placenames with the element 'Welsh' (such as Welsh Road) and corruptions of Welsh names for fields. Similarly place-names associated with London (Llundain in Welsh) and the River Thames can be found in Wales.

By the mid-eighteenth century upwards of 30,000 cattle and very many sheep travelled annually through Herefordshire to south-east England. Droving gradually died out with the coming of the railways in the mid-nineteenth century, although skilled stockmen were still required to move animals carefully around the sidings and trucks. The droving of sheep, however, continued until quite recently within Wales.

Born just after the turn of the century, Dai Jones of Abergwesyn, Brecknockshire is one of the two surviving drovers still living in mid-Wales. He drove sheep to Brecon from the Upper Teifi Valley. With two to four other drovers (and two dogs to help) he would drive up to 1,200 sheep 16 miles / 25 km a day for several days, through all kinds of weather. They stayed overnight at houses and inns along the way and might collect more sheep from farms to take to market.

'It was certainly a hard life, but it was also enjoyable. I was lucky because I had a good pair of boots and a good employer. The late Mr John George was good to us and treated us as men should be treated, plus we always had good food and a good bed waiting for us on the journey.

'Bad weather sometimes delayed us. I remember one Thursday I went on without my leggings, it poured with rain and I got soaked. I went to bed soaking wet, got up and there was a cold white frost outside. It wasn't very pleasant but I was young and I could take it – I never had a cold. By the time I got home on Saturday I was quite dry again.

'There was a lot of robbery in the meantime before the bandits stopped. There was one man though, Edgar Morgan, who had been in the Indian Army for 15 years and he slaughtered a lot of these highway robbers. Luckily they had all gone by the time I started droving'.

Turnpike roads

In the seventeenth century roads were generally poor, unmaintained by the parishes and unsuitable for long-distance travel. The landed classes started to realise that communications had to be improved to develop trade, and a solution was developed when powers of erecting barriers and levying tolls were vested in local bodies called 'Turnpike Trustees'.

Potential trustees had to have an income of at least £80 a year from rents or own real estate worth £2,000. They and other interested people would then advertise in the local press their intention to establish a turnpike and invite interested parties to meet and discuss the matter. If they agreed among themselves they subscribed towards the passage of a private Act through Parliament (which would normally be renewed every 21 years). If successful, the trustees then had to buy land, build toll-houses and appoint surveyors and toll-collectors. The difficulty of financing these initial capital developments and borrowing large sums of money meant that many trusts soon got into difficulty.

In the early years the trustees themselves arranged for the collection of the money but eventually the toll-gates were leased by auction for periods of up to three years. The original toll-houses were flimsy huts or cabins, made out of wood and sometimes mounted on wheels. Later more permanent toll-houses were erected, many like ordinary roadside cottages, although in the nineteenth century some were specially-designed and can be seen in various parts of Wales.

Toll-collectors were not popular. Although some turnpike trusts improved the roads by making diversions round the steepest hills, lessening the gradient and upgrading road surfaces, some trusts did little but collect income. Different tolls were charged for different users of the road and these varied from trust to trust, depending on the extent it was believed that a certain vehicle would damage the surface. Discrimination was particularly hard against narrow-wheeled vehicles, although the narrow-wheeled mail coaches were exempt from toll. Other travellers exempt were military horses, wagons and coaches, travellers to and from church and chapel, funeral corteges, horses going to be shod, livestock going to water, vagrants with passes and citizens going to vote at Parliamentary elections.

Drovers in particular would often try to pass round a gate across unfenced common land. The trustees replied with long wide trenches to prevent them leaving the highway, and chains across any side roads.

An early exemption for vehicles carrying dung, timber and lime for agricultural purposes was discontinued in the first decade of the nineteenth century. This was extremely unpopular as Welsh farmers needed large amounts of lime to neutralise their acid soils. Those near the Cardigan Bay coast managed to avoid the tolls by obtaining it from beachside kilns, such as at Mwnt, which fired limestone landed in the bay.

Dissatisfaction with the turnpike system grew during the 1830s and 1840s in central and south-west Wales. There was a series of poor harvests in the 1840s and the economic depression meant low prices for the crops. This, together with Chartism, the effects of the New Poor Law and Tithe Commutation, increased the rural population's anger and frustration which eventually exploded in the Rebecca Riots of 1843–44.

Rioters disguised in women's clothing and with blackened faces attacked the gates and the toll-keepers, symbols of repression. They called themselves 'Rebecca and her Daughters', taking their name from the Bible where it says in Genesis, 'And they blessed Rebeka, and said unto her, "Thou art our sister, be thou the mother of thousands of millions, and let thy seed possess the gate of those which hate them."'

Rioters also took the opportunity to settle other scores, attacking the property of unpopular magistrates and clergy. Few rioters were arrested but two ringleaders were transported to the colonies for 20 years.

Rhayader, lying at a turnpike crossroads of six routes, experienced several outbreaks of rioting in 1843. The route to Aberystwyth from Presteigne via New Radnor, Cwmystwyth, and Devil's Bridge (to be replaced later by a less precipitous route from Kington via Llangurig and Ponterwyd, the route of the A44), crossed the north-south route here. Travellers could hire post chaises at the Red Lion Inn, Rhayader for these journeys.

A Royal Commission was finally appointed to investigate the situation and made many recommendations. One was to halve the toll on lime, which eased matters slightly.

From the 1850s to 1907 the name of Rebecca and her Daughters was adopted by salmon poachers. They were acting in defiance of the unpopular Fishery Laws which removed local people's right to take and dry salmon for the winter, once part of the staple diet.

The turnpike trusts became increasingly impoverished and in 1841 an Act empowered justices to levy rates in order to relieve them. Gradually, over the next fifty years, the toll-gates disappeared as railways were built and in the late 1880s the County Councils took over responsibility for the roads.

The Heart of Wales line

The Heart of Wales line (also known as the Central Wales line) was completed in 1868 and travels through ever-changing scenery of green hills, lush river valleys and rolling uplands from Shrewsbury to Swansea. The leisurely cross-country railway journey lasts three and a half hours. As well as travelling for short distances up and down the line, you can buy a circular ticket from your starting point and travel out via Shrewsbury and back via Swansea.

Despite being proposed for closure by Richard Marsh, the then Labour transport minister, the Heart of Wales route survived when George Thomas, Secretary of State for Wales, made his celebrated remark, 'But Prime Minister, this railway runs through six marginal constituencies!' The support of the Heart of Wales Travellers Association now assists the line, which acts as a through route from West Wales to the north and is a vital link for dozens of small communities.

At *Craven Arms*, south of Shrewsbury, the line enters the Central Wales single-line section and travels past the villages of the Clun valley described by A E Housman as 'the quietest places under the sun'.

From *Bucknell*, where the station has a splendid triple-gable porch and steeply pitched roof, the railway was originally built as the Knighton Railway.

Knighton is the first and last station in Wales, the River Teme which marks the Welsh border flowing between the station and the town.

The next section of line was called the Central Wales Railway; its company built the impressive *Knucklas Viaduct* with thirteen masonry arches and castellated towers and parapets.

The line then climbs at a gradient of 1:70 with fine views to the highest point on the line, *Llangynllo* summit (980 ft / 298 m). This and the next halt are the most remote along the line: ideally situated for ramblers and cyclists to explore the many country lanes and tracks in this sparsely populated area of rural Radnorshire. Just over three miles / under five km to the north-west of Llangynllo lies Beacon Hill (1796 ft / 547 m) from where the rambler will have outstanding views of the surrounding area. Far down the Lugg valley are communities which depend entirely on the train as their public transport link.

Emerging from the Llangunllo tunnel the line falls with extensive views via *Llanbister Road Halt* (several miles from Llanbister), *Dolau* (on the River Aran) and

Crossgates (on the River Ithon). *Llandrindod Wells* is the principal station on the line. The town really came into its own as a spa town with the coming of the railway in 1865. A recently installed passing loop enables trains to work safely and cheaply on the line which has to be worked economically in order to survive. The stretch beyond Llandrindod Wells was built by the Central Wales Extension Railway.

At *Builth Road* station the traveller may notice the platform of the former low-level Mid Wales railway station which had a connecting lift.

Cilmeri has a granite monument to Prince Llywelyn ap Gruffudd who was killed nearby on 11 December 1282. It is an ideal starting point for walks in isolated surroundings.

Garth is a tiny spa village once known for its magnesium waters, near to Llanelleonfel in whose church Charles Wesley was married.

To the south of *Llangammarch Wells* (in a wooded landscape at the confluence of the Rivers Cammarch and Irfon) and *Llanwrtyd Wells* (beside the River Irfon) lie the military ranges of Mynydd Epynt.

The line then climbs a gradient of 1:80 to pass the Sugar Loaf Halt, a very remote place built to serve a small community of railway men. After going through the Sugar Loaf Tunnel the railway then travels across the *Cynghordy Viaduct* (283 yds / 259 m long, 18 arches with a span of 36 ft / 10.9 m up to 102 ft / 31 m high). *Cynghordy* is an isolated halt ideal for the enthusiastic walker before the railway goes on to *Llandovery* and through the wide valley of the Tywi to *Swansea*.

Llandrindod Wells station on a busy summer Saturday

Country churches

Sacred enclosures and yew trees

Many churches in Wales were originally founded during the fifth and sixth centuries when Christianity was primarily monastic with an emphasis on spartan asceticism. This may account for churches' often isolated position, high in the hills or on the banks of a river. They may even be on the site of an even older religious site. Small burial grounds, enclosed by a circular or oval wall or earthwork, can be seen today in many circular and even raised churchyards. The Welsh word *llan* describes these early religious enclosures and place-names beginning with *llan*, usually followed by the name of a saint, may indicate the very early sites of many existing Welsh churches and religious foundations. In areas like this part of the Welsh March, controlled or influenced by Norman strongholds like Clun and Hereford, dedications were often changed to St Mary and to St Michael.

From the eighth to the ninth centuries the early monasteries began to decline and the more important ones evolved as Celtic mother or *clas* churches. These had a community consisting of an abbot or bishop, priests and hereditary canons. They were centres of scholarship and in turn responsible for a group of daughter or lesser churches.

The circular walls of the llan, often bordered with yew trees, are said to offer no corners for the devil to hide in.

Allen Meredith, who has done much research on all aspects of the yew tree, explains its importance:

'Years ago the yew tree was considered the tree of immortality by the Celtic people and their Druids as it can live for thousands of years by regenerating itself. Records prove that it can stand dormant for many hundreds of years until an aerial branch descends inside the hollow trunk and takes root. People living thousands of years ago would have realised the yew's significance by its ability to resurrect itself from within, from apparent decay and even "death".

'In ancient societies it was used as a form of protection. Neolithic and Celtic people planted it on the northern side of burial mounds to protect the souls of the departed. (The north side was the dark side, the evil side, the side of the devil.) As the yew can regenerate itself when struck by lightning, it must have been taken as a sign from the gods. Even as recently as 1822, the Reverend Bree said, "As long as a yew tree is on that sacred spot it could remain there as long as the world continues," indicating the continued belief in the yew tree's importance and connection with human life.

'There are many old yew trees left in Wales. It is difficult to say which is the oldest but one or two are certainly around 5,000 years old. The tree at Discoed in Radnorshire is around this age and significantly, is on the north side of the churchyard.

'The saints who came over from Brittany appear to have planted yew staves in the ground. At Llanerfyl (Montgomeryshire) St Erfyl was supposed to have planted a staff in the ground and from it grew a yew tree which, if the story is true, would date back some 1,600 years. I have seen the tree which is still there and it is certainly of that age.

'The connection of the robin with the yew could have a practical explanation as robins eat the berries and spread the seed. Grave diggers also see them looking for worms in the churchyard. There is, however, a legend that associates the robin with the crucifixion of Jesus. Apparently the robin was once a plain sparrow but a drop of blood from the Cross dropped onto it, giving it a red breast and so turning it into the robin'.

Circular churchyards around *Builth Wells* are at St Michael, Bryngwyn (in sparsely populated hill country at 1,174 ft), St David, Cregina (in the upper reaches of the River Edw), St David, Glascwm (thought to be a Dewi foundation from the sixth century and a former *clas* church), St David, Rhulen (in a remote hill setting, white-painted and shaped like a hull with outward-leaning walls), St Bridget, Llansantffraed in Elvel (within a smaller near-complete ring of old yews), St Teilo, Llandeilo Graban (high above the Wye), St Matthew, Llanelwedd (overlooking the Wye) and St Mary, Llanfaredd (a small single chamber).

Circular churchyards around *Knighton* are at St Michael, Beguildy (single-chamber and larger than usual in a Radnorshire valley), St Mary Magdalene, Bleddfa (where the tower is built into a mound), St Michael, Casgob, Pentre (the tower is also built into a mound), St Michael, Discoed (with very old yews), St Mary, Kinnerton (a raised churchyard), St Stephen (or the sixth century St Ystyffan), Old Radnor (overlooking the Radnor basin) and St David, Whitton.

Circular churchyards around *Llandrindod Wells* are at St Michael and All Angels, Llanfihangel Rhydithon (a raised churchyard), St Llŷr, Llanyre (a raised churchyard), St Michael, Llanfihangel Nant Melan (with a close ring of large yews), St Cewydd, Disserth (beside the Ithon), St Cynllo, Llanbister (on hilly ground with an unusual layout), St David, Llanddewi Ystradenni and St Tecla, Llandegley (a raised churchyard).

Circular churchyards around *Rhayader* are at St Michael, Llanfihangel Helygen (church on a simple rectangular plan), St Cynllo, Nantmel and St Garmon, St Harmon (the oldest Christian foundation in Radnorshire, founded in the early fifth century and site of a *clas*).

Rood-screens and lofts

Many late-mediaeval carved wooden rood-screens and lofts in England were destroyed during the Reformation but in parts of Wales they have been preserved. This could be due to many churches' isolated position or to the strong Welsh singing tradition.

Rood-screens, sometimes with recesses for carved statues, divide the chancel from the nave of the church. The often intricately-carved and decorated rood-loft is above it, a singing gallery intended to carry a rood (a cross or crucifix), flanked by figures of the Virgin and St John. They appear to have been carved by local craftsmen, who may have also worked for the abbeys, so that each region has its own distinctive characteristics. Those of the Severn Valley are bold and rich for example, and those in the Black Mountains are generally more delicate and restrained.

The most famous screen in the Heart of Wales is that of the fifteenth and sixteenth century at Llananno, near Llandrindod. The beautiful screen and loft, thought at one time to have come from Abbey Cwmhir, is the best example of the work of the imaginative Newtown school of screen carvers. The detail is intricate and exuberant with trails of vines, serpents and pomegranates. The 25 figures on the loft parapet are late-nineteenth century replacements.

Old Radnor church has a splendid late-fifteenth century screen of an English type spanning the whole width of the church. The church also houses the oldest organ case in Great Britain; it is from the sixteenth century with linenfold panelling and Tudor roses.

Detail of rood screen, Llananno Church

Other rood-screens and lofts to be seen are at Aberedw and Cregina, near Builth Wells, at Beguildy, Heyop and Casgob near Knighton, and at Cefnllys and Llandegley near Llandrindod.

In the Brecon Beacons rood-screens and lofts worth seeing are at Llanfilo, the early sixteenth century screens at Llandefalle and Partrishow and the rare fourteenth century screen at Llaneleu. On Cardigan Bay the sixteenth century screen at Llanegryn, near Tywyn, is one of great variety. In Montgomeryshire parts of the screen from the old church of St Mary's are now at St David's, Newtown, and in Montgomery a Welsh screen has been put together with an English one from the Augustinian priory at Chirbury.

Rood-screen and rood-loft at Partrishow

Highlights of the rural calendar

Royal Welsh Show

The Royal Welsh Show, usually held in the third week of July, is one of the cultural highlights of the Welsh summer, sandwiched between the Llangollen International Eisteddfod in early July and the National Eisteddfod in the first week of August.

The four-day show of the Royal Welsh Agricultural Society is held on its permanent site at Llanelwedd, across the River Wye, from Builth Wells. The showground hosts many other events during the year but during July farmers and others can view some of the best livestock animals in Britain, dogs, fur and feather, poultry and pigeons and exhibitions of skill in their handling. There are also demonstrations of rural crafts which have been practised for centuries, machinery, horticulture and forestry, home produce and country pursuits.

Trotting races

Trotting, or harness racing, is a sport in which horses or ponies drawing light gigs or 'sulkies' compete at the trot round an oval track. It has been in existence in Wales for many years and is becoming increasingly popular in Britain and abroad. In America, Australia and New Zealand trotting is as well-established as flat racing is in Britain and is administered under strict rules.

In mid-Wales trotting owes its origins to farmers and tradesmen who made long journeys to market and to outlying farms and villages for which they needed a good trap-horse like the Welsh Cob with its strong legs, natural trotting action and extreme staying power. Over the years a specific type of trotting horse has been developed in different parts of the world. The dominant British breed is the Norfolk Roadster, bred in 1729 from an Arab stallion crossed with a Yorkshire mare. The American trotter originated in the early nineteenth century from thoroughbred and half-bred stocks. Over the years the signs of a good trotter have become a small elegant head, a long back and neck, fine legs, a prominent windpipe and a height of between 14.2 and 15.2 hands. There is an international trade in these horses. Most trotters do not come into racing maturity until they are six or seven years old.

The trotting action is all important as any horse or pony pulling a sulkie with a faster action, such as a gallop, is liable to be dangerous and to overturn its sulkie. Trotting describes both pacing (moving both legs on one side of the body at the same time with a rocking action, also known as ambling) and trotting (a diagonal action with the left front and right rear legs moving forward simultaneously, followed by the right front and left rear legs). Pacers are very marginally faster than trotters. The horses are owned by farmers and local enthusiasts and their riders are usually members or friends of the family, rarely professional drivers. Those owned by hill farmers may be used for shepherding, good exercise for the legs and lungs.

Although at some meetings there is racing of horses under saddle (with a rider), sometimes in mixed races with sulkies and some Galloway racing (ridden galloping races), at the larger meetings all horses are raced in sulkies. This is a light two-wheeled vehicle, formerly made of wood and wickerwork, now of light alloy but otherwise little changed in design. American sulkies have solid alloy wheels whereas in Britain they tend to be spoked, similar to bicycle wheels. Sulkies were introduced in 1829 but in mid-Wales were not adopted until about 1918, traps and other vehicles being used until then. To draw the sulkie horses wear a light harness, pacers wearing a leg harness and head check to discourage them from breaking into a gallop. If horses should break into a gallop they must be pulled back within 20 yds / 18 m or risk disqualification.

At first spontaneous affairs, the races developed into more organised 'matches' on the roads over distances of up to 13 miles / 21 km. The earliest regular race meeting probably took place at Knighton at the beginning of the nineteenth century where there were four different race-tracks. The first of the annual mid-Wales trotting races takes place at one of these, Monaughty Poeth, near Knucklas, just before the Knighton May Fair.

Penybont races have the longest continuous history in Powys, being described as 'old' in 1850, and have attracted some 6,000 spectators. This, in a hamlet of less than a hundred people, gives some idea of trotting's popularity in this part of Wales. The Dol-yr-Ychain racetrack near Pontrhydfendigaid in the upper reaches of the Teifi Valley was the location in 1988 for the first harness racing to be shown live on Welsh television.

The most common distance for racing is the mile. Horses are handicapped for each race on a time basis, the lowest handicapped horses starting a given number of seconds before those with a higher handicap. Prize money is on the increase and there is vigorous on-course betting. Meetings in Wales, held in beautiful natural surroundings, some with the American-style colourful harness, sulkies and razzamatazz, are great social occasions and regularly attract between 1,000 and 3,000 spectators from all walks of life, men and women of all ages.

Birds of Mid Wales

The red kite

The magnificent red kite is the only British bird found solely in Wales. Although still common in parts of Europe notably Germany and Spain, it has declined through much of north-west Europe and Britain during the last two or three centuries. Up to the middle of the eighteenth century, red kites hunted over most of Britain, even scavenging on the streets of London. Persecution by shooters and egg collectors caused the population to dwindle so that by the turn of the century, it was restricted to perhaps a dozen birds in the hills of mid-Wales. Here a tiny population has held on despite continued pressure from unscrupulous egg collectors.

The guarding of nests by a determined and dedicated band of birdwatchers early this century and before and after the World Wars helped ensure the kites' survival in Wales. The Royal Society for the Protection of Birds, the Nature Conservancy Council and keen kite supporters now form the Kite Committee which organises nest protection, research and monitoring. Due to the efforts of many people, not least the sympathetic landowners on whose land the kites nest, the mere handful of birds in 1900 has increased to at least 150 individuals, with forty or more pairs now attempting to breed each year. Sadly many are unsuccessful, kites being very prone to disturbance and to the vagaries of weather. However, about forty young were reared in both 1987 and 1988.

The red kite is unmistakeable. It has long, angled wings, a long, deeply-forked tail and in good light, the striking reddish-brown colour of the body and tail is very evident. The wings have black tips and a pale patch close to the tips.

It is a beautiful and spectacular bird, circling, gliding and soaring effortlessly,

Red kite, Milvus milvus

steering with its long tail. In spring kites may indulge in aerobatics in their courtship displays. When feeding with crows, buzzards and other birds at carrion or at a refuse tip, they show best their aerial skills. They dive, twist and swoop, snatching morsels from other birds or chasing them to make them drop their prey in piratical fashion.

Apart from carrion and slaughterhouse offal, red kites feed on rodents and other small mammals, birds, frogs and even fish, as well as worms and insects.

In the spring, each pair of kites establishes a territory. This must include a suitable wood for the nest site, usually a hanging oakwood, and sufficient open hill and valley fields for the pair to find food for their brood. Kites build a bulky stick nest lined with mud, sheepswool, hair and rubbish such as paper and polythene bags. In April or early May they lay two to three eggs which the female incubates for over four weeks. The nestlings fly after about seven weeks.

Red kites in Wales are largely sedentary, unlike their European relatives which migrate south each autumn. Young Welsh birds do however, wander into England with occasional birds spotted from Northumberland to Cornwall. Although for much of the year birds tend to live alone or in pairs, kites congregate at good food sources and when roosting, up to fifty birds may gather together during the winter. This is a spectacular sight.

The buzzard

Mid-Wales is very much a stronghold for the buzzard (boncath in Welsh). Although it is widespread throughout Wales from the wooded rolling country of Gwent across to Pembrokeshire and up through central Wales and the Borders to Gwynedd, nowhere is it more common than in mid-Wales. Here a mosaic of open hills, valleys and wooded areas provides ideal nesting and feeding habitat.

Sadly persecution by gamekeepers still continues, and illegal shooting, trapping and poisoning may explain why this large bird of prey does not expand into England.

The buzzard is readily identified in flight by its broad, rounded wings and by its broad, short, often fanned tail. It may be seen soaring and gliding, occasionally hovering into the wind in the manner of a kestrel, all the time scanning the ground below for prey. Sometimes a buzzard may be spotted perched up on a telegraph post or perhaps on a fence post by the roadside when its plumage is more readily visible. Birds may vary greatly from dark-brown individuals to those with much white in their plumage, especially on the underside. Their feet are yellow as is the cere, the skin at the base of the dark bill.

The prey of buzzards is very varied. It includes small mammals such as rodents and rabbits, birds and even lizards and snakes. In spring, frogs are a favourite food,

Common buzzard, Buteo buteo

along with worms and other invertebrates, carrion, particularly dead sheep, also attracts them; and in winter, when they feed on lower ground, they may gather at slaughterhouses for a free meal.

Superb aerial displays, sometimes involving up to eight birds, occur from mid-February. Soon the pair constructs its large stick nest high in a tree or sometimes on a cliff ledge. The nest is 'decorated' with leafy green twigs or seaweed. The clutch of two or three eggs, occasionally up to six, is laid during April and after a long incubation of four to five weeks, the chicks emerge. These remain in the nest for about six weeks, with both parents bringing them food. For a month after leaving the nest, they still depend on their parents. By the autumn the family breaks up, the adults remaining on their breeding territory and the young dispersing to find a nearby empty territory. Buzzards may live for twenty or more years.

Few sounds can be more typical of the Welsh hills than the plaintive mewing made by buzzards in the spring. Similarly, the sight of a buzzard being mobbed by other birds, particularly crows, is commonplace when you are walking in mid-Wales. Usually the buzzard flaps steadily on, ignoring the attacks. If it is pestered too much it may turn over in flight and extend its talons towards its persecutors. Although the buzzard is our commonest bird of prey, it is well worth a second glance.

Brecon Beacons

The Brecon Beacons take their name from the peaks at their centre; the highest, Pen-y-Fan, in the care of the National Trust, rises to 2907 ft / 886 m. This forty-mile-long range includes the highest mountains in South Wales and is formed of four mountain blocks: the Black Mountain in the west, Fforest Fawr, the central Brecon Beacons and the Black Mountains in the east. We follow the normal practice in referring to all of the mountains as the 'Beacons' and to the specific mountain block as the Central Brecon Beacons. In general, those parts which lie outside the Borough of Brecknock (the Black Mountain, Abergavenny and Merthyr Tydfil, for example) are not included in any detail. Llandovery is an exception because of its strategic position between the Beacons and the Teifi Valley.

Old Red Sandstone rocks form an east-west 'backbone' of high ground across the Beacons from the English border. This is deeply cut by the broad and fertile valley of the Usk between Brecon and Crickhowell, followed by the Monmouthshire and Brecon Canal. The Old Red Sandstone outcrops in horizontal beds and provides a purple-grey material for local buildings. Along the southern edge of the Beacons there are narrow bands of Carboniferous Limestone and Millstone Grit which produce dramatically different scenery, with remarkable cave systems and fine waterfalls. Brecon water is amongst the purest natural low-mineral waters derived from ecologically protected sources. Glaciers have also played their part in sculpturing the landscape. Mynydd Epynt to the north of the Beacons is smooth, barren and remote. The military range there means that this area is often out-of-bounds with red flags flying. The Beacons abound with other activities: gliding, canal and river boating, walking, pony trekking, fishing. Scenic mountain roads offer an interesting challenge to motorists and cyclists.

The towns and villages are historic and charming. Brecon is an ancient town with an imposing cathedral. Crickhowell and its ruined castle lie below the limestone peak of Pen Cerrig Calch, the only such peak in the Beacons. Hay-on-Wye is well-known as the capital of the second-hand book trade. Llandovery was formerly a cattle-droving centre where David Jones set up an early bank, the Bank of the Black Ox. Talgarth is situated where old routes converge in the good agricultural tract of the gap between Usk and Wye.

Small fields, hedgerows and walls are characteristic of the Beacons; forestry and reservoirs also make their mark on the landscape.

Standing stones, stone circles and ruined castles are just part of the historical interest of the Beacons. Rural mid-Wales changes abruptly to industrial South Wales along their southern boundary. The Beacons' raw materials of iron ore, limestone, wood supplies and water played a key part in the development of industry between the sixteenth and nineteenth centuries and the reservoirs continue to supply the urban areas. Limestone was also quarried and burnt for use as a fertiliser, carried with other materials by the Monmouthshire and Brecon Canal. The Brecon Mountain Railway follows part of the route of the scenic Merthyr Tydfil-Brecon line, closed in 1962, 99 years after opening.

Brecon

Modern Brecon with a population of 7,470 people has an even longer history than its busy market, passageways, narrow streets and pleasant Georgian and Jacobean shop-fronts might suggest. It lies at the confluence of the Usk and the Honddu rivers at a strategic point. There is some protection from the gales between the Beacons and Mynydd Epynt and so it has been a good place of settlement for many centuries. This is reflected in its Welsh name *Aberhonddu*, place at the mouth of the Honddu, *honddu* meaning pleasant or easy. Brecon derives from the personal name Brychan, that of a fifth century prince of Irish descent with many sons and daughters. One of these was the martyr Tydfil whose name is commemorated in the placename Merthyr Tydfil.

The Iron Age hillfort of Pen y Crug overlooks the town. The Romans built one of the largest and most important forts in the Wales network at Y Gaer, two and a half miles / four km to the west at the confluence of the Rivers Usk and Yscir. From AD75 to 100 it was garrisoned by a 500-strong Spanish cavalry regiment but now only stone gateways in the east, south and west remain to the eye of the untrained observer.

In 1094 Brecon was captured by Bernard de Neufmarché, a half-brother of William the Conqueror. He was granted numerous rights as Lord of Brecon in return but felt the need to build a heavily fortified castle, now adjoined by the Castle Hotel and which can be seen from the grounds. Bernard then sent masons to build a Benedictine priory of which Giraldus Cambrensis was archdeacon in 1188 when he travelled through Wales with Archbishop Baldwin. The priory was developed in the thirteenth and fourteenth centuries into the fortified Priory Church of St John

Brecknock Museum

the Evangelist, 'half church of God and half castle against the Welsh', standing high above the River Honddu on the northern outskirts of the town. In 1923 it became the cathedral of the newly created Diocese of Swansea and Brecon. Outside the cathedral within embattled walls is the most complete group of monastic buildings in Wales. There is a pleasant walk along the banks of the Honddu past the cathedral.

Around the castle and the priory the walled town of Brecon grew up, an important seat of power in the Middle Ages. In the eighteenth century it became a fashionable place to winter for the rich. There is a charming and elegant theatre in the Guildhall, as befits the birthplace of the famous actress Sarah Siddons, who was born in an inn in the town in 1775.

Parts of the mediaeval town walls can be seen at Captain's Walk, named after the Napoleonic prisoners of war who used to exercise there. Nearby in a building resembling a neo-Grecian temple is the Brecknock Museum with its excellent displays of local history, including an Edwardian gentleman-naturalist's study and a fine collection of lovespoons.

Brecon has continued to be linked with military activity over the years. The regimental museum of the South Wales Borderers includes a commemoration of the 1879 Zulu War and the Battle of Rorke's Drift which involved 140 Welsh soldiers and 4,000 Zulu warriors.

The Monmouth and Brecon Canal which was begun in 1797 to form a link with Newport starts in the town and today it is possible to navigate as far as Pontymoile near Pontypool. Not far outside Brecon, a mile north of Llanfrynach, there is a fine stone aqueduct carrying the canal over the River Usk on its way through the Vale of

Usk. Boating is also available in the town. Llangorse Lake with its many watersports is within easy reach.

There are a number of interesting churches near Brecon such as Llanfeugan Church with huge old yew trees in the churchyard and Llanddew, originally a *clas* or Celtic religious community.

The area offers a variety of wonderful walking. More information about the National Park can be found at the Brecon Beacons Mountain Centre at Libanus on the A470 south-west of the town. Mynydd Illtud common behind the centre has gentle walking with views of Pen y Fan which may beckon the hardier.

Further south just off the A470 north of Merthyr Tydfil is the Garw Nant Forest Centre complete with adventure area for children. The Brecon Mountain Railway starts its four-mile / 6.4 km trip into the National Park from Dowlais, also near Merthyr.

Brecon market is on Tuesday and Friday and the Women's Institute co-operative market is held on Friday mornings from February to December in the Market Hall.

For more information, including accommodation, contact the Wales Tourist Information Centre, Market Car Park, Brecon, Powys.
Telephone (0874) 2485 or 5692 (seasonal).

Brecon Beacons National Park Information Centre, Watton Mount, Brecon, Powys LD3 7DF (seasonal).

Brecon Beacons National Park Information Centre, The Mountain Centre, Libanus, Brecon, Powys LD3 8ER. Telephone (0874) 3366.

Crickhowell

Crickhowell, a charming town with a population of 2,010 people, is named after the Iron Age hillfort of Crug Hywel which lies at the end of the ridge above the town, otherwise aptly known as Table Mountain. Pen Cerrig Calch (2,302 ft / 701 m) is the only limestone summit in an area dominated by sandstone mountains. The town lies in the valley of the Usk and has a long history. The Neolithic Gwernvale long cairn was excavated to show a four chambered tomb and can be seen from the roadside on the outskirts of town. There is a ruined castle of which only the mound and two broken towers remain, in a large public park, scene of a leek-throwing competition in May. The Bear Hotel is an old coaching inn with a cobbled courtyard through the entrance arch. Sir George Everest, after whom the Himalayan mountain was named, was born here in 1790 at Gwernvale Manor.

In August there is a tug-of-war across the Usk, crossed also by a seventeenth century bridge with thirteen arches. Fine fishing and pony trekking are available in the area. The general market is on Thursdays.

There are many places to explore round and about Crickhowell. Llangynidr village map, devised by the Women's Institute, shows places of interest within the village, including the charming narrow bridge dating from about 1600 and five of the six locks on the Monmouthshire and Brecon Canal. Tretower Court is a well-preserved mediaeval manor house with the remains of a motte and bailey castle nearby. The remote mediaeval Partrishow church is full of interest with a famous carved rood screen and loft of about 1500. At Cwrt-y-Gollen army camp there is the Welsh Brigade and Regimental Museum. Llanfihangel Court at Llanfihangel Crucorney is a fine gabled house with Tudor and seventeenth century features.

Cwm Clydach National Nature Reserve is a semi-natural beech wood at the extreme west of its distribution, set in a spectacular gorge. There is also an industrial archaeology trail here. Beech and the rare small-leaved lime and lesser whitebeam grow on the limestone outcrop of Craig y Cilau National Nature Reserve near Llangattock which also has an interesting large cave system, Agen Allwedd. Dany-wenallt is the small Brecon Beacons National Park study centre at Talybont on Usk.

For more information, including accommodation, contact the Wales Tourist Information and Brecon Beacons National Park Centre, 2 Lower Monk Street, Abergavenny, Gwent NP7 5NA. Telephone (0873) 3254 or 77588 (seasonal).

Hay-on-Wye

This small market town north-east of Brecon originated as a fenced-in hunting ground. The Welsh name of Y Gelli (or, in full, Y Gelli Gandryll) means literally 'the broken grove', implying the same fencing-off of the woodland. Extensive hunting forests existed in the eleventh century, stretching from the Herefordshire borders to Talgarth and on across Fforest Fawr.

Before the building of the Elan Valley reservoirs with their elaborate water control system, many miles upstream, this area was particularly prone to flash flooding by the River Wye. The ferry and ford were badly affected until a bridge was built in 1763, this was swept away, and so was its successor. A high-level Hay Bridge is now in place. Angling is available on the river.

A gentle riverside walk for all ages was presented to the population of Hay in 1884 by Sir Joseph Bailey. Sauntering and picnicking are popular pastimes for which seats and tables have been built. The Offa's Dyke long-distance footpath passes through the town, over Hay Common and south to Monmouth.

The streets and alleys of Hay offer many surprises such as the two-storey Cheese Market with its deep-eaved pediment and the Butter Market, an 'uncouth Doric temple, three bays by nine'. There are ruins of the Norman motte and the thirteenth century castle and many bookshops holding the largest collection of secondhand books in the world.

Nearby Clyro was once the site of a Roman fort and from 1865 to 1872 the home of priest and diarist Francis Kilvert.

The Forest Road over Bwlch yr Efengyl / Gospel Pass (1778 ft / 542 m) through the Black Mountains leads to Capel y Ffin. Father Ignatius founded a monastery here in 1870, later to be the home of artist Eric Gill. A few miles further on are the ruins of thirteenth century Llanthony Priory.

Market day in Hay-on-Wye is Thursday.

For more information, including accommodation, contact Hay-on-Wye Information Centre, Oxford Road, Hay-on-Wye, Powys HR3 5AE.
Telephone (0497) 820144 (seasonal).

Llandovery

Llandovery lies at the confluence of the Brân, Gwydderig and Tywi (Towy),
described by its Welsh name of Llanymddyfri, as 'the church by the water'. As
George Borrow wrote, it is a 'water-girdled spot'. The delightful little town of 1,700
people is the market centre of the Upper Tywi valley.

The town has a long history as befits a settlement at the control point of several
valleys. The ruined Norman castle was built on a rocky knoll above the River Brân
and now lies in the grounds of the Castle Hotel, overlooking the cattle market.
There are pleasant Georgian and Victorian buildings and a remarkable number of
public houses. These stem from the charter granted in the reign of Richard III giving
Llandovery the sole right of keeping taverns in the area. Until 1909 Lloyds Bank was
the famous Bank of the Black Ox, founded in 1799 by David Jones for the drovers
who gathered here with their cattle on the way to English markets. Cattle markets
are still held frequently today. The Saturday general market is held in the Market
Hall, a low nineteenth century building capped with a turret.

Natives of Llandovery and area have secured for it a place in the history of
non-conformism. Rhys Pritchard wrote the simple verses of The Welshman's
Candle, as popular as the Pilgrim's Progress in seventeenth century Wales. Pan-
tycelyn, the farm of William Williams who wrote 'Guide Me, O Thou Great
Redeemer' and many other hymns, is nearby. Today the Llandovery Male Voice
Choir rehearses on Wednesday at the County High School. Llandovery College, the
public school, was founded in 1848 expressly to provide education completely in
Welsh. Llandovery Theatre can be found in Stone Street.

This area was significant in Roman times. As the legions marched from Brecon
against the fiercely resisting Silures, they built Y Pigwn, a temporary camp on a ridge
three miles / 4.8 km to the east of Llandovery. The Roman road takes the higher
ground running south of the modern A40. Dolaucothi, to the north-west, is the only
place in the country where the Romans are definitely known to have mined gold
and is one of the most technically-advanced Roman mines. The site, owned by the
National Trust, is set on wooded hillsides overlooking the beautiful Cothi valley and
was last worked in 1938. There is a Visitors' Centre and a self-guided trail along the
Miners' Way which provide information on the history and geology of the mine. In
mid-summer underground tours are available.

On the A40, near the village of Halfway, is the Mail Monument, a simple stone
obelisk commemorating a coach and its passengers which were driven off the road
and over a 121 ft / 39 m precipice by a drunken driver in 1835. Although no lives
were lost and the mail was retrieved by the Post Office guard, the driver was fined £5
with costs. The Inspector of Mail Coaches erected the memorial as 'a caution to all
mail coach drivers to keep from intoxication.'

To the north is Llyn Brianne, a huge reservoir built in the early 1970s to supply
water to Swansea. This area was previously considered to be one of the most
remote and beautiful in Wales. Gwenffrwd and Dinas RSPB reserves are here and
there is a nature trail past the cave of Twm Shon Cati. Dolauhirion Bridge is on the
way to Gwenffrwd, a single arch built of stone in 1773 with a span of 84 ft / 25.6 m

over the River Tywi. Cilycwm is a bright village with a thirteenth-to-fifteenth century church and a Methodist chapel reputed to be the first meeting house established in Wales. At Cynghordy the Heart of Wales railway line (formerly the London and North Western Railway) traverses a magnificent eighteen-arch stone viaduct, 283 yds / 259 m long and up to 102 f / 31 m high.

Westwards are the ruins of Talley Abbey, built for canons of the Premon-stratensian order in the early thirteenth century and surrounded by beautiful countryside and the Talley Lakes.

To the south-west, between Llandovery and Llandeilo, on a 700 ft / 213 m ridge high above the Tywi valley near Bethlehem, is Carn Goch, one of the largest Iron Age hillforts in Wales.

Southwards is the village of Myddfai, the home of the doctors of Myddfai, an ancient family who held the secret of healing and who were known throughout Wales for their cures. The Usk reservoir lies above the village on Mynydd Myddfai.

For more information, including accommodation, contact the Wales Tourist Information and Brecon Beacons National Park Centre, Central Car Park, Broad Street, Llandovery, Dyfed SA20 0AR. Telephone (0550) 20693 (seasonal).

Talgarth

Talgarth is an interesting town of about 2,000 people, situated between Brecon and Hay-on-Wye in the western foothills of the Black Mountains. The old town with its narrow streets and mainly nineteenth century architecture has many historic associations. Hywel Harris, the eighteenth century revivalist, had his great religious vision at St Gwendoline's Church. The town and its footpaths are well worth exploring. A stream makes its way through the centre of the town and there are sudden views of the hills.

The late-twelfth or early-thirteenth century tower house is one of only two in mid-Wales, although there are many in Scotland and Ireland. The main rooms were built above each other on the first and second floors for defensive purposes.

There are a number of castles and other historic sites within easy reach. Old Gwernyfed is a large stone Jacobean manor house probably built between 1600 and 1613. Bronllys Castle is a well-preserved round keep, built in the early thirteenth century to guard the border territory against the Welsh.

There are many fascinating churches. Bronllys has a large sixteenth century screen which includes a portrayal of the 'Green Man', a human head with leaves sprouting

from the mouth. Remote Llanelieu, 800 ft / 244 m up on the slopes of Rhos Fawr, has a little thirteenth century church with a rood screen, loft and wall painting in a large round churchyard. Llandefalle and Llanfilo are other interesting churches.

Maesyronnen Independent Chapel was formed in 1696–97 and is the oldest unaltered nonconformist meeting-place still in use in Wales. The chapel is in a converted barn attached to a farmhouse, a not-untypical arrangement and deliberately discreet so that dissenters could meet to worship with privacy. Astonishingly, the chapel has survived intact, complete with its original eighteenth- and nineteenth-century furniture.

The area around Talgarth has good angling and walking along the ridges and foothills or the forested Grwyne Fawr trackway in the Black Mountains. Pony trekking and horse-drawn caravans are also available. Llangorse Lake has a range of watersports and there is canoeing on the River Wye at Glasbury.

Talgarth has a stock market on Fridays.

For more information, including accommodation, contact Wales Tourist Information Centre, Market Car Park, Brecon, Powys. Telephone (0874) 2485 or 5692 (seasonal).

Talgarth Tower

Ancient mountains

Geology and ecology

The rocks known as Old Red Sandstone form most of the central, northern and eastern parts of the Beacons. They were deposited mainly by large meandering rivers which flowed slowly over vast floodplains during the Devonian period, 395–345 million years ago. Some rock surfaces display ripple marks like those of sandy river beds, and former river channels filled with sand, mud and gravel can be made out.

These red, brown and purple sandstones and interbedded red marls are the Brownstone sub-division of Old Red Sandstone. The Brownstones are layers of resistant rock 1200–1400 ft / 366–427 m thick, particularly noticeable on the north-facing escarpments, especially the steep north face of Pen y Fan.

The very resistant sandstones and conglomerates known as Plateau Beds are responsible for the characteristic 'table-top' appearance of the Beacons' summits such as Pen y Fan (2907 ft / 886 m) and Corn Du (2863 ft / 873 m) in the central Beacons and Waun Fach (2660 ft / 810 m) and Pen y Gadair Fawr (2624 ft / 800 m) in the Black Mountains in the east. Looking at the northern scarp more closely a stepped profile can often be made out. Each step shows rocks slightly more resistant to the weathering process, culminating in the Plateau Beds.

Heath and moorland

Up above the cultivated and wooded lowlands, the Brecon Beacons are dominated by heath and moorland. Above 1000 ft / 300 m cultivation gives way to rough grassland and heath which, with increased altitude, gives way to bog and moorland. The monotonous appearance of this upland landscape belies its complex vegeta-

Craig y Cilau

tion structure. Different types of plant communities with cotton-grass, heather or bilberry may dominate. The complex jigsaw is in a long-term state of flux, with succession from one type of plant community to another determined by such factors as climate, rainfall, erosion and sheep grazing.

Sphagnum bog is made up of extremely wet and spongy areas where up to 30 different species of sphagnum moss overlie deep layers of peat. This can give way to cotton-grass moor and this, in turn, can lead to four other peat-based plant communities.

	→ *heather moor* → *upland heath*
	→ *bilberry moor* → *upland heath*
sphagnum bog → *cotton-grass moor*	
	→ *fescue moor* → *matgrass moor*
	→ *purplegrass moor*

In the drier Black Mountains in the east, heather and bilberry moorlands overlying deep peat are common, whereas in the western part of the Beacons, with higher annual rainfall and freer drainage, sheep's fescue, a plant which thrives on poor, well-drained shallow soils, has created fescue moorland. This can become matgrass moor through overgrazing by sheep, which much prefer to eat fescue than matgrass. In poorly-drained areas of the central Beacons another type of moorland, the tough wet areas known as purplegrass moor, can develop.

These peaty moorlands are acidic, so their range of flowering plants is limited, but close inspection can reveal surprises like heath bedstraw, tormentil and heath milkwort. In the wetter, spongier areas there are delights such as bog asphodel, bogbean and the fly-catching sundew and butterwort.

Other upland places
Where lime-rich Brownstones from the Old Red Sandstone come to the surface and form craggy well-drained slopes, an extremely interesting flora can develop. Rare arctic-alpine plants such as purple saxifrage and roseroot are at their southernmost British limit here in the Beacons. The north and east-facing scarps of areas such as Craig Gerrig-gleisiad and Cwm Du, in the north-east corner of Fforest Fawr, are where these plants are to be found but they should not be picked or otherwise disturbed.

The limestone which outcrops in the south gives rise to another type of plant community, typified by yew and whitebeam. One particular type of tree, Ley's whitebeam, is unique to the Brecon Beacons.

Upland animals
Animals living in this harsh and varied upland environment include over 200 bird species. There are birds of prey such as the buzzard and kestrel, more rarely the small, fast merlin and peregrine falcon and, occasionally, the majestic red kite. Other upland birds include curlew, snipe, ring ouzel, the red grouse and its rarer relative, the black grouse. Among the mammals can be seen the occasional polecat,

stoat and several species of bat. Some of the more bizarre inhabitants of caves within the Carboniferous Limestone include several types of blind, white crustaceans specially adapted to a totally subterranean life.

Caves and waterfalls

In the south of the Beacons Old Red Sandstone succeeds to Carboniferous Limestone overlain by Millstone Grits (280–345 million years old).

These rocks produce dramatic and spectacular scenery, different from that further north, with remarkable cave systems and fine waterfalls. This river scenery is most notable along the southern edge of Fforest Fawr where the rock band is at its widest and the headwaters of the Neath plunge down a seven mile / 11 km band of the rocks in a varied and abundant series of falls and rapids, amongst the most impressive anywhere in Wales. There are delightful opportunities for walking.

Carboniferous Limestone is formed of material laid down in warm shallow seas (including corals and shellfish whose skeletal remains can often be seen in the rock). It is permeable to rain and river water which cut through the many fissures and joints to form steep-sided gorges and ravines, sometimes disappearing completely in swallow holes and cave systems.

The Millstone Grit series (formerly used in millstones) includes the Twelve Foot Sandstone of the Middles Shales, responsible by its superior hardness for some of the waterfalls on the rivers that cross it, and the Farewell Rock, a massive sandstone lying below the Coal Measures in which almost all workable coal seams occur. On meeting this rock miners knew they had bade farewell to the coal seams.

As the rivers cross the Millstone Grit some of the rivers cut gorges and plunge as waterfalls over the edge of the harder upper sandstone beds to erode the softer shales below, forming rapids and waterfalls. This type of erosion has produced a narrow ledge of rock behind the 70 ft / 21 m drop of Sgwd yr Eira (the Spout of Snow) on the River Hepste. It is possible to stand and admire the waterfall from behind, imagining the fully-laden packhorses which once travelled this way. Sgwd yr Eira is claimed to be the most spectacular of all the falls in the valleys of the Mellte and Hepste, just south of the village of Ystradfellte. Approach can be made from Ystradfellte, Penderyn or Pontneddfechan.

The lesser rivers have not yet cut down to the water-table below and may have underground watercourses in places. This is a common occurrence in the headwaters of the Neath. Near Ystradfellte the Mellte flows beneath a usually-dry pebbly stream for about a mile, and at Porth yr Ogof (Cavern of the White Horse) enters the cave at the base of a cliff. The cavern's English name comes from the calcite streaks like a horse's head on a rock a short way inside. The river Mellte disappears into the cavern to flow through caves and fissures, emerging 33 yds / 30 m away in a deep pool. There are often many potholers to be seen around the cavern.

Beyond the cave the Mellte flows south and on meeting the Millstone Grit, tumbles into a series of spectacular waterfalls: Sgwd Clun-Gwyn (White Meadow Fall), Sgwd Isaf Clun-gwyn (Lower White Meadow Fall) and Sgwd y Pannwr (Fall of the Fuller). It then joins with the Hepste.

Other falls can be found on the River Pyrddin, a tributary of the Neath. Sgwd

Gwladys with its pronounced overlying ledge can be reached by following a path from Pontneddfechan. Sgwd Einon Gam, further upstream, is more difficult of access.

Travelling westwards towards Coelbren, Henrhyd Falls in their deep wooded ravine are accessible from the car park, down a good, if steep, path. The Nant Llech falls in an unbroken stream for 90 ft / 27 m, the highest waterfall in the National Park. The fall, together with nearby Graigllech Woods, is owned by the National Trust.

Near Abercraf in the Upper Tawe (or Upper Swansea) valley on the A4067 are the Dan-yr-Ogof showcaves, the largest showcave complex in western Europe. Guided tours are available through part of the huge cave system to see stalagmites and stalactites, narrow passageways and very large chambers. Cathedral Cavern is 150 ft / 46 m long and 70 ft / 21 m high. Nearby Ogof-yr-Esgyrn (the Bone Cave), occupied by human beings in prehistoric times, today has a display illustrating the bones discovered and people and animals associated with the caves.

Ogof Ffynnon Ddu, across the valley, is a National Nature Reserve, protecting the internationally important cave system. This is by far the largest, and biologically the best studied, cave system in Britain with more than 19 miles / 30 km of cave passages.

Glaciation and Llangorse Lake

The huge glaciers of the Ice Age also left their mark on the Beacons' landscape. As the ice moved slowly forward it collected rock material underneath which scratched the underlying rock. These marks, known as striations, indicate the direction of the flow of glaciers and can be seen in the Millstone Grits around Ystradfellte.

Moraines of gravelly boulder clay were dropped by the glacier as the ice melted. Such moraines can be seen clearly at the head of the Tarell valley from the A470 near the Storey Arms. Where the moraines were deposited at the ends of the

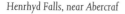

Henrhyd Falls, near Abercraf

valleys, lakes formed behind such as Llyn Cwm Llwch below Pen y Fan and Corn Du in the central Beacons.

Llangorse Lake (Llyn Syfadden in Welsh), five miles/eight km east of Brecon, is another lake dammed by moraines and, at over one mile / 1.6 km in length, the largest natural water body in South Wales. A moraine of boulder gravel and clay deposited by the melting ice in the area of Llanfihangel Tal-y-llyn and Talgarth increased the depth of the waters which collected in a rock basin scooped out by a glacier.

The waters are the noted haunt of a variety of birds because of the amount of fish. They are also a watersports venue for both novice and expert. In the reeds of a shallow part of the lake there are flocks of ducks, geese, moorhens and other birds, safe from the disturbance of speed boats. Coarse fishing is available for pike, perch and roach, as well as the lake's fabulously long eels. Boats can be hired for fishing, rowing or sailing. There are launching facilities for sailing boats and canoes, water skiing, power boating and board sailing. Many other outdoor activities such as camping, pony trekking, caving and walking are catered for in the area.

In 1925 a primitive dug-out canoe was found in the lake. It was thought to be mediaeval, used for getting to the artificial island near the north shore for fishing. Some archaeologists suspected that the island was an Iron Age 'crannog', an artificial island improved with stakes as a lake dwelling like those at Glastonbury and Meare in Somerset, or even a prehistoric site dating to the first millenium BC.

Exciting new finds in 1988, however, have given credence to persisting Welsh legends handed down by word of mouth from the early tenth century. Archaeologists from the University of Cardiff have discovered by diving that the island was originally 100 ft / 30 m wide, surrounded by two rings of vertical oak planks, of a type common in Scotland and Ireland. Using a tree-ring method of dating timber, the site fits neatly into the historical record. According to the Anglo-Saxon Chronicle, in AD911 the palace of a Welsh king was sacked by King Alfred's oldest daughter, Aethelflaed. (She was to become sole ruler of Mercia and known as Lady of the Mercians). The AD916 Anglo-Saxon Chronicle tells us that 'Aethelflaed sent an army into Wales, destroyed *Brecenan Mere* (Llangorse Lake) and took prisoner the king's wife and 33 others'.

More than 250 years later, in 1188, Gerald of Wales in his *Journey through Wales* recorded a possible folk memory of the violent destruction of the island palace: 'The local inhabitants will assure you that the lake has many miraculous properties. It sometimes turns bright green and in our times it has been known to become scarlet, not all over, but as if blood were flowing along certain currents and eddies'.

Some local people still believe that there is a town beneath the waters of the lake. One folk tale recorded by an Oxford academic is that the town grew 'to be another Sodom' and was destroyed 'in a mighty cataclysm which produced the present lake'. Could this be the disapproving verdict of Welsh people on the rule of the 'foreign' dynasty founded by the powerful Irish king Brychan, whose name is commemorated in Brecon and in the lake's name, Brecenan Mere?

Forests, reservoirs and parks

Forests and reservoirs

The name of Fforest Fawr, the lonely stretches west of the A470 cut across by the Roman road Sarn Helen, can be confusing. As in other areas of upland Britain, Dartmoor and Exmoor Forests for instance, 'forest' refers to open treeless hunting country rather than wooded country. The use of the word goes back to early mediaeval times and the Latin word 'forestis' meaning 'outside'. All lands lying outside the fences of estates or parks, forested or not, were called forests or 'outside lands'.

The Norman lords established a hunting ground, the Great Forest of Brecknock, later to become a royal hunting ground, on this area of bare moor and mountainside with its few settlements in the wooded valleys. At one time this included all the land from the Usk in the north and the Pyrddin and Mellte in the south and from the Carmarthen Fans to the Tarell. A code of forest law was introduced, preserving deer and other game. Royal hunting forests have been among the most hated official institutions because the laws administering them were so restrictive and severe.

The 1815 Enclosure Act ended the hunting laws, the lower and peripheral land was sold off and the remainder divided between Commoners and Crown.

In the twentieth century the development of forestry in the Beacons has come to mean conifers for timber production. Their planting has made an enormous impact on the landscape. By 1924 only 3% of Wales was being used for growing trees and more were needed. Land available for planting was poorer, less fertile ground between 500 ft / 152 m and 1,000 ft / 305 m with a heavier rainfall and shorter growing season than the lowlands. Hundreds of years of sheep grazing and grass burning to encourage new growth in spring had meant a decline in the fertility of the hills. The coniferous sitka spruce thrives in wet, cold climates and at relatively high altitudes which made it, and other conifers, an easy choice for financial return on new upland planting.

The first of this new planting began in the 1920s and was followed by further plantings in the 1930s and in the 1950s and 1960s, largely along the southern dip-slopes of the Beacons. Large plantations such as Coed y Rhaiadr in the Neath valley, Taf Fechan, Taf Fawr and Talybont are now mature and being harvested.

Since the 1970s the Forestry Commission has developed its policies. Forests are now better landscaped, with irregular edges fitting in with the contours of the land. Species of trees are more sympathetic to the landscape, particularly along the edges of plantations. Broad-leaved trees are more likely to be retained. Imaginative recreational facilities for the public have been developed with waymarked forest walks, picnic sites, car parks and interpretation of the forests. The forest of Coed Taf has the Garw Nant Forest Visitor Centre north of Merthyr Tydfil, off the A470. Pleasantly situated at the gateway to the Beacons, the Forest Centre has displays and interactive exhibition materials including video. There are forest walks, a picnic site and adventure play area and nesting boxes have been put up to encourage bird-life.

Travellers on the A470 cannot fail to notice the reservoirs of Llwyn-onn, Cantref and Beacons, built to supply Cardiff. There are many others in the Beacons: Talybont, Pontsticill and the Usk reservoir to name but three. The heavily-populated conurbations to the south of the park all demand water for domestic and industrial use. The deep valleys which are possible to dam and the heavy rainfall of the Beacons help to meet that demand and nowadays provide sailing and fishing facilities as well.

National Parks

The Brecon Beacons National Park is one of ten in England and Wales set up in the 1950s. They were established to protect the finest landscapes from inappropriate development and to provide local people and visitors with opportunities to use and enjoy the open countryside. Unlike other countries where vast tracts of land are in public ownership, in Britain most of the land within the parks is privately owned. The Brecon Beacons National Park Committee, however, has recently bought Black Mountain with funds from the Countryside Commission, the National Heritage Memorial Fund and the Brecon Beacons Natural Waters Company (which wished to help protect the quality of the water supplying its bottling plant near Llandeilo).

The two other national parks in Wales are Snowdonia (set up in 1951) and the Pembrokeshire Coast (set up in 1952). All the parks are valuable for their scenic beauty, landscape character, wildlife, historical and cultural associations, archaeology, education and for recreation and relaxation.

National parks are administered by their authorities with financial support from central government (75%) and local government (25%). Their employees include national park officers, planning, conservation and estate management staff, rangers, information officers and administrative staff. Visitors most frequently come across information staff and rangers, who often wear a distinctive uniform and drive vehicles marked with the National Park's logo.

BRECON BEACONS
NATIONAL PARK

History in the Beacons

Stone circles and standing stones

Walkers exploring the countryside often choose a route which passes some form of prehistoric monument. Visiting such monuments can raise questions about changes in climate and land-use, rituals, how society is organised, as well as survival techniques.

With the retreat of the glaciers there was a gradual improvement in the climate and from 10,000 to 4,000BC the mountains and coasts of Wales were reoccupied by people. These Mesolithic (or Middle Stone Age) people's most distinctive relics are small worked flint microliths. Inset into handles of wood and antler they served as the points and barbs of specialised hunting and fishing equipment. During an excavation at Gwernvale, just outside Crickhowell, some of these flint points and scrapers were found at the probable site of a temporary camp in a clearing in the forest. The Mesolithic people may have caught deer coming to the river for water as well as fish from the river itself.

In the Neolithic period (4,000–3,000BC) small bands of people began to arrive in Britain in search of new land for the developing agricultural way of life. Their most common surviving structures are the communal vaults of megalithic tombs. Chambers and passages of large upright stones are combined with dry walling, roofed with massive capstones or smaller stones overlapping inwards as corbelling. The large covering mounds have often been entirely robbed or eroded leaving the main chambers standing alone as cromlechs (wrongly associated with the activities of the Druids). The Gwernvale neolithic long cairn (visible from the road) and several others in the Black Mountains are of this period. Gwernvale is higher and broader at one end where there is a large slab of stone like a door, perhaps symbolic of entry to the Other World. The cairn would once have been about 148 ft / 45 m long, rising in height from that of a child at one end to that of a tall man at the other. The sides were walled with stone which curved inwards to meet the imitation door. Inside were four burial chambers with walls and a roof made of large slabs of stone. Each had a separate entrance from the sides of the mound, allowing people to crawl inside to the darkened chamber.

The Neolithic Beaker people, who moved to Britain from the continent and used distinctive drinking vessels, were involved in religious developments involving henge monuments and stone circles. They came to Pembrokeshire for the bluestones for Stonehenge. Some of the smaller stone circles and alignments in the mountains are almost certainly their work or their ideas passed on to the early Bronze Age.

Less is known about the numbers and distribution of standing stones than almost any other type of prehistoric monument, although they are fairly common in Wales. In addition, not all standing stones are prehistoric; they may, for example, have been put up as rubbing stones in the centre of a field, preferable to stock knocking down fencing. Some of the most obvious circles are those found in public parks in towns up and down Wales: the *Gorsedd* stones, erected for their part in the modern-day Druidic ritual associated with the National Eisteddfod. Older standing stones (in Welsh *maen hir*, plural *meini hirion*) were, in many cases, isolated burial markers but were also associated with cairns or circles or used as trackway markers.

The pair of stone circles at Mynydd-Bach Trecastell, on the same ridge as the Roman camps of Y Pigwn near Llandovery probably mark a place of Bronze Age religious significance. In the more hospitable climate of the Bronze Age good grazing would have been found at this height. There is a larger circle (75 ft / 23 m in diameter) with a low mound at the centre which may be a burial place. The smaller circle is 144 ft / 44 m to the south-west, once of ten stones but now only five, rather taller than the other circle. Four stones once formed an alignment continuing 115 ft / 35 m to the south-west.

Nant Tarw circles are about three miles / five km to the south of Mynydd-Bach Trecastell. They lie by the Nant Tarw, one of the headwaters of the Usk, on level platforms 360 ft / 110 m apart, just over 60 ft / 18 m in diameter. About 15 stones survive of the original 20 or so. Outside the western circle there is a massive outlying stone, 377 ft / 115 m further west and two small uprights beyond it, presumably part of the same group.

Cerrig Duon is formed of about 22 low standing stones in a fairly regular circle with perhaps eight missing. They stand on a shelf projecting from the hillside on the west of the Tawe near its source in wild empty moorland in the foothills of the Black Mountain. The circle can be seen from the mountain road from Trecastle to the A4067 to Craig-y-Nos. None of the stones is over half a metre high but the circle is more prominent than the two almost parallel lines north-east of the circle. The lines and the six ft / 1.8 m high single Maen Mawr to the north must be in association with the circle.

Maen Llia, a single stone, six miles / 9.7 km south-west of the Brecon Beacons National Park Mountain Centre, at the top of the mountain road, seems to invite you into the Fforest Fawr. At Battle, to the north-west of Brecon, is a monolith 12 ft / 3.7 m high on a low cairn. Cwrt y Gollen Menhir, south-east of Crickhowell on the A40, is the most impressive of several Bronze Age standing stones in the Usk valley and is in full view from the road. It is about 12 ft / 3.7 m high and presumed to be of Bronze Age date.

Alignments of standing stones are not common in Wales. As well as the one at Mynydd-Bach Trecastell, the short alignment of Saeth Maen, seven stones at Craig-y-Nos, is worth the climb up the slopes of Cribarth. The line is 45 ft / 13.7 m long with an outlier on the same alignment about 26 ft / 7.9 m to the south-west. The alignment appears to point in the direction of Cerrig Duon, three miles / 4.8 km away in the next valley.

Finally, eight miles / 12.9 km south-west of the Mountain Centre there is a Roman memorial stone known as Maen Madog. It stands, in typical Roman fashion, at the edge of the Roman road from Brecon to Neath and is thought to date from the fifth century, after the official withdrawal of the Romans in AD410. The stone states simply, in Latin, 'Dervacus, son of Justus, lies here'.

Castles

Nothing like the Norman castles had been seen before. They were heavily-defended administrative centres which controlled the areas in which they stood and were the symbol of oppression. The classic timber castle stood on a mound of bare earth, sometimes revetted with stone later for extra protection. The bailey of one or more courtyards was crammed with all kinds of residential buildings and workshops, the whole being surrounded by ditches and ramparts crowned with turreted palisades. Although William of Normandy (the Conqueror) had some claim on England, this claim did not extend to Wales and inevitably the Welsh reaction to a Norman invasion was hostile. To control the Marches the Normans established three great earldoms at Chester, Shrewsbury and Hereford. Later these so-called Marcher Lords grew in number and established more strongholds at Clun, Abergavenny and elsewhere. The coastal plain of South Wales was penetrated as far as Pembroke in 1093–94 and secured by the planting of castles; those on the Welsh March were begun around 1097. The pattern of settlement established during this time still dominates the landscape of the Brecons with open, unimproved common land on the hilltops and the lower slopes and valleys enclosed and improved for grass and other crops.

Tretower Castle and Tretower Court

The remains of Tretower Castle and Tretower Court stand at the head of the Rhiangoll Pass in the lovely Usk valley off the A479, north-west of Crickhowell. The first stronghold was a Norman motte, unusually revetted in stone as it was being built. The castle blocked and controlled the Rhiangoll Pass through the Black Mountains from Talgarth and guarded the Usk valley from any hostile Welsh activity. This early and strong defence was founded by a Norman knight called Picard, one of the men of Bernard de Neufmarché, half-brother of William the Conqueror. It was captured by the Welsh in 1233 but reverted to the English when the uprising was crushed. The bailey was probably added then – a stone wall with three round towers, two of which enclose the gate. Though reinforced, the castle succumbed to the Welsh again in 1322 for a limited period. In 1404 Sir James Berkeley successfully withstood an attack by Owain Glyndŵr. The castle then passed into the possession of Sir Roger Vaughan who rebuilt the fourteenth century manor house, now one of the finest examples of a fortified manor house in Wales. As often happened the manor house replaced the castle as the lord's residence and with its impressive gatehouse, spacious gallery and hall and stout oak timbers it is as great an attraction as the castle ruins. Cassette-taped tours are a feature of the site, bringing it alive with commentary and music.

Bronllys

At Bronllys, near Talgarth, stands the remains of a small castle, probably a knight's stronghold, of which there were many in the thirteenth and fourteenth centuries. The keep is now a ruined circular tower, standing on an earlier steep Norman motte thrown up against a rock outcrop. The castle had two baileys, the main one walled, and a small domestic block probably added in the sixteenth century. Accommodation in this type of castle was limited but at Bronllys a nearby church with a detached tower could have provided additional shelter, a last resort and sanctuary for women, children and livestock.

Crickhowell

Ivy now covers the ruined towers of Crickhowell Castle which, at its height, had a shell keep on a motte, a shell gatehouse and stone wall with towers circling the outer ward. The stone keep was probably built on a Norman motte and bailey castle in the thirteenth century. The gatehouse and two towers of the outer ward were probably built in the fourteenth century for a knight, Sir Grimbald Pauncefoot. The castle was abandoned in the fifteenth century and mostly pulled down in the nineteenth century. Although much of its history is uncertain it is a pleasant spot. A leek-throwing competition is held there in May.

Hay-on-Wye

There are traces of a Norman motte at Hay, probably started by Revell, the first Norman in this area, soon after Henry I came to the throne in 1100. The present remains were built much later, probably by King John after he captured and burnt the original castle in 1216. The building was apparently carried out under the direction and supervision of one of the most reviled and treacherous Marcher Lords, William de Braose. There is also an old tradition that his formidable wife, Matilda, built it with her bare hands. Gerald of Wales wrote of Matilda as an excellent woman, prudent, chaste and a marvellous housekeeper. This was a most flattering description of a woman whose reputation as a baby-eating, demon-conjuring witch persisted in Breconshire seven centuries after she died in King John's dungeons at Corfe Castle in Dorset.

Brecon

Brecon Castle, in the grounds of the Castle Hotel was attacked six times and

Bronllys Castle

captured three times in the thirteenth century alone. Bernard de Neufmarché first built a motte and bailey fortress here in a commanding position at the confluence of the Honddu and Usk rivers at the end of the eleventh century. De Neufmarché had captured the kingdom of Brycheiniog from Welsh princes in 1094 and was granted numerous rights as Lord of Brecon in return. His fortification at Brecon shows his determination to hang on to his gains. The polygonal shell on the motte was added in the twelfth century, a hall and round tower in the thirteenth century and a semi-octagonal tower early in the fourteenth century. It was in this tower that Morton, Bishop of Ely was imprisoned by Richard III for supporting the young Welsh Henry Tudor's (Henry VII) claim to the throne. The gaoler, Duke of Buckingham and Lord of Brecon, who arranged for the bishop to escape, was beheaded in 1521 for treasonable action against his king. It is yet another of the castles attacked by the followers of Owain Glyndŵr, this time in 1403.

Trecastle

Castle Tump at Trecastle, ten miles / 16 km west of Brecon, is now the scanty remains of a probable Norman motte and bailey castle, an outpost of Brecon Castle. It would have had an important role as the town was once of considerable stature, an important stop on the road from Brecon to Fishguard and Milford Haven. It is a good example of twelfth century fortification: the steep motte is 30 yds / 27.4 m broad on top and ditched all round; the 200 ft / 61 m long bailey is raised and protected with a counterscarp bank.

Llandovery

Of the Norman castle, established by Richard Fitz Pons, which once dominated the district, only the ruins remain in the grounds of the Castle Hotel on the south edge of Llandovery. It was captured by the Welsh in 1116, almost before the mortar had dried, and held until it was won back again in 1272. The next 15 years saw it change hands four times. In 1403 it was attacked by the followers of Owain Glyndŵr.

Crickhowell Castle

Transport in the Beacons

Monmouthshire and Brecon Canal

Isolated from the main canal network of England and Wales, the Monmouthshire and Brecon Canal runs along the side of the Usk valley through remarkable scenery. The tree-lined banks have tranquillity as well as breath-taking views of rugged landscapes.

At Brynich an imposing stone aqueduct carries the canal over the fast-flowing River Usk and at Pencelli the canal was built through the castle moat, a former Norman stronghold. Kingfishers breed, there is a variety of bats, and Llangattock Park has exotic trees and rhododendrons. The wharf of Govilon, stands beneath the mountain of Blorenge (1,833 ft / 559 m), a barrier between rural and industrial Wales.

The Monmouthshire and Brecon Canal of today began as two canals, both surveyed by Thomas Dadford Junior. The Monmouthshire Canal from Newport to Pontnewydd, north of Pontypool, was opened in 1796. In 1797 work began on the Brecknock and Abergavenny Canal which included a junction with the other canal at Pontymoile. After many delays the whole route from Brecon to Newport was opened in 1812.

The canal was built to transport coal, iron ore and limestone to the industry of South Wales or for export by sailing ship from Newport Docks. The extensive horsedrawn tramroad networks brought the materials to canal wharves to be transferred to barges. Local market towns and farms were also supplied with household coal and lime for mortar, whitewash and fertiliser, produced by burning limestone in canalside lime-kilns. Local farmers sent produce, including sheep and cattle, to market by canal.

The development of the railways meant competition, and eventually ownership of the canal passed to the Monmouthshire Railway and Canal Company and then to the Great Western Railway Company. A small amount of local trade continued until the 1930s but ended in 1938.

Today, supported by the Brecon Beacons National Park, the British Waterways Board has restored the 33 miles / 53 km of canal between Brecon and Pontypool. Towing-path walks vary from short strolls to watch the boats go by to a walk the length of the canal. Public rights of way, including many of the old tramroads linking ironworks and quarries to the canal, often join the towing-path to provide circular walks. There are plenty of opportunities for photography, painting, sketching and bird watching.

There is excellent coarse fishing with a plentiful supply of roach, perch and dace. The stretch of canal between Llangattock and Llanover is restocked with bream and mirror carp.

Several companies have holiday hire boats available for the day, short breaks and longer holidays. It is easy to appreciate the gentle pace of life on the canal with only six locks and a 22 mile / 34 km lock-free stretch, a tremendous feat of engineering and the longest in the country. The canal is also used for canoeing, both touring or just gentle exploring.

Brecon Mountain Railway

The Brecon Mountain Railway is a narrow-gauge steam railway which follows the route of the old Brecon-Merthyr Tydfil line for two miles / 3.2 km into the National Park at Pontsticill. The main station is at Pant, near Dowlais (well-signposted from the A465 Heads of the Valleys road and the A470) where the locomotive workshop and running shed show how old steam locomotives are repaired. There is also a visitor centre and refreshment facilities. The round trip from Pant to Pontsticill takes 50 minutes including a stop of 20 minutes for a picnic or a walk beside the Taf Fechan reservoir.

Musical landscape
Welsh choirs and the Methodist Revival
The Methodist Revival of the eighteenth century brought enormous spiritual joy and satisfaction to many people. The emphasis on soul-searching preaching, intimate fellowship and fervent hymn-singing made Methodism an attractive religion, especially among pious and relatively well-to-do farmers and craftsmen in rural communities. According to the doctrine of Calvin, followed by the Methodists, only the elect will be saved, so energetic missionary activity is necessary in order to win souls to Christ.

Hywel Harris (1714–73) was one of the great revivalists. In 1735 he had his great religious vision at St Gwendoline's, Talgarth when, he wrote, '(I) felt suddenly my heart melting like before a fire, with love to God my saviour'.

Harris showed remarkable staying power and resolution as, despite toothache, piles and gout, and with only a few hours sleep at night, he travelled from place to place with a slack rein so that he could read, and from his mobile pulpit preached a form of charismatic evangelism.

His relationship with 'Madam' Sidney Griffith, who claimed to have second sight, became a public scandal and caused a rift with many of his religious brothers, particularly Daniel Rowland. In 1752 Harris assembled about a hundred of his Welsh supporters in a 'Family' at Trefecca. The members of the religious community, sometimes known as the Connexion, pooled their possessions for the common good. They became self-sufficient in the building trades, in agriculture and in the manufacture of clothing. In 1755 Harris founded the Brecknockshire Agricultural Society and his scientist brother Joseph promoted new farming methods and some new mechanical devices.

The Howell Harris Memorial Chapel at Coleg Trefecca, near Talgarth has an exhibition including relics of the Harris circle and the evangelist himself, a great letter-writer in a tiny, close-written and barely decipherable hand.

Another of the great revivalists was William Williams, Pantycelyn (1717–91) from a farm near Llandovery. He was converted after hearing Hywel Harris and became an itinerant preacher. His works of inspirational prose and more than 860 hymns expressed the Revival's visionary instinct. He described pre-Methodist Wales as a 'valley of dry bones' and using striking images of light and heat he portrayed Methodism as a movement which brought passion and energy into the national life of Wales.

'Guide me, O Thou Great Redeemer' is one of Williams' hymns known in its Welsh and English versions across the world, thanks to chapel congregations. Hymns played a vital part in spreading the Methodist Revival across eighteenth century Wales.

The singing in harmony of the Welsh has been remarked upon for centuries. Gerald of Wales wrote in 1188, 'In their musical concerts they do not sing in unison like the inhabitants of other countries, but in many different parts: so that in a company of singers, which one frequently meets with in Wales, you will hear as many different parts and voices as there are performers'.

This tendency was nurtured in the fires of the Revival and the developing non-conformist tradition. The *cymanfa ganu* (singing festival), when different chapel congregations of the same denomination would get together to sing hymns and psalms, was one of its expressions. The great choirs of the industrial parts of Wales, male voice, mixed and female, are also part of this tradition. Most choirs welcome visitors at their weekly rehearsals, a marvellous opportunity to look behind the scenes.

Craig-y-Nos and Adelina Patti

Today the grounds of Craig-y-Nos Castle are a 40 acre / 16 ha country park managed by the Brecon Beacons National Park Committee, a lovely spot for picnics, walking or studying wildlife.

In 1841 T H Wyatt (the designer of the Shire Hall in Brecon, now Brecknock Museum) designed a baronial chateau for the wild and romantic site of Craig-y-Nos, the 'rock of the night' in the Upper Tawe valley.

It was bought and extended by the prima donna, Adelina Patti, as an elegant, private retreat for herself and her second (and subsequently third) husband. At the height of her career she could easily command £1,000 for one performance, and at Craig-y-Nos she provided every 'civilised' delight for her friends and guests, including royalty. Society gossip columns marvelled at the plumbing, heating and lighting systems and the generating plant on the premises. There was good shooting which suited her second husband, Ernesto Nicolini, who was keen to live the life of a country squire. In 1891 a tiny private theatre was opened.

Craig-y-Nos Castle

Although Mme Patti's lifestyle was lavish – to reach Craig-y-Nos she took a special train to Penwyllt with its luxuriously furnished waiting room – the local area did benefit from her charity. In 1887 the 'Patti-Nicolini Fund' was set up for the benefit of the poor of Brecon.

In 1917 the elaborate Winter Gardens from Craig-y-Nos were transported to Victoria Park, Swansea where they are now known as the Patti Pavilion. Mme Patti died in 1919 and the castle and grounds were bought by the Welsh National Memorial Association to be converted into a hospital.

The heyday of the estate and Mme Patti's 'Home, sweet home' was in the 1890s. The rebuilt pavilion overlooking the tennis courts and a number of introduced features are reminders of this time. The beechwood with its many birds and shade-tolerant plants was probably first laid out then and has now been thinned and replanted with young trees. Specimen trees selected for their colour, fragrance or fruit were planted, rather like an arboretum, on flat open land to the east of the main bridge, with the rugged limestone outcrop of Craig y Rhiwarth beyond. The ornamental pond and lake with an island in the centre attract species different from the rivers and there are introduced fish and wildfowl. The meadows are now less heavily grazed in order to promote the natural regeneration of typical plants. This renewed care and interest in the grounds would no doubt have pleased Mme Patti who apparently used to sing to her plants in order to make them grow.

Jazz at Brecon

The first Brecon Jazz Festival was organised in 1984 by a group of local enthusiasts who had been to the Breda Festival in Holland. Held over the third weekend in August it has been developed annually and now attracts an estimated 30,000 people from all over Britain to hear a wide range of jazz. The Festival is different from others in that it takes place throughout the town itself, at nine indoor and three large outdoor venues. There is also street music (including marching bands) under coloured tensile canopies, fringe music in many of the pubs and a packed Cathedral jazz service on the Sunday morning. The Krukke marching band from Breda opens the Festival together with the Adamant Band from Cardiff. Overseas-based bands and musicians are a significant part of the programme. The Festival sees itself as a community-based Welsh festival which regards jazz as an international language.

Teifi Valley

This chapter covers not only the valley of the Teifi but other nearby countryside. From its source high in the Cambrian Mountains the Teifi goes through many stages from mountain stream to mature river, passes through Tregaron Bog (where the red kite can sometimes be seen), over Cenarth Falls and through Cilgerran Gorge to reach Cardigan Bay beyond the town of Cardigan.

The area has many small towns each with its own character: Tregaron, well-known for horses and pony trekking; Lampeter (despite its small size), a university town; Llandysul, home to the Gomer Press; Newcastle Emlyn with its large Friday market; and Cardigan, former county town of Cardiganshire standing above the estuary. Other towns include Dre-fach Felindre, famous for its woollen mills, and Llanybydder where the monthly horse market is held.

Many people have made a living from the river whether by fishing (often from the famous Teifi coracle), corn-milling, spinning, weaving and finishing in the woollen industry or boat-building. Different forms of husbandry take place on the land bounding the river and beyond in the hills: dairying in the flat meadows of the lower reaches, keeping sheep on the great sheepwalks of the uplands, organic farming and wildlife gardening.

The Teifi has been an inspiration to at least one poet. The bard Cynan wrote of the river,

Mae afon sy'n groyw a gloyw a glân
A balm yn addfwynder a cheinder ei chân.

A river that is pure and clear and clean,
A balmy gentleness and elegant song.

where

... llif yno'n ddiog, a'r dolydd yn las
A'r brithyll a'r sewin a'r samon yn fras.

... the flow there is lazy and meadows green,
the trout and sea-trout and salmon are fat.

Cardigan

Cardigan with a population of 3,840 people, is the former county town of
Cardiganshire and the main shopping centre of South Ceredigion. It takes its name
from Ceredigion, the land of Ceredig, who was one of the sons of the fifth century
founder of Gwynedd, Cunedda. Situated on the north bank of the Teifi estuary, as
its Welsh name *Aberteifi* indicates, it is the lowest crossing point of the river.

When Ceredigion was conquered by the Norman Roger Montgomery in 1093 he
chose a strategic site on the north bank of the river for his fortress. It gave easy
access both to the Irish Sea and inland to the fertile Teifi valley. Today there is a
ruined castle dating from 1240, but it was probably in an earlier one that the Lord
Rhys of Deheubarth hosted in 1176 what is regarded as the first national eisteddfod.
A great feast for many visitors was organised a year in advance and entertainment
was provided by the poets and musicians of Wales who competed amongst
themselves for the prize of a chair. Today the Eisteddfod is one of the most

celebrated cultural events in Wales, held annually in August at different towns throughout the country.

The Teifi Bridge is a splendid multi-arched structure with pedestrian passing-places dating from 1726, a remarkable technical achievement for its age. Nearby is the bronze otter, sculpted by Geoffrey Powell and presented to Cardigan by David Bellamy on behalf of the Dyfed Wildlife Trust to mark its Golden Jubilee, 1938–88.

At one time 300 ships were registered at Cardigan and the port was considered to be the second most important in Wales. It was a centre for ship-building and the warehouses on the quays speak of the town's past. During the first half of the nineteenth century it was a point of departure for emigrant ships, especially to New Brunswick in Canada and to New York. The arrival of the railway in 1885 and the silting up of the estuary brought the decline of the port.

Pleasant walks along the river, narrow streets and old-fashioned shop-fronts encourage exploration. The Market Hall is one of the best in Wales, built in 1859 with stone arches picked out in black and white against the red brick. Outside the 'Gothic' Guildhall is a cannon.

Theatr Mwldan is to be found in Bath House Street. The national shrine of the Catholic Church in Wales with a statue of Our Lady of the Taper is in the town and on the other bank of the Teifi is St Dogmael's Abbey. The Normans founded it in the twelfth century for the Benedictine Order of Tiron on the site of a Welsh seventh century abbey sacked by the Vikings. The famous Sagranus Stone recording Sagranus, son of Cunotamus is in St Thomas's Parish Church nearby, a Celtic 'Rosetta Stone'. Notches in ogham along the stone's edge and the Latin inscription on its face provided the key to deciphering the ogham alphabet of the Goidelic-speaking Irish people who migrated to this area in the fifth century. There is a working water mill, Y Felin, in the village producing stone-ground flour.

Cardigan Wildlife Park, near Cilgerran, three miles / four km from Cardigan, houses several species of rare animal as well as some native to this area.

The thirteenth century ruins of Cilgerran Castle are set spectacularly in a strong position on a promontory overlooking the deep gorge of the river, an inspiration to many artists, including Turner. Accessible to large ships, this was the lowest crossing place of the river at all states of the tide. Coracles are often seen in the pools below and there is a renowned annual coracle festival in August. The Teifi has good fishing for salmon and sea trout. Further upstream there is an attractive late-nineteenth century arched bridge at Llechryd.

The coastline and its beaches, such as the National Trust's sheltered cove of Mwnt, beckon. There are boat trips from St Dogmael's to Cardigan Island, reserve of the Dyfed Wildlife Trust and home to birds, seals and Soay sheep.

General market days in Cardigan are on Saturday and Monday, with a livestock market on Monday. The Women's Institute co-operative market is held on Friday morning at the Senior Citizen Centre in the Market Place.

For more information, including accommodation, contact Cardigan Tourist Information Centre, Prince Charles Quay, Bridge Street, Cardigan, Dyfed SA43 1HY. Telephone (0239) 613230 (seasonal).

Lampeter

Lampeter was known originally in Welsh as Llanbedr Talybont Steffan ('the church of Peter at the end of Stephen's Bridge') but is referred to more usually today as 'Llambed'. Stephen would have been the man appointed to look after the bridge in mediaeval times, an important job when a bridge was a link to the outside world and the way by which an enemy could enter. Lampeter has a population of 1,980 people and a distinctive Welsh character. Lying at the meeting point of several main roads, it is the shopping centre for much of the central Teifi valley.

St David's College is Wales's oldest University College. It was founded in 1822 by an Englishman, Bishop Burgess, so that Welsh students, prohibited by expense from attending Oxford or Cambridge, could get a university education. The oldest building was put up in 1827, based on the design of an Oxford or Cambridge college. There is a stuccoed quadrangle with small cupola towers at the corners, a fountain, chapel, student accommodation and an arched entrance gateway. The library includes mediaeval manuscripts and first editions and there is the occasional art exhibition at the Arts Hall. The remains of a Norman keep are in the college grounds and on the opposite bank of the Teifi is the course of the Roman road, Sarn Helen.

During the eighteenth century Lampeter became an important droving centre, where cattle were gathered before being driven to England. The Black Lion Hotel was built as a coaching inn about 1790 and most of its stables, loose boxes and the coach house still stand in the two inner courtyards beyond the archway entrance. The Harford family of Blaise Castle built the mansion at Falcondale (now a hotel) early in the nineteenth century. The Harfords also donated land and money for St David's College, the fountain at the centre of the town and the Town Hall, built in 1881.

There are many opportunities for walking in the area: by Falcondale Lake off the A482 Aberaeron road, past the college into Mount Pleasant woods for panoramic views of the Teifi valley and beyond and along the Teifi itself which has marvellous salmon, trout and sea trout fishing.

In the War Memorial park are the Gorsedd stones from the National Eisteddfod and picnic tables. The local Eisteddfod is held during August Bank Holiday and the annual Agricultural Show is also in August.

Theatr Felinfach is to be found in the village of Felinfach in the Aeron valley, seven miles / 11 km north-west of Lampeter on the A482 Aberaeron road. At Cellan, a few miles along the B4343 Tregaron road which runs beside low-lying meadow-

St David's University College, Lampeter

land, can be found the Brooklands Model Aircraft Museum, a collection of 350 model aircraft. Further afield are the Roman goldmines at Dolaucothi, now owned by the National Trust, with guided tours of the underground workings in summer, and the thirteenth century Talley Abbey, situated in beautiful countryside.

Lampeter's fatstock market is held on alternate Mondays followed on Tuesdays by the dairy, calves and general market alternating with that of Tregaron. The Women's Institute co-operative market is held every other Tuesday at the Football Club in Drovers' Road.

For more information, including accommodation, contact Lampeter Tourist Information Centre, Ceredigion District Council Offices, Town Hall, Lampeter, Dyfed SA48 7BB. Telephone (0570) 422426 (seasonal).

Llandysul

The small town of Llandysul lies on the hillside above the bosky valley of the Teifi with its renowned salmon fishing. Although a small town by today's standards, it was the early mediaeval centre of a *cwmwd*, a local administrative area where the local Welsh prince had a lesser courthouse. This may explain the large size and importance of the church of St Tysell which had six 'chapels of ease' associated with it in the seventeenth century. A sixth century stone with the vertical inscription 'Velvor(ia) / Filia / Brohomagli' ('Velvoria, daughter of Brohomaglus'), previously part of a churchyard stile, has been built into the inner face of the north wall of the tower.

The 1933 lych-gate of the churchyard celebrates Calan Hen – the centenary of the victory of religious propriety over cnapan, a brutal mass football game previously played between the men of Llandysul and those of Llanwenog, eight miles / 13 km away. The object of the game, found in other parts of the British Isles, was, after a large and alcoholic meal, to knock the ball against the door of the opposing side's church. Struggling to get the wooden ball from one territory to another involved a great deal of fighting and kicking, violence and blood. In 1833 the Reverend Enoch Jones, vicar of Llandysul, decided that this barbaric game should be replaced by a more religious activity. With the co-operation of all churches within eight miles / 13 km a Sunday School-type competition in answering catechisms, singing anthems

and reciting the scriptures was introduced in celebration of the old calendar's New Year's Day on 12 January.

Other reminders of past rituals are found on Mynydd Llanybydder where there is a stone alignment of at least 18 stones, set almost exactly east-west. There are a number of hillforts. Castell Gwynionydd, a ringwork enclosure above the minor road linking Capel Dewi and Llandysul, has panoramic views of the countryside on both sides. In the 1930s a Celtic stone head was found in the area. Its coarse-grained sandstone with hollow eyes and swollen lips is reminiscent of the Celtic cult of the severed head as found, for example, in the West Riding of Yorkshire.

The area's woollen mills, so important in the nineteenth century economy, all welcome visitors. Gwasg Gomer / Gomer Press which publishes a variety of books of Welsh and wider interest is in Llandysul. The West Wales Farm Park at Plwmp has rare breeds of cattle, sheep, pigs and poultry.

Llandysul general market is on Tuesdays with the Women's Institute co-operative market in the Wilke's Head, Llandysul on Tuesday mornings. Llanybydder general market is held on alternate Mondays and the famous Llanybydder horse market on the last Thursday of the month.

For more information, including accommodation, contact Lampeter Tourist Information Centre, Ceredigion District Council Offices, Town Hall, Lampeter, Dyfed SA48 7BB. Telephone (0570) 422426 (seasonal).

St Tysell's Church, Llandysul

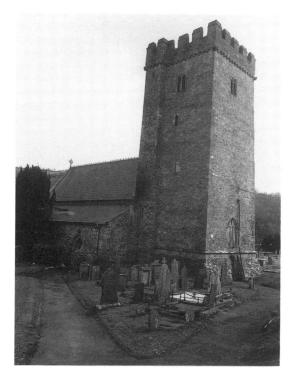

Newcastle Emlyn

Newcastle Emlyn is a friendly little market town of under 1,000 people. The many pubs and former pubs, together with the big main square dominated by the Cawdor Hotel, are indications of the days when the place was busy with dealers, drovers and their stock. However European Community milk quotas have adversely affected the area and some farmers are diversifying into specialised foods with 'added value', like cheese or smoked fish for which the area is becoming well-known.

The town's Welsh name is Castell Newydd Emlyn. 'Emlyn' derives from the Welsh *am glyn* ('round the valley'), the descriptive name of the mediaeval cantref or district here. This castle, probably overlying earlier remains, was built in 1240 within a bend of the river which provides an almost complete natural moat. It regularly changed hands until it was severely damaged by followers of Owain Glyndŵr. Little remains today except parts of the walls and the ruined gatehouse.

A plaque placed in a shop wall near the Teifi bridge in 1912 by the Committee of the Happy Winter Evening Entertainments commemorates Wales's first official printing press which operated nearby in the early eighteenth century. The town has a splendid Bethel chapel, parish church and Town Hall, built in 1892.

The hills south of the town are notable for large numbers of surviving Bronze Age cairns, several of which may be seen from small country roads.

Downstream are the Cenarth Falls, once famous for their coracle fishing, and Cenarth Mill, formerly owned by the Cawdor estate. To the north-east, near Cwm Cou, is Felin Geri Mill, built in 1604 and still producing stone-ground flour. Visitors can see every stage of the production process.

Upstream at Dre-fach Felindre is the Museum of the Welsh Woollen Industry, the National Museum of Wales's working record of a great industry with the looms which produced the tweed and flannel which made this area famous. The Henllan narrow-gauge railway which brought anthracite from South Wales to power the mills and to take away their products in the nineteenth century has been restored for tourist use.

Market day (livestock and general) is on Friday with the Women's Institute co-operative market to be found in the morning at the Plough Hotel.

For more information, including accommodation, contact Cardigan Tourist Information Centre, Prince Charles Quay, Cardigan, Dyfed SA43 1HY. Telephone (0239) 613230 (seasonal).

Tregaron

Tregaron ('the town of Caron') is an attractive small town in the Upper Teifi valley, known today as a pony trekking centre. The church is set on a mound in the centre of the town and set low into the tower's outside south wall is a small inscribed stone from the nearby Roman fort of Bremio. In the square is the statue of Henry Richard MP (1812–88), an outspoken supporter of disarmament who became known as the Apostle of Peace. He founded the European Peace Union, the forerunner of the League of Nations and the United Nations Organisation.

Before 1900 Tregaron was an important droving town where drovers and their animals gathered before their journey across the mountains to the markets of England. A branch of the Aberystwyth and Tregaron Bank was opened in the town. It issued its own banknotes from 10 shillings (50p) to £20 which had a black sheep on them and so the bank came to be known as *Banc y Ddafad Ddu*, the Bank of the Black Sheep. Like many other small banks it collapsed after the Napoleonic Wars. The mountain road, taken by the drovers into the eastern unpopulated uplands, through the Cwm Berwyn pass to Abergwesyn and thence Llanwrtyd Wells, can be travelled by car today. It is a delightful 13 miles / 21 km, one of the most beautifully scenic roads in Wales. One branch of the road leads past Llyn Brianne and Twm Shon Cati's Cave eventually to reach Llandovery. Other mountain roads lead to the Teifi Pools, the source of the river, high above Pontrhydfendigaid, and to Soar y Mynydd chapel, built in 1822 with the chapel, a house and a stable all under one roof.

Besides pony trekking, the Tregaron area has a long history of Welsh Mountain Pony and Cob breeding. Trotting races are popular and the Endurance Horse and Pony Society and British Horse Society also organise events.

The Craft Design Centre of Wales, in the middle of the town, sells crafts from all over Wales including gold and silver 'Rhiannon' jewellery made on the premises, pure wool garments and pottery.

Nearby are a number of places of interest. Llanddewibrefi, an attractive small village, once Lampeter's rival for the site of St David's College, has a thirteenth century church situated on a hillock, like that of Tregaron. Apparently when St David preached here he could not make himself heard and miraculously the ground rose up into a natural pulpit under his feet. The ruins of the Cistercian Strata Florida Abbey are beautifully situated in Ystrad Fflur, the Vale of Flowers. A permit from the Nature Conservancy Council is required to enter Tregaron Bog, the largest raised bog in Wales but visitors can walk across a corner of it along the Old Railway Walk.

Tregaron market is on Tuesday, alternating with Lampeter. The Women's Institute co-operative market is on Tuesday mornings in the Committee Room at the Memorial Hall. Côr Meibion Caron Male Voice Choir meets on Sundays at Capel Bwlchgwynt Chapel.

For more information, including accommodation, contact Tregaron Tourist Information Centre, Ceredigion District Council Offices, Dewi Road, Tregaron, Dyfed SY25 6JN. Telephone (09744) 248 (seasonal and office hours).

The River Teifi

Teifi Pools

Llyn Hir, Llyn Teifi, Llyn y Gorlan, Llyn Egnant and the other lakes of the Teifi Pools are deep pools near the source of the River Teifi, brown and sparkling by turns. They were famous in mediaeval times for the excellence of their trout and eels, serving as the mountain fisheries of the monks of Strata Florida. At least one lake was reputed to be unfathomable.

Around the Pools is uneven rocky country with grassy ridges, part of a fine stretch of high fertile sheepwalk. One of the specialities of mid-Wales, bog rosemary, can also be found here in wetter hollows. When ungrazed it decorates whole patches of bog with tiny pink bells in early spring and sometimes again in the autumn.

The lakes are five miles / eight km north-east of Tregaron, on the mountain road from Ffair-rhos.

Tregaron Bog

Tregaron Bog is a complex of three large raised bogs lying between Tregaron and Pontrhydfendigaid at a height of 500 ft / 150 m. The 1,957 acres / 792 ha are now a National Nature Reserve, Cors Caron, mostly owned by the Nature Conservancy Council. It is the largest peat bog in Wales and reputedly the largest outside Ireland. Its Welsh name Cors Goch (the 'red bog') probably refers to the way in which sedges on the bog turn red in winter.

During the last Ice Age movements of ice created the broad basin of the Teifi. This was then dammed by a moraine behind which a shallow lake formed. This moraine was eventually breached by the lake's outlet stream, the Teifi, which today sluggishly makes its way through the bog and its peaty pools.

The open-water plants of the lake were succeeded by reed which led to the formation of fen peat. Continued accumulation of peat eventually dried out the surface encouraging trees including alder, birch, oak and pine to grow. Later, rainfall increased, water levels rose and the trees died out. Constantly wet conditions encouraged the development and growth of sphagnum mosses and an acid moss peat. This build-up raised the level of the ground almost 30 ft / 9 m above the level of the lake.

Tregaron Bog is a classical site, the first raised bog in Britain to have its development described in detail. The botanical evidence coincides in a startling way with the historical record. Before 404BC the inhabitants of the area had been involved in a shifting pattern of land clearances. This then changed to a long period of pastoral activity on more open grassland, coinciding with the occupation of the Tregaron area by Celtic tribes who are known to have pastured large flocks and herds. Around AD1182 this pastoral period ended and the botanical record shows predominantly arable farming and its weeds: buttercups, daisies, Good King Henry and fat-hen. Such a significant change coincides neatly with the settlement of Cistercian monks at Strata Florida in 1164 and their development of agriculture.

In the past, parts of Tregaron Bog were grazed by livestock, its rushes used for bedding, and peat cut for fuel which drained it around the margins. The peat was

Teifi Marshes

cut in early summer to a depth of six ft / two m, stacked to dry and carted away in autumn before the bog's rising water levels turned paths to mire. Small-scale peat-cutting continued until cheaper alternative fuels were introduced in the 1950s. A plan in the 1920s to excavate the peat mechanically did not succeed; nor did one to produce oil, paraffin and ammonia gas commercially.

The western bog suffered little from peat cutting and is still 'living', of great value as an undisturbed site. The management of the reserve allows for some agricultural rush-cutting and grazing, the creation of shallow pools to encourage wildfowl and the control of invasive scrub. Much research is still being carried on into the vegetation, hydrology and nutrient status of the peat, making population studies of several insect groups, birds and otters and detailed recording of the climate.

The bog has a range of relatively undisturbed habitats, home to many insects, birds, animals and plants.

The centre of the bog has hummocks and hollows which are a permanent feature of a developing bog where the surface is still growing upwards. The vegetation is dominated by bog mosses in the hollows and deer grass, sedges, heathers, hare's tail, crowberry, bog rosemary, cranberry and sundews on the hummocks.

The lagg (the wet depression between the edge of the bog and the valley side) offers a different habitat for red canary grass, meadowsweet, yellow flag and kingcup.

The rand (the sloping margin of the raised bog) is yet another habitat, dominated by purple moorgrass and some cotton-grasses, their fluffy tufts white in summer. Higher up are deer grass, bog ashphodel, sedges, sundews, heather and some bilberry. There are also small birches which do not develop because of the constantly wet conditions and the low nutrient status of peat.

Insects include the marsh fritillary, small pearl-bordered, small skipper and green hairstreak butterflies. The large heath butterfly is at the southernmost limit of its range. It overwinters in the larval stage, eats the white beak-sedge as its main food and is on the wing from mid-June to late July. July also sees horse flies in the sunshine and thousands of mosquitoes at dawn and dusk.

The common frog, common lizard, slow worm, common toad and adder live here and the British black adder is confined to this area. There are polecats, stoats, weasels, otters, shrews, woodmice, water voles and some mink.

Over 160 species of birds have been recorded here and about 70 species breed on the reserve or in its immediate surroundings. The open water is an overwintering area for many duck, a few dozen whooper swans and some white-fronted geese (but not in their hundreds as in the 1950s). Buzzard, red kite, sparrowhawk, barn owl and short-eared owl hunt over the bog, joined by hen harrier in winter. In the spring the loud cries of curlew and plover can be heard. Kingfisher and heron prey on the fish.

The high ground on the east gives the best views of this great stretch of bogland, shining with water when the Teifi has flooded over its banks. Bog habitats are easily affected by trampling and so access is limited by permit, available from the Warden or from the Nature Conservancy Council. One corner of the bog, however, can be crossed by following the Old Railway Walk, a self-guided trail along the route of the old Manchester–Milford Haven railway line. Opened in 1866, this linked Tregaron and Lampeter with Aberystwyth and Carmarthen until the tracks were finally removed in 1966. The trail begins from the car park on the B4343, two miles / 3.2 km north of Tregaron and leads to an observation tower overlooking wide areas of the northern part of the bog. It does not require boots, is never flooded and can be managed by partially disabled people with a little help.

Cenarth Falls

At Cenarth, a charming riverside village set in a broad gorge with oak and ash woods and bluebells in season, the Teifi cascades over a series of rocky ledges. These are the famous Cenarth Falls which also serve as a salmon leap. The swirling pools between the bridge and the waterfall provide good sport for fishermen, who used to fish here with coracles before new licences were limited in 1935 to the tidal section of the river below Llechryd Bridge. These pools were traditionally the place where sheep were washed before being shorn, coracles waiting downstream to catch any swept away by the current.

The finely-proportioned narrow bridge dates from the eighteenth century and spans the old county boundary between Carmarthenshire and Cardiganshire. The seventeenth century water-powered corn mill here is being restored and a coracle museum is being developed.

The Lower Teifi

Twice a day the tide floods brown through the arched bridge spanning the Teifi, hard beneath the remains of Cardigan's once-proud castle. Twice a day it ebbs, revealing a thin band of mud which, as you look upstream, soon turns out of sight, seemingly lost. This is an area well worth exploring on foot.

Between Cardigan and the next bridge, some four miles / six km upstream at Llechryd, is a tract of spectacular countryside whose only link is the river. Here the river is everything. It shaped the countryside, mostly in glacial times when, instead of meandering across a plain to the south, it carved a gorge nearly three miles / five km in length. The river hurries through Cilgerran Gorge to this day and you can walk beside it.

Llechryd is a good access point. From the south side of its bridge a path leads past Castle Malgwyn Hotel and on to Cilgerran. This village is also a good start for an exploration of the gorge, but first visit the castle. From the curtain walls and towers of William Marshall's thirteenth century castle reconstruction the views are outstanding.

The woodlands clinging to the gorge sides below Cilgerran seem to climb ever

River Teifi at Cilgerran

higher above the path. Oak is dominant but there is a range of other species including ash and birch and close to the water's edge, fine alders. On some rocky knolls and screes a small number of wild service trees may be found, a scarce species here in the far west. The maple-like leaves turn a rich red in autumn and draw immediate attention to their presence. Look earlier for the brown berries and in spring the clusters of white flowers.

Shut your eyes and cast back 800 years or more. The woodlands would have looked much as they do today, but in the water you may well have glimpsed a beaver. Giraldus Cambrensis reported beavers here in 1188, the last known British haunt of this animal with such a valuable skin. Perhaps this led to its early extinction in Great Britain.

Beavers have passed into legend and only their ghosts remain here. Almost as elusive are otters but they are still with us; the Teifi and its tributaries form one of their strongholds. Mink are also resident along the banks.

River birds like grey wagtails are frequent, their upper-parts contrasting with bright sulphur-yellow below. Dippers, in a handsome livery of brown and white, go about feeding as no other British birds do: they simply disappear below the surface to walk along the river bed seeking caddis and other invertebrates from amongst the stones. Kingfishers sometimes fly by, a flash of ultramarine and vermillion. Equally resplendent is the agrion damselfly. The male has metallic greenish-blue wings and body, the female is a rich brown and equally handsome.

Passing the remains of the slate quarries, you eventually emerge from the gorge to see the reedbeds, alder and willow carrs and marshes and, not far away, the roofs of Cardigan itself.

Grey herons stalk or stand at the water's edge waiting for the opportunity to take some unsuspecting fish. Cormorants swim on the river or stand on the shore with wings outspread. Waders feed on invertebrates, prised, probed or deftly picked from the mud. Curlew, lapwing, redshank or dunlin, each has its own particular method.

The marshes on the west side of the Afon Piliau, the hidden watercourse which meanders across to join the Teifi, are one of the Dyfed Wildlife Trust's nature reserves. On a gorse-covered knoll on the outskirts of Cardigan the Trust has built an observation hide with excellent views overlooking the marshes. There are always birds to be seen: the resident mallard, moorhen and coot, the migrant swallows and martins and perhaps rarer visitors such as purple heron and little egret.

From late August the marshes are at their best. Sometimes, in hard weather, there are up to a thousand each of wintering teal and widgeon. The shrill whistling of packs of widgeon on a still frosty day carries right across the marshes. Smaller numbers of other duck like shoveler and gadwall occur, and on the river, goldeneye, tufted duck and pochard. Among birds of prey are kestrels and sparrowhawks, while peregrine falcons regularly hunt here and wintering hen harriers are not infrequent visitors.

Cilgerran Castle

Getting a living from the river

Otters

A delightful aquatic gymnast with its characteristic long, slender brown body, strong, muscular tail and short muzzle can occasionally be seen on the Teifi and other Welsh rivers. Mud slides, footprints and spraints (droppings) are clues to the presence of the European otter (*Lutra lutra*), an elusive and mainly nocturnal member of the weasel family.

Once persecuted by fishermen and otter hunts, we now know that it lives mainly on eels, supplemented by sticklebacks, pike, gudgeon and other coarse fish. Crabs, crayfish, frogs, toads and a few species of mammals and birds also feature in its diet. Despite appearances, the otter actually spends very little time fishing and is normally underwater for only a short period, 40 seconds at most and normally less than 15 seconds.

Survey work since the 1970s has indicated that the otter is widespread in small numbers over large parts of mid- and West Wales, which, along with the West Country, constitute its heartland in England and Wales. The north of Scotland is its other main British stronghold. Since 1982, some concern has arisen over numbers on the Teifi; the number of spraints found on Tregaron Bog appears to have declined, and more recent work on the stretch of river between Lampeter and Tregaron seems to confirm this. The work of the Otter Haven Project has been invaluable in protecting the animal's habitat and in creating artificial holts out of log piles and brick, where it can safely lie up and breed.

Otter cubs may be born at any time of year in the Teifi Valley, although in harsher northern climes such as Sweden, they are restricted to the spring. Mating takes place in the water and after a gestation period of about two months, two or three cubs (sometimes four or five) are born. At birth they are covered in pale grey fur and their eyes do not open until they are about five weeks old. Weaned at eight weeks, they leave the holt for the first time. After three months they have learnt to swim, but stay with the mother for a further seven to nine months.

The home range or territory of the otter varies considerably, but for the average female it is about ten miles / 16 km and for a large male up to 25 miles / 40 km. The total length of the river Teifi is 87 miles / 140 km and a large male can therefore theoretically range from Cardigan as far inland as Llandysul.

One of the most likely indicators that otters are about is their spraints, usually oily-black or greenish-black when fresh, turning a brown-grey colour with age. They are normally full of tiny fish bones, having a characteristic sweet musky smell, useful in marking out territory. Spraints are usually found on riverbanks, under bridges, on islands in the river, on fallen trees or prominent rocks and have even been discovered on the top of molehills.

Tracks are another sign of otter activity, especially in soft mud or clay. They are distinguished by five toes radially arranged around a central pad, but beware, sometimes when the ground is hard only four can be seen and these can easily be confused with the paw marks of a fox or small dog.

The best time to see an otter is the hour or so before sunset when it leaves its holt, usually a cavity in a river bank or in the roots or hollow trunk of an ash, oak or sycamore, to begin its night's activity. The most likely sites for seeing otters or their tell-tale signs in the Teifi Valley are along the river in the Tregaron Bog area, between Lampeter and Tregaron and beyond the top end of the valley, in the Vale of Rheidol.

Otters now enjoy full protection by the law and are covered by Schedule 1 of the Conservation of Wild Creatures and Wild Plants Act 1975 and, more recently, by the Wildlife and Countryside Act 1981.

Coracle fishing

The coracle is a keel-less, bowl-shaped fishing boat specifically designed for use in swiftly-flowing streams. It was formerly used on most Welsh rivers and is well documented on the Spey in Scotland and the Boyne in Ireland. Today it is restricted in Wales to the rivers Teifi, Tâf and Tywi. It is likely that the design has altered little in the last 5,000 years. In 1807 the traveller Malkin described the shape of coracles as resembling 'the section of a walnut shell, their length is generally five feet and their breadth seldom less than four.'

Julius Caesar in 40BC described very similar hide-covered sea-going craft in the south-west, considering them 'very artful'. These were larger than the coracle and probably keeled boats, similar to the Irish curraghs.

The design of coracles differs to meet the conditions of a particular river (whether it is swift or slow-moving, whether there are rapids, whether the water is shallow or deep) and according to the preference of the individual fisherman. The Teifi coracle is short and broad with a waist where the deal seat is inserted, the Tywi coracle is longer and more elegant and the Ironbridge Severn coracle was almost completely oval.

Coracles were known on the Teifi from at least the last quarter of the eighteenth century. In 1781 H P Wyndham mentions them being used at Cilgerran for ferrying people across the river as well as fishing. They vary little from one part of the river to another and are built to withstand the river's rough handling.

The strong and supple framework is made of willow strips cut by hand, preferably from seven-year-old willow. Willow grows in profusion along the Teifi and in the past, when there was considerable demand for withies, the trees were pollarded at regular intervals. Today harvesting is irregular and coracle builders have difficulty in finding the correct material. The framework is tied together with a plait of several layers of young hazel saplings as a gunwale. Originally it would have been covered with hide but this was replaced by the first half of the nineteenth century by calico or flannel, waterproofed with hot pitch. The use of flannel or calico meant that the coracle was much lighter. This was a distinct advantage as coracle fishermen usually had to carry the boat on their back for a considerable distance, since they fished by drifting with the flow of the river. Flannel was thought more durable than canvas, easier to prepare, and able to keep out water longer. It would have been easy to obtain from the woollen mills of the area. For the last 80 years canvas or calico covered with pitch and linseed oil has been used. Coracles have a short life and most Teifi fishermen believed in replacing their craft every two years.

The ash paddle is held by the right hand at the top end and the left hand at the lower quarter point. The boat moves, as in sculling, from side to side by describing a rough figure of eight.

One of the coracle's great advantages is its manoeuvrability and its shallow draught, only 3–4 in / 8–10 cm water. It is useful in shallow or rock-strewn waters both for netting and angling.

Coracle fishing is surrounded by mystery. Its secrets, language and code of practice have been handed down through the centuries and learning to fish from a coracle takes many years of apprenticeship.

When coracle fishing was unrestricted during the nineteenth century the river was divided into four sections: Cenarth, Aber-cuch, Llechryd and Cilgerran. Fishermen from one of the four villages had the sole right to fish in those sections of the river.

The Teifi method of fishing is to paddle two coracles downstream with a long net between them. When the salmon is caught the net is drawn into one coracle and the fish then hit on the head with a wooden cosh called a 'priest'. On reaching the end of a section the fishermen carry the boat back to the beginning and repeat the operation. The size of the net in this oldest form of trawling cannot sweep the river clean every time. More particularly, fish, especially salmon and large sea-trout (sewin) can only be caught one at a time because the net is too small and there is no room in the coracle to handle two fish of more than 10 lbs / 4.5 kg in weight. H P Wyndham remarked: 'The dexterity of the natives who fish in these coracles is amazing, though it frequently happens to the most expert, that a large fish will pull both the boat and the man underwater.'

The use of the coracle as a fishing craft even on the Teifi, Tywi and Tâf is declining. The 1923 Salmon and Freshwater Fisheries Act put an end to coracle fishing on many rivers and subsequent river authority bye-laws caused an even more rapid decline. Legislation in 1935 prohibited the issue of new licences to fishermen in the non-tidal section of the Teifi above Llechryd Bridge. In 1861 there had been more than 300 coracles on the river with about 28 pairs of fishermen. Cenarth was once regarded as the centre of coracle fishing but there is none there today, the last licence holder being unable to work after 1970. In the nineteenth century an observer wrote: 'There (is) scarcely a cottage in the neighbourhood of the Tivy, or the other rivers in these parts, abounding with fish, without its coracle hanging by the door.'

Bernard Thomas, coracle fisherman

Below Llechryd Bridge the river is classified as tidal. Until 1987 coracles were not registered but since then the number of licences has been limited under a net limitation order imposed by the Welsh Water Authority and they are not transferable. At Cilgerran five licensees are allowed to fish from coracles.

Annual coracle races were established in the 1830s under the patronage of Lewis Gomer, attracting many entrants and onlookers. These continue today in August at Cilgerran as part of a watersports festival. Regular coracle demonstrations take place during the summer on the Teifi at the Cardigan Wildlife Park. At Cenarth the coracle centre shows visitors the art of coracle making and there are plans to open a coracle museum showing types of coracle from all over Britain.

Corn mills

As elsewhere, the corn mills of the Teifi Valley generally served the needs of the immediate locality and were of great importance in the peasant economy before the Industrial Revolution. Most corn mills were owned by the local lord of the manor until well into the nineteenth century. Tenants were obliged to take their corn to be ground at the lord's mill rather than to another and were also expected to help with tasks such as thatching the mill and scouring the mill-pond. Remains of corn mills can be found throughout Wales and there are a number of working examples in the Teifi Valley. Some have much of their original machinery and are open to visitors.

Grain is usually raised to the upper floors of the mill with a hoist and then lowered into the grain bins. The bins are then opened to release the grain onto the rotating pair of millstones. Water drives the wheel which in turn drives the mill's grinding machinery.

Felin Geri flour mill

Felin Geri Flour Mill, near Cwm Cou, north-east of Newcastle Emlyn
This mill was built in 1604 and is well-known for its stoneground flour. It is still grinding on a commercial basis in the traditional way with all the original means of production and water from the River Ceri. Visitors are able to see every stage of the production process and stone-ground flour can be purchased at the mill shop. The bakery provides bread and scones for visitors at the café alongside the mill. There is also a rare example of a nineteenth century water-powered sawmill, a craft workshop, restaurant, museum of domestic industry (including bread and butter-making) and exhibition of the fishing history of the Teifi Valley. Set in 40 acres / 16.2 ha of unspoilt river valley and woodland, the estate also has a replica eighteenth century fort as a giant adventure playground, a farm of rare breed animals, trout pools, picnic areas and miles of nature walks.

Cenarth Mill, Cenarth, near Newcastle Emlyn
This mill beside the Cenarth Falls, a place formerly well-known for coracle fishing, probably dates from the eighteenth century and is currently being restored to full working order. There is an undershot timber and cast-iron water-wheel which drives two pairs of stones, one for barley and the other for oats. Cenarth Mill was formerly owned by the Cawdor Estate.

Y Felin / The Mill, St Dogmaels, near Cardigan
The present mill was probably built in the late-eighteenth or early-nineteenth century with new machinery installed in 1819. The overshot water-wheel incorporates a cast-iron rim brought from St David's mill and rebuilt in 1981 as part of the restoration of the mill. There are three sets of millstones, a flour bolter (for sifting the meal) and an oatmeal kiln which produce wholemeal and speciality flours. Situated near the ruins of St Dogmaels Abbey, the mill, tea-room and shop are open daily.

The woollen industry
Carding, spinning and weaving of wool took place in people's homes for centuries but the last decade of the eighteenth century saw the introduction of machinery and the consequent setting up of woollen factories. They were generally small family concerns powered by water and using local wool.

After 1880 and the introduction of power looms, the villages of Teifiside became the most important woollen manufacturing area in Wales, replacing Newtown by the turn of the century. From 1880 to 1920 the area enjoyed a period of unprecedented prosperity with the industry attracting workers from other areas both to provide work in the mills and, until about 1905, to build them. Up to 70 workers might be employed in the factories which were owned by Victorian industrial capitalists. The mills were no longer dependent on local farmers for their wool: some came from Welsh dealers but wool was also obtained from Dorset and New Zealand.

Most villages in the area had at least one woollen mill but the industry centred on

Llandysul, Pentre-cwrt and the twin village of Dre-fach Felindre. In 1899, a local historian writing in Welsh, remarked of Dre-fach Felindre,

'In all probability there are no two parishes in Wales producing as much flannel as these. Nearly all the power of the streams and rivers has been harnessed to drive machinery. There is hardly a spot on the river bank where it would be convenient to build an additional factory or mill.'

A number of factors contributed initially to the Teifiside industry. Water was easily available to drive machinery and to scour and wash the raw wool and fabrics. A plentiful supply of raw material came from the nearby hill sheep farms. The Teifi Valley was within reasonable reach of the industrial markets of South Wales. Expertise in spinning and the preparation of yarn already existed.

The smaller mills continued to rely on water (Rock Mill, near Llandysul still uses its water-wheel to turn some of its machinery) but most of the bigger factories went over to the more reliable gas engines. These were fuelled by anthracite from the western part of the South Wales coalfield, brought by train via Henllan, now the centre for the Teifi Valley narrow gauge railway. The railway also linked the mills to their South Wales markets. Power looms were installed to deal with all processes of textile manufacture, secondhand machinery often being purchased from Yorkshire mills.

A large proportion of the trade was in supplying flannel and shirts, underwear and shawls to the large, flourishing wholesale market of industrial South Wales. Certain mills concentrated on certain areas: Ogof Factory at Dre-fach Felindre, for example, in the 1890s sold at the fairs in and around Swansea. Maesllyn Mill supplied drapers in South Wales and also in London, Birmingham and Glasgow. Even the small mills served markets other than the local agricultural community and Welsh flannel was exported to clothe the slaves of North America.

The majority of people in the Teifiside villages were concerned with some aspect of textile manufacture. Most worked in a local mill but others wove cloth in their own homes or were engaged as 'outworkers' making up clothes for one of the mills. Children were expected to follow their parents to the mill as soon as they were ten years old. Within each factory, except the smallest, there was a distinct division of labour between those involved in spinning, weaving, carding, dyeing and finishing.

The people of Dre-fach Felindre did not see themselves as countryfolk and had a more urban outlook, like the people of the industrial valleys of South Wales with whom they traded. Their interests were similar: brass bands, soccer teams and male voice choirs.

The golden age of the industry, when the mill-owners made fortunes, lasted until the end of the First World War and the dramatic market collapse in the 1920s. The end of the war meant the end of War Office clothing orders for the troops and the dumping of surplus stocks on the market. Wool prices dropped quickly, within a few weeks and at the same time the home market in South Wales was gripped by depression. Weavers were dismissed because wages could not be paid and many people moved away to the towns and industrial regions. Chapels, grocery stores, public houses and craft workshops closed and choirs, dramatic societies and brass bands ceased to exist. Out of the fifty mills in Dre-fach Felindre in 1900 at least twenty closed around this time. Fourteen mills had disastrous fires and only two were rebuilt afterwards.

Today most mills are ruined and unrecognised although there are still about twenty working woollen mills in Wales. About half of these stand within a 12 mile / 19 km radius of the Cambrian Mills, Dre-fach Felindre, now the Museum of the Welsh Woollen Industry.

These mills employ far fewer people today. The majority are dependent on dyed yarn from Yorkshire, and are just specialised weaving mills unconcerned with carding, spinning and cloth finishing.

It was in the 1950s that the double-woven 'tapestry' cloth and bedcovers made its widespread appearance. Far from being a traditional Welsh design (though some similar patterns were woven on hand looms in the eighteenth century in north-east Wales), the pattern is equally well-known in Scotland, Kentucky, the north-west of Canada and among the American Indians.

In the Teifi Valley there are still a number of mills to visit, all with different aspects of the woollen industry to show.

Melin Teifi and the Museum of the Welsh Woollen Industry, Dre-fach Felindre
The original mill on this site was founded in the 1840s as the weaving shop of Doldywyll. It was rebuilt and re-equipped in the early years of this century as the Cambrian Woollen Mills, typical of the large-scale enterprises of the industry's heyday, employing over fifty people.

There is a comprehensive collection of old machinery and equipment, photographs and documents. These form the basis of an exhibition tracing the technological history and regional development of the Welsh woollen industry. An interpretative exhibition traces wool from fleece to fabric, there are regular demonstrations of hand-carding, spinning, handloom and power loom weaving and an exhibition of the products of contemporary woollen mills.

Within a mile of the museum all the stages in the development of the industry can be followed on a factory trail, from fulling mill through to weaver's cottage. The museum has a café and shop.

Double-width overshot water wheel, Rock Mill

The adjoining Melin Teifi was re-opened as a woollen mill in 1984, its seven looms producing cloth for garments on sale at the mill.

Rock Mill, Capel Dewi, Llandysul
Rock Mill was built in 1890 by John Morgan, the great-grandfather of the present operator. The River Cletwr, a tributary of the Teifi, is used to drive a rare double-width overshot water-wheel which powers the carding and spinning operations inside the factory as well as producing electricity via an alternator. This provides lighting for the factory and, before the coming of mains electricity, it supplied the neighbouring church. All woven articles and yarn produced in the mill are for sale in the shop.

Maesllyn Woollen Mill
Established in 1880, this privately-owned working museum preserves the atmosphere of a nineteenth century woollen mill. The changes from hand spinning and weaving to various types of powered machinery, some driven from the restored Pelton wheels, are shown here. In the renovated machinery hall there are displays of items and photographs from the nineteenth and twentieth centuries, including collections of sewing machines, laundry equipment, writing instruments and the largest collection of vintage wireless and television sets in Wales. There is also an audio-visual presentation. The museum has a shop, café and nature trail and is to be found between Croeslan on the A486 and Penrhiwal on the B4571.

Other woollen mills nearby are:
Siwan Woollen Mills in the old school building at Llanybydder
Curlew Weavers, a family firm established in 1961 at Rhydlewis, near Llandysul
Dyffryn Mills, Felindre – established about 1835, gutted by fire in 1926 and now re-opened
Dol-werdd (Ceredig), Felindre – built in 1899, closed in the 1920s and re-opened in 1970.

Use of the land

Strata Florida Abbey and its lands

When the Normans arrived in Britain they invited a number of Continental monastic orders to settle here. Of all the new orders the Cistercians seemed to fit in best with the Welsh tradition. Like the old Celtic saints they were ascetics, governed by strict rule, living a simple life with hard practical work. They chose to settle in the harshest and loneliest places of Wales and eventually identified themselves with Welsh ways and found patrons amongst the Welsh princes. In mid-Wales the Cistercians founded Strata Florida, its sister foundation of Abbey Cwmhir, near Llandrindod Wells and the latter's daughter Cymer Abbey, near Dolgellau and Strata Marcella near Welshpool (of which hardly anything remains).

In 1164 a group of monks from the Abbey at Whitland in Dyfed established a foundation on land provided by Robert Fitz-Stephen, Lord of Pennardd. It was barren and inhospitable, lying between the Red Bog of Tregaron to the west and the Cambrian Mountains to the east. In 1184 it attracted the enthusiastic patronage and support of the Lord Rhys of Deheubarth and so began the Abbey's entire rebuilding on a new site nearby, work which continued until 1235. The monks were granted vast tracts of upland grazing right across the mountains to Rhayader and from Plynlimon to Llanddewi Aberarth, just north of Aberaeron on the Cardigan Bay coast.

Much of the hewn stone for the construction of the new Abbey was brought by sea from Somerset to Aberarth and then dragged by oxen and manhandled the 12 miles / 19 km to Strata Florida. Aberarth later developed as Strata Florida's port for exporting wool and other agricultural commodities from its estates.

Little remains of the Abbey now, much of the site being covered by a group of eighteenth century farm buildings. The Celtic-Romanesque west door is an exceptional survival, remarkable for its uncharacteristic embellishment which includes triskel motifs. The design is Celtic, a direct link back over many centuries to the art of the Iron Age, before the coming of the Romans.

The monks illuminated manuscripts and encouraged Welsh language and literature. Much of the famous *Brut y Tywysogion* (Chronicle of the Princes), which recorded the history of Wales and the feats of many of its princes, was written at Strata Florida. Nine minor princes of the twelfth and thirteenth centuries are buried here, including two of Rhys' sons; rows of ancient tombstones can be seen to the east of the church. It is said that Dafydd ap Gwilym, the fourteenth century poet and bard whose repertoire was wider than that of almost any other mediaeval love poet, is also buried in the Abbey.

During the reign of Edward I the monks were known to have a sympathy for Welsh causes. In 1238 Llywelyn the Great called together all the Welsh princes here to swear allegiance to his son Dafydd and to confirm Dafydd's heredity as the sovereign Prince of Wales, as previously recognised by England and Rome. The Abbey served as a garrison for royal troops in the early fifteenth century when they were pursuing Owain Glyndŵr.

Although Strata Florida Abbey was in an unpromising and initially barren place it

became a major cultural and economic centre as well as a spiritual one. Strata Florida means 'flowery road' in Latin and the Welsh name of Ystrad Fflur means Vale of Flowers, both names probably referring to the flowers of Tregaron Bog.

The Cistercians were well-known for their agricultural ability. They made a major contribution to the area with their farm, gardens and orchards, and granges throughout Cardiganshire and in Brecknock and Radnor. When the Abbey was at the height of its power in the thirteenth century it ran huge flocks of sheep on the areas of mid-Wales under its control. It is said that the monks' success with sheep so impressed the Welsh that they gradually changed to sheep from a cattle-dominated economy. The monks became major exporters of wool and had several fulling mills. They bred trout and eels in the pools of the Teifi and created weirs in the streams passing through their lands. Their fishtraps on the coast caught herring and other fish. They grew wheat, oats and barley, especially on the coastal strip, and there were several corn mills. Peat was cut from the bog. They mined silver-lead and iron-ore, smelted it, had their own ships and built roads and bridges.

The monks are thought to have established the great fairs of Ffair-rhos to sell their own and peasant tenants' surplus farm produce and as a source of income from tolls. The fairs (and those at Ystradmeurig established under the patronage of the

Knights Hospitallers) were very attractive to hundreds of visitors who combined their visit with a pilgrimage to the Abbey. Strata Florida could be visited by making a short detour from the pilgrim route along the Cardigan Bay coast from Bardsey to St David's. The routes the pilgrims took often have distinctive place-names with the elements *yspyty*, *ysbyty*, *spite* or *spital*, possibly derived from the Latin *hospitium* (inn or hospitality). Hospitality to travellers was a basic duty of monastic bodies.

Pilgrims were also attracted by the fabulous relic of a small well-worn wooden cup, claimed to be a fragment of the true cross or even the chalice used at the Last Supper. The cup was reputed to have marvellous healing properties and many people visited the Abbey to be cured of a range of ills by drinking from it. It eventually came into the possession of the Powell family of Nanteos, near Aberystwyth and came to be known as the Nanteos Cup.

In later years there were quarrels amongst the monks and with other Church officials. This, together with the break-up of the traditional mediaeval economy, meant that at the Dissolution, there were just six monks and an abbot with a rental income of only £150.

Strata Florida stands in magnificent countryside, the starting point for walks into the surrounding hills. The routes used by the monks and the pilgrims remain today as roads and trackways. The Abbey's remains, a small museum and the neighbouring nineteenth century parish church of Pontrhydfendigaid can be reached by the B4340 or B4343 from Pontrhydfendigaid (the 'Bridge over the Blessed Ford').

Markets

There is a range of markets to visit in the Teifi Valley. Each has its own personality, whether a busy general stallholders' market or a livestock market, an extension of the business world of farming. Many market towns hold both markets on the same day and there is usually at least one pub or hotel with a special market-day licence.

The Teifi Valley's specialist market is the Llanybydder West Wales Horse Sales, held on the last Thursday of the month. This small town at a boundary point between the old counties of Carmarthenshire and Cardiganshire attracts buyers and dealers from all over the world. Up to 400 horses (and ponies, cobs, hunters and foals) are sold every month. The market was originally known for Welsh Ponies and Cobs which were used in the mining industries and in droving. They are no longer demanded for these tasks but they are important in the pony trekking business and their strong constitution, courage and kind temperament make them a popular stock from which to breed.

Markets are held weekly or fortnightly, alternating with a nearby town. There are also seasonal sheep sales.

Cardigan: Mondays (livestock), Saturdays and Mondays (general)
Lampeter: alternate Mondays and Tuesdays (livestock), alternate Tuesdays (general)
Llanybydder: alternate Mondays (general) and last Thursday in the month (horses)
Llandysul: Tuesdays (general)
Newcastle Emlyn: Fridays
Tregaron: alternate Tuesdays

Organic farming and diversification

In the past farmers produced a whole range of produce, from eggs and chickens to milk and cattle, sheep and wool. They grew timber and supplemented their income with other activities such as wood turning, spinning and weaving. For many this was a self-sufficient economy, like that of the monks at Strata Florida, but for others it was a subsistence lifestyle with occasional years of famine.

After the Second World War, concentration on agriculture for maximum food production resulted in intensive farming, drainage and ploughing, and the increased use of fertilisers and pesticides. With the United Kingdom's entry into the European Community and its Common Agricultural Policy, guaranteeing a fixed price for any amount of grain, beef, sheepmeat and other foodstuffs, farms tended to specialise even more, with cereals in the east, sheep on the marginal land and cattle on the fertile lowlands.

Lately, there has been a growing interest in organic and healthy foods. An increasing number of people would prefer to eat food which has been grown without the use of chemical fertilisers or pesticides. Alongside this is an increasing concern about the harm these may be doing to the environment. A number of farmers have begun, or continued, to control weeds and pests without using chemicals. The growth in this trend has coincided with a change in the face of farming and, to a lesser extent, agricultural landscapes.

Population levels in Britain and Europe have become more or less static, causing wide-scale over-production of food at huge cost to the tax payer. In an attempt to stem this over-production the EC has imposed milk quotas, sheep quotas and 'setaside' policies. Quotas put limits on the number of livestock units per farm, and 'setaside' is an attempt to take land out of production and use it for other purposes, such as nature conservation and country sports.

As a result of EC milk quotas, dairy farmers in many areas like the Teifi Valley have gone out of production – and with them the associated industries of creameries, agricultural machinery and other services. The creamery at Aberarad near Newcastle Emlyn closed in 1983, with the loss of 132 jobs.

In the lowlands some farmers have begun to keep sheep again and the EC is now introducing a limit on sheep numbers. This in turn will badly affect hill farmers whose marginal land has only been profitable with the sheep subsidy.

In this economic climate, farmers are being encouraged to diversify. This involves producing a range of products rather than relying on one or two, perhaps more like former times. Farmers are also looking to products with 'added value', where raw materials have gone through an additional process on the farm which adds to the price the customer will pay. Examples of diversification and added value in the Teifi Valley are organic vegetables, speciality cheeses and smoked fish. Caws Cenarth (or Cenarth Cheese) is a natural product made exclusively from the milk of pedigree cows with no artificial colour, preservative or fertiliser. Fferm Glyneithinog, Pontseli at Boncath near Cardigan is open most weekdays for the sale of this special cheese.

Organic Farm Foods near Lampeter claims to be the biggest organic food company in Britain, marketing for producers from as far away as Somerset, the

Midlands and Scotland. The demand is so great that 65–70% of their food has to be imported; 150 tons of produce are handled every week.

Organic farming is no recent fad: concern about the effects of industrial methods of agriculture was voiced in the late nineteenth century and arguments about soil management were fairly sophisticated by the 1950s. Along with diversification and the efforts of such food promotions as 'Taste of Wales' and the Dyfed Food Initiative, the Teifi Valley is one of the areas leading the way.

Wildlife gardening

There are a number of places to see wildlife gardens in mid-Wales including the Brimstone Wildlife Centre at Penuwch, near Tregaron and the six-acre Winllan Wildlife Garden, nine miles / 14.5 km north of Lampeter on the Talsarn-Llangeitho road, open to the public on certain days of the week. This garden is situated on the banks of the unpolluted River Aeron along which one can see herons, moorhens, mallards, dippers, kingfishers and damselflies. There is a pond, and orchids grow in the marsh. An organic hay-meadow created by good management is rich in wildflowers and the mini-cornfield has red poppies and corncockles. On the dry bank, ox-eye daisy, cat's ear and bird's foot trefoil attract large numbers of insects and butterflies. Native trees grow in the wood, many planted by the Callans, the custodians of Winllan.

Twm Shon Cati

Twm Shon Cati, according to tradition, was the illegitimate son of Sir John Wynne of Gwydir and Catherine Jones of Tregaron. He was born at Ffynnon Llidiart near Tregaron some time in the sixteenth century. Unusually for the time he had some education as his mother taught him to read and write, but to free them from poverty he became a thief between the ages of 18 and 19. His clever and daring exploits as a rogue, especially as a horse and cattle thief, became legendary throughout Wales. He was particularly renowned for disguising himself as an ancient crone, a begging cripple or a wounded soldier. He was also able to disguise his stolen animals so well that he could sell them back to their original owners. The forces of the law found it difficult to arrest him: Twm was either never at home when they called or, being in disguise, he did not look at all like the man they had come to arrest.

Nevertheless, at one time the law got too close for comfort and Twm went to live in a cave in the Upper Tywi valley, near Cilycwm. The cave is more like a narrow cleft in the rock, set up high on a tree-covered outcrop and surrounded on three sides by rivers. When Twm was at home he always had a sword handy to cut off the head of anyone stooping low to enter. Twm Shon Cati's Cave can be found along a marked path in the Dinas bird reserve, beyond Llyn Brianne on the mountain road.

Despite his reputation as a thief Twm was on good terms with his neighbours, both the poor to whom he gave away money, and with the rich since he knew or invented their pedigrees and had a gift for composing odes.

Eventually Twm married a wealthy lady. Legend tells that her father would not agree to the marriage and locked her up in a barred room. Twm got her to put her hand through the bars and then threatened to cut it off if she did not marry him. He slipped a ring on her finger (luckily a priest was nearby) and they waited until the father died, when they inherited his estate.

Money enabled Twm to obtain a general pardon and also a commission as a Justice of the Peace where his previous experience stood him in good stead. Some stories tell that he became High Sheriff of Carmarthenshire. He retired as Thomas Jones, poet, antiquarian and JP.

George Borrow points out in *Wild Wales* that many of the actions attributed to him are those attributed to legendary rogues everywhere from Delaney, the Irish thief, to Klim, the Russian robber.

Cardigan Bay

The long sweep of Cardigan Bay between the northern peninsula of the Llŷn and the southern one of the old county of Pembrokeshire is a favourite place for many people.

The coastline changes constantly. In the north there are miles of golden sandy dunes and beaches with the mountains of Snowdonia in the background. There are low-lying meadows, the bracing steep cliffs and headlands of the southerly part of the coast, rocky shores and small and secluded beaches. And, however well you think you know the coast, you can always be caught unawares by the glorious estuaries of the Glaslyn, Mawddach and Dyfi or the noise of the sea on shingle beaches or just by the changing weather and light.

Many small rivers also make their way down to the coast from the Cambrian Mountains. In their clear waters, in the rock pools and on the shore there is much to discover as well as keeping a lookout for the grey seals which live in the area from New Quay to Cardigan.

These shores and further inland have been the scene of great industry in the past. The tradition of maritime activity reaches from the earliest settlers of prehistoric times to the fishing and pleasure craft of the present day. The western seaways were the highways of the Celtic saints, the herring caught from small smacks was part of people's staple diet and the bigger boats built in the shipyards travelled all over the world. Lime was imported and prepared in kilns on the shore to fertilise the poor acidic clay soils; silver and lead mined inland contributed to the area's wealth in other ways. Today many of those activities have gone but there is much to see and do or just to dream and consider.

This has been an area of holiday resort for many years developing with the arrival of the railways in the nineteenth-century. The towns and villages are a joy to explore – the stone-built villages of Meirionnydd, Barmouth with its panoramic views from the cliffs above, Tywyn, town of the sandy shore, Aberystwyth, the focal point of the coast, the planned pastel town of Aberaeron, and New Quay, once full of the activity of shipbuilding.

Myths and legends persist – of the lost domain under the sea, the beautiful Branwen who lived at Harlech, the wicked robbers who lay in wait at Devil's Bridge and the many itinerant saints who travelled by sea.

Cardigan Bay is a coast to explore and a place to delight in the beautiful views of both land and sea. There is much to discover in an area of great historical interest and many pursuits for the active – bathing, boating, fishing, water skiing and more. There is a choice of quietness or wildness according to your mood.

Aberaeron

Aberaeron is a pastel-painted, neat town at the mouth of the River Aeron, as its name suggests. Aeron means, basically, 'battle', referring to the goddess who was believed to live in its crystal-clear waters. The earliest recorded settlement was Castell Cadwgan, a fortification built in 1145 whose name has been recorded by the SS *Prince Cadwgan*, the ketch *Cadwgan*, Cadwgan Square and, nowadays, a pub. The town has a population of 1,445 people and is the only one in mid-Wales to have been deliberately planned. There are many buildings of historical or architectural interest.

In 1805 the small fishing hamlet was part of the large estate of Lewis Gwynne of Mynachdy. When he died he bequeathed most of his estate in Cardiganshire to the Reverend Alban Thomas Jones and his wife Maria, on condition they took the surname Gwynne.

In the eighteenth century spirit of improvement Reverend Gwynne decided to develop the harbour. Between 1807 and 1811 breakwaters were built and Aberaeron soon developed into a flourishing trading port (exporting butter, corn, cattle and wool) with a busy ship-building industry. Development continued with the building of the open square around the harbour and the adjacent grid of terraces, the fine Harbour Master's house, and in 1835 the elegant Town Hall facing the harbour. From the beginning, builders who applied for leases had to conform to an overall plan in which John Nash, the architect of Buckingham Palace, is reputed to have had a hand. The repeated keystone patterns seen above many doors and windows show the trademarks of different builders. There is a feeling of space and neatness with wide main streets and larger buildings at the end and centre of terraces avoiding monotony. There are deeply-marked quoins or corner stones and decorated lintels and porches. Every dwelling had to have its walls painted with a terracotta limewash every two years. The town's pavements were cobbled decoratively with pebbles from the beach, still to be seen in places such as Belle Vue Terrace, outside the Magistrates' Clerk's office in Alban Square and opposite the County Court.

Alban Square was built in 1840. In the 1900s the public green had a cycle track, parts of the embankment of which can still be seen.

Although Georgian in appearance, much of Aberaeron was not built until well into the reign of Victoria. Waterloo Street and Wellington Street were built soon after 1815 and Princess Street, Queen Street, Albert Street, Victoria Street and Regent Street much later. There are also small cottages in Drury Lane and Masons' Row, for example. Chalybeate Well House covers a mineral spring: Aberaeron could have been a spa town.

Today Aberaeron is an elegant and unspoilt holiday resort with two safe beaches, the more pleasant of which is South Beach. There is ample opportunity for walking, whether along the riverside or the old railway line, enjoying the birds and flowers, a pleasant stroll around the town or energetic hikes along coastal footpaths.

The harbour is a colourful place, full of yachts and small fishing boats. There are weekend yacht races. There is good angling for brown trout, sea trout (sewin) and salmon, especially in the deep pools below the four weirs. The pool below Lovers' Bridge was formerly used as a baptism pool. On the old wharf the Hive on the Quay has honey, icecream and a honey-bee exhibition. This is also the starting point for the recreated Extraordinary Aerial Ferry – the Aeron Express. This device, a four seater carriage, moved across by hand-powered pulleys on each quayside, was first built in 1885 by Captain John Evans and operated for 46 years. Further along is the Marine Sea Aquarium and Animal Kingdom where the wildlife of the coast is on display.

For more information, including accommodation, contact the Ceredigion District Council Information Centre, The Quay, Aberaeron, Dyfed SA46 0BT. Telephone (0545) 570602 (seasonal). The building is the former mortuary.

Aberystwyth

Situated in the centre of Cardigan Bay and at the mouth of the river Rheidol, Aberystwyth is the principal sea-resort on the western coast of Wales. The town's name refers to the old site of the town, 1.5 miles away in the valley of the River Ystwyth. 'Ystwyth' means 'winding' describing the river as it flows to the sea.

It lies between two headlands. To the south is the double hillfort of Pen Dinas, one of the largest and best-preserved Iron Age earthworks in Wales, a trading centre controlling inland routes and with easy access to the sea. It reached its full development about 100BC but would have been abandoned soon after the arrival of the Romans in AD75. Nowadays the Wellington Monument stands on the top, a landmark for seafarers. To the north lies Constitution Hill and the Camera Obscura on the summit. There is a stiff climb to the top or a ride on the Aberystwyth Cliff Railway, the longest electric cliff railway, but whichever you choose you are rewarded by spectacular views of Cardigan Bay. On a clear day you can see Snowdon (44 miles / 71 km to the north).

The harbour was a significant factor in Edward I choosing this site for a castle, begun in August 1277 at the end of his first campaign to conquer Wales. Situated in pleasant gardens above the mouth of the Rheidol it is now in a ruinous state having seen a number of hostile sieges. The castle suffered most at the hands of Owain Glyndŵr in the fifteenth century, was home to a Mint just before the Civil War (using silver mined nearby) and was blown up in 1649 by Parliamentary forces. Laura Place has eighteenth and nineteenth century buildings from the prosperous time when lead was the most valuable commodity leaving the harbour. The fantastic neo-Gothic building near the Royal Pier started off as a hotel but when funds ran out was taken over as the University College building. There is safe bathing north of the pier.

The Old College, University of Wales, Aberystwyth

The history of the district of Ceredigion (broadly the former Cardiganshire) can be traced in the Ceredigion Museum, housed in the restored Edwardian Coliseum Theatre whose atmosphere has been carefully preserved.

Today Aberystwyth has a population of 11,170 people. The modern buildings of University College, Aberystwyth (part of the University of Wales) are on Penglais Hill where the fine building of the National Library of Wales can also be found. A copyright library, it houses over two million volumes including a collection of priceless ancient Welsh books and manuscripts, some of which are displayed in the exhibition halls. Aberystwyth Arts Centre and the Theatr y Werin are also in Penglais.

The general market is held on Monday (as it was in Edward I's thirteenth-century walled and gated town) and the Women's Institute co-operative market is on Thursday morning in the Market Hall.

The former village of Llanbadarn Fawr, now a suburb of Aberystwyth, was the settlement of St Padarn in the sixth century. Inside thirteenth-century Llanbadarn Fawr church is a visual celebration of the history of the village including two Celtic memorial stones and a cell typical of St Padarn.

To the north is Brynllys organic farm, Ynyslas National Nature Reserve and Visitor Centre, spectacular dunes and beaches, Borth Bog, the National Museum of Wales at Yr Hen Gapel / The Old Chapel, Tre'r Ddôl (a museum of nineteenth century religious life), Ynyshir RSPB reserve, Dyfi Furnace and restored water mill.

To the east a narrow-gauge steam railway runs along the Vale of Rheidol to Devil's Bridge running for 12 miles from sea-level through picturesque wooded glens and past waterfalls up to 680 ft / 207 m near Devil's Bridge. This was once the main coach road to Rhayader via Devil's Bridge and Cwmystwyth. Further up these valleys are lead, copper and silver mines on which the prosperity of the whole area depended. The Llywernog silver-lead mine on the A44 near Ponterwyd is open to visitors. Bwlch Nant yr Arian Forest Visitor Centre is high above the Rheidol Valley, eight miles east of Aberystwyth, just off the main A44. Cwmrheidol hydro-electric Visitor Centre has a trout lake and nature trail. Nanteos, built in 1739 in Palladian spirit and former home of the Powells who made money through the mines, is open to the public and lies four miles east of Aberystwyth, off the A4120.

For more information, including accommodation, contact the Ceredigion District Council Information Centre, Terrace Road, Aberystwyth, Dyfed. Telephone (0970) 612125.

Barmouth

The name of this popular holiday town on the Mawddach estuary is a mixture of both English and Welsh. The name of the river is probably derived from *Mawdd*, which was then rendered into English as 'mouth'. In Welsh the town is known as Abermaw or Abermo and also, incorrectly, Y Bermo. With a population of 2,142 people the town is built against steep cliffs with a long sandy beach and wide promenade. Views across the beautiful estuary are to Cader Idris and its foothills. To the north are the Rhinog mountains. From the busy harbour, where the lifeboat and the RNLI museum are housed, there are ferries across to Fairbourne and boat trips up the estuary. The town also boasts the Dragon Theatre.

There are older houses, such as Tŷ Gwyn, an originally mediaeval house on the harbour, reputedly where Jasper Tudor met supporters to plot to overthrow Richard III and put Henry Tudor, the Earl of Richmond (Henry VII) on the throne. Barmouth, though, only really grew in the railway age. Before the road along the estuary was built, Panorama Walk, above the town, was the only way from

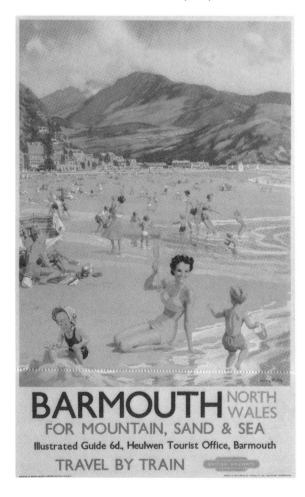

Dolgellau. Dinas Oleu, the first piece of land to be owned by the National Trust, given in 1895, is also above the town.

There are tall eighteenth and nineteenth century houses built up the steep slopes and the 1889 church, designed by John Douglas, a Chester architect and built, not from local stone, but red sandstone imported by rail from Chester.

In June, Barmouth sees the start of the Three Peaks International Yacht Race. Hardy competitors sail to Fort William, stopping en route to run up to the summits of Snowdon, Scafell Pike and Ben Nevis.

The wooden railway bridge, now reopened after its battle with the teredo worm, is the first bridging point of the estuary. There is a footbridge for pedestrians to enjoy the views of Friar's Island and the tidal estuary – feeding ground for many birds – and perhaps to continue on to the Cregennen Lakes above Arthog. For cars there is an attractive timber toll bridge at Penmaenpool, three miles / five km west of Dolgellau.

Within easy reach are the 'Roman Steps', Dyffryn Ardudwy megalithic long cairn, Harlech Castle and the National Nature Reserves of Morfa Dyffryn and Morfa Harlech as well as the other interesting villages of the Meirionnydd coast.

General market day in Barmouth is on Thursday.

For more information, including accommodation, contact the Wales Tourist and Barmouth Publicity Information Centre, The Old Library, Station Road, Barmouth, Gwynedd LL42 1NL. Telephone (0341) 280787 (seasonal).

New Quay

This busy holiday and yachting resort on the leeward side of New Quay Head developed as a fishing port and an important shipbuilding centre in 1835 with the construction of the new harbour. It replaced an older smaller one which had provided shelter for smugglers in the eighteenth century. The Welsh name Ceinewydd translates exactly as 'new quay' and this gave the only safe harbour along this stretch of coast. The population is about 800 people but there are many more in summer months as people come to stay near this village with its narrow, hilly streets. A famous visitor of the past was Dylan Thomas who stayed in the 1940s and found some of his inspiration for *Under Milk Wood*.

New Quay is still a fishing port today. Lobster pots can be seen on the quayside and local boats sell their freshly-caught fish. Anglers catch pollack from rocks near the headland. There is a choice of beaches including the deep sand, safe boating and bathing of the harbour beach, and the undeveloped, fairly peaceful Cei Bach beach. The lifeboat station is open to the public in the summer, ready to help pleasure craft and other boats. Boat trips are available. The coast (part of the Heritage Coast) offers fine walks and wonderful views. To the south, at yet another Bird Rock (Craig yr Adar) you can see a multitude of seabirds, and the National Trust own Caerllan Farm at Cwmtudu as well as the rocky headland hillfort of Lochtyn which give views of the entire coast. To the north of New Quay is Llanina Point and the 150 ft / 46 m cliffs of Craig Ddu, which has a waterfall over the edge after rain.

The New Quay Bird Hospital, set up in the early 1970s to clean and rehabilitate oil-coated seabirds is nearby at Cross Inn. With the help of local vets it now treats all kinds of wild creatures with the aim of getting them fit and released back into the wild.

On Fridays from April to December the Women's Institute co-operative market can be found from 11.00 am to 1.30 pm in the Memorial Hall.

For information, including accommodation, contact Ceredigion District Council Information Centre, Church Street, New Quay, Dyfed SA45 9NZ.
Telephone (0545) 560865 (seasonal).

Tywyn and Aberdyfi

Tywyn is surrounded by the foothills of the Cader Idris range and lies in the plain of the Dysynni river just south of Broad Water, a wildfowl haunt. The older part of the town lies about a mile inland but it has gradually grown to meet the sandy beach and dunes which its name describes. There is a population of around 3,000 people, more in summer. Tywyn may be the place where St Cadfan from Brittany founded his first settlement in the seventh century. The seventh-century St Cadfan's stone, about 7 ft / 2.1 m high, with the oldest known Welsh inscription is in the church. Although the building is mainly nineteenth century, the nave, arcades and part of the north transept are late eleventh century and there are two fourteenth-century effigies.

The Tal-y-llyn railway, originally built in 1866 to carry slate from the quarry above Abergynolwyn, starts from Tywyn Wharf, where there is a railway museum, shop and café, and ends at Nant Gwernol. You can stop en route and explore – three waterfalls in a wooded ravine are just a short distance from Dolgoch Halt. Travelling further up the valley you come to Tal-y-llyn lake, formed during the Ice Age, at the foot of Cader Idris.

Craig yr Aderyn (Bird Rock) and Castell y Bere, the Welsh castle, are near to Tywyn. Trefrifawr Farm trail, overlooking the Dyfi estuary, will enable you to find out more about a Welsh hill farm.

The Holgates Honey Farm and Factory Shop is on the outskirts of Tywyn. Market day is Wednesday, during the summer.

Three miles of footpaths through the dunes lead to nearby Aberdyfi (Aberdovey) on the shores of the Dyfi estuary, a National Nature Reserve and across the water from Ynyslas, a duneland and bog National Nature Reserve. Aberdyfi is another historic town where Llywelyn the Great came to a settlement with the other princes of Wales in 1216, and which used to be one of the most important ports on the Welsh coast. Today there is a small nautical museum and a strong Outward Bound presence as well as boat trips to see the estuary and Cardigan Bay. There are many pleasant early-nineteenth-century buildings.

For information, including accommodation, contact Wales Tourist Board, High Street, Tywyn, Gwynedd LL36 9AD. Telephone (0654) 710070 (summer only).

The Snowdonia National Park Centre, The Wharf, Aberdyfi, Gwynedd LL35 0ES. Telephone (065 472) 321 (seasonal).

The Dynamic Coastline

For over 30,000 years, until 14,000 years ago, most of mid-Wales was covered by dense ice sheets and glaciers. Where those glaciers (some over 1,000 ft / 300 m thick) centred over the Harlech Dome and Plynlimon and moving slowly westward met the south-flowing ice-masses of the Irish Sea, the great earth-wrenching forces involved gouged out the basic shape of what we today know as the coast of Cardigan Bay.

Some 10,000 years ago, this Ice Age came to a fairly abrupt end when for some still not fully understood reason, air temperatures rose causing the ice sheets and glaciers to melt and retreat northwards. At the end of this period sea-level was about 200 ft / 60 m below its present level and the coastline about 7.5 miles / 12 km further west and nearer to Ireland. As the ice retreated, where the harder underlying rock lay, it left behind cliffs, glaciated valleys and a rich covering of glacial debris. The erosion of the softer rocks produced a mineral rich 'till'.

This glacial material was ideal for colonisation by the wind-dispersed seeds of plants which had survived the glacial winter in the extreme south of Wales and certain parts of mid-Wales, beyond the limit of the enshrouding ice. Arctic-alpine grassland developed, soon to be followed by a succession of shrubs and trees such as birch, willow, pine and elm. By about 7,000 years ago, most of Wales was covered in forest.

As sea-level rose to its present level, some of these forests along the coast were gradually submerged and evidence of this can still be seen between Ynyslas and Borth where the stumps of a submerged forest of birch, alder and Scots Pine can still be seen.

The dynamic coastline did not stop there – it continues to shift and change to this day. The constant coastal erosion and deposition by tides, currents, longshore drift (a particularly constant shift of sands in one particular direction) and wind, is continually reforming the edge of Cardigan Bay. You have only to look at Harlech Castle – which in the thirteenth century overlooked the sea from its dominant clifftop location and now, only seven centuries later, is more than half a mile inland – to appreciate the shifting nature of the shoreline. Or visit Llandanwg a short distance away, where moving sand-dunes are even now threatening to engulf the small fifteenth-century stone church. Further south, the storm beach at Borth has extended northwards by some 1,000 ft / 300 m in the last 20 years, and no more dramatic example of the forces of nature is needed than the catastrophic collapse of part of Aberystwyth's northern promenade in the last century.

Estuaries

Perhaps the two most beautiful and dramatic features of Cardigan Bay are the twin estuaries of the Mawddach and the Dyfi, both products of glacial over-deepening and rising sea level.

The Mawddach estuary extends from the toll bridge at Penmaenpool to the seaside town of Barmouth. The mouth of the estuary is straddled by an impressive railway viaduct and pinched by a sand spit which extends almost across from nearby Fairbourne. One of the best places to start exploring the estuary is the RSPB's

Penmaenpool Wildlife Information Centre, a converted signal box on the A493 south of Dolgellau. A railway walk runs along the track of the disused Aberdyfi to Dolgellau Great Western Railway by the edge of the estuary. From this can be appreciated a wide range of habitats from the oak woodlands covering the slopes to low-lying saltmarshes and sandbanks, hazards to shipping and haven for wading birds.

The Dyfi estuary, further south, has a similar shape, extending some 5 miles / 7.5 km inland and 1.5 miles / 2.5 km at its widest point at high tide. Its mouth is also

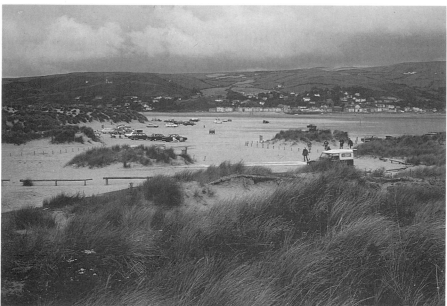

TOP *Mawddach estuary, Barmouth.* BOTTOM *Ynyslas sand-dunes*

restricted, this time by the sand-dune complex at Ynyslas. Nestling in these sand dunes is the Nature Conservancy Council Wildlife Information Centre, again a good starting point for exploring the estuary and its features. For those primarily interested in wading birds, the RSPB's bird hides at Ynyshir on the A487 south of Machynlleth are worth a visit.

Both estuaries are constantly shifting bodies of seawater and freshwater, of mud, silt and sand. Generally speaking, where currents are strong only the larger, heavier particles can settle and finer silts and clays are held in suspension. The coarse, sandier sediments thus tend to be found at the mouth of the estuaries, while mudbanks and associated saltmarshes are found in the stiller waters of the upper reaches.

Dunes and sandy beaches

Cardigan Bay can boast a number of large sand dune complexes and fine sandy beaches. Two of the best dune systems can be found at Morfa Harlech and Morfa Dyffryn, both designated National Nature Reserves. Access to the fragile dunes themselves is restricted, but they have good car parks and access points to the beach. Boardwalks laid down on the sand help to protect the dunes and provide a solid path down to the shore.

An interesting feature of sand dune complexes is their zonation, that is, the way they change in structure from the beach to their inland limit. The *embryo dune* is the seaward beginning, where sand-bearing winds are intercepted by plants such as sea rocket and prickly saltwort which begin the process of binding the sand together and laying down the dunes. Next come the *foredunes*, often characterised by stiff grasses such as marram which have the important characteristic of being able to grow almost without limit both horizontally and upwards through blown sand. After about 10 years, these foredunes develop into the taller, more species-rich *yellow dunes*, which in turn give way to *grey dunes*, so called because of the colonisation of their bare sand by grey colouring lichen. It is possible to record over 30 different types of plants (if one includes mosses, liverworts and lichens) in one metre square of such dunes. Finally the *dune slacks* are low lying, often submerged, areas between the grey dunes where some types of orchid find ideal conditions for survival. Such dune systems are very fragile and disturbance can cause catastrophic 'blow-out', where the protective vegetation is stripped and large volumes of sand are literally blown away. Less dramatically, but no less seriously, unprotected and unbalanced dunes can rapidly advance inland and smother farmland and buildings. (The church at Llandanwg is a good example.)

However, there are plenty of safe sandy beaches all along the coast, starting at Harlech with its 4 mile / 6.5 km stretch of sand, sweeping round to Llandanwg and Talybont and another 15 miles / 24 km of unspoilt golden beach. Barmouth, Fairbourne, Tywyn (which means sand dune in Welsh), Aberdyfi and Borth all have busy sandy beaches, but check locally for bathing safety.

Further south, New Quay has three beaches. Two of them, the harbour beach bounded by the stone pier and Traethgwyn, are gently sloping and sandy. The small village of Llangrannog has two fine sandy coves which nestle at the base of

Morfa Dyffryn

impressive cliffs. Penbryn has three-quarters of a mile / 1.2 km of golden sand which merges with the beach of nearby Tresaith at low tide. Finally Mwnt, near Cardigan, has a fine sandy beach which with its southern aspect forms a natural suntrap.

Shingle beaches

For those who prefer the crunch of pebbles underfoot, shingle beaches abound, notably near ready sources of eroded rock and where wave action and currents are particularly vigorous. Borth has a broad shingle spit separating the sea from the inland bog. Tanybwlch south of Aberystwyth has perhaps the finest example of a storm beach, with its steeply-shelving curve of shifting stones. Aberaeron's two pebble beaches are separated only by its fine stone-walled harbour. Cwmtudu near New Quay has a predominantly shingle beach with a small area of sand exposed at low tide. Here, pebbles are often thrown up by storm waves to block the mouth of the stream and create a large freshwater pool popular with children.

Cliffs, rocks and islands

Broadly speaking, the southern half of the Bay has the most striking cliff scenery and clifftop walks. Particularly impressive is the stretch of coast from New Quay south to Cardigan, which includes Cwmtudu, Llangrannog, Aberporth and Mwnt. Further north, Wallog and Morfa Bychan near Aberystwyth have fine craggy cliffs and rocky shores.

Islands possess their own particular magic and small gems occur along the coast. Shell Island or Ynys Mochras, near Harlech, is really a sand spit which is easily

Ynys Lochtyn, near Llangrannog

reached along a causeway at low tide. It has a sheltered harbour, camping facilities, café and shop. Its name derives from the large accumulations of shell material built up along its margins. The tidal island of Ynys y Brawd (Friar's Island) at Barmouth can also be easily reached on foot at low tide.

Ynys Lochtyn near Llangrannog stands at the tip of the Lochtyn Peninsula, and can be distinguished by its distinctive band of white quartz. Both it and Mwnt are now in the care of the National Trust. It was formed by progressive and continual erosion by the sea which first of all carved caves out of the rock, then a sea-arch and finally the islet of Lochtyn.

Cardigan Island is the only true island along this coast and during the summer months, boat trips can be taken around it from neighbouring Gwbert on Sea. Now managed by the Dyfed Wildlife Trust, it has good soil and a deep grass cover, but until very recently, few birds because of rat infestation. Attempts have been made to remove the rats, to introduce shearwaters and even to attract nesting puffins by using wooden decoys!

What lives on Cardigan Bay?

Grey seals

The type of large colony of grey seals associated with the Farne Islands and islands around Scotland is not to be found in Wales. Grey seals require an undisturbed breeding area, and in Wales this will mean isolated sea caves and small bays, often backed by steep cliffs preventing access from the land. The size of these sites means that they can often accommodate only one or two pups at a time.

Although the main seal-breeding sites are further to the south in Pembrokeshire, and most notably the Pembrokeshire islands, there are breeding sites in mid-Wales to the north of Cardigan. The coastline from Cardigan Island to New Quay provides suitably undisturbed caves and beaches, and it is likely that 20 to 30 pups are produced in this area every year. Travelling further north from New Quay to Aberystwyth the coastline becomes less suitable and more accessible from the land, so there are very few breeding sites. North of Aberystwyth there is a preponderance of open sandy beaches popular with holidaymakers, and cliffs give way to gentle slopes and sand dunes, providing an environment totally unsuited to seals. It is not until the more rugged coastline of the Llŷn Peninsula is reached that conditions are once again favourable.

The main breeding season is between mid-September and mid-November, but pups may be born at any time from late August through to early spring. Seals however do not come ashore only to breed, and seals of both sexes will come ashore throughout the year. These haul-out sites will change through the year, some being used mainly in winter, others in summer. Groups of seals will often gather on small offshore rocks and islands. Seals are extremely nervous on land, and if disturbed will usually make straight for the sea.

Given this sensitivity to disturbance and the inaccessibility of mainland breeding and haul-out sites, the greatest chance of seeing seals is probably either in the water or on offshore rocks. Seals are seen offshore occasionally throughout the length of Cardigan Bay, but the greatest concentration will be found in the Cardigan to New Quay area. The nervousness displayed by seals on land is not matched by their behaviour in the water. Whereas on land their movements are slow and lumbering leaving them vulnerable, in the water they are quick and agile making them completely at ease. In their own environment they can afford to be curious, and will often show great interest in people watching from the cliff tops.

Bull and cow seals are easily distinguished, even when they are in the water and only the head is visible. The cow is altogether smaller, slimmer and more delicate in appearance, a fully grown cow averaging about 7 ft / 2.1 m in length compared to around 8 ft / 2.4 m for a bull. The face shape is a distinguishing characteristic, with the cow having a gently concave bridge to her nose. A typical cow will have a coat of mid-grey, paler on the underside, with large, dark-grey markings scattered randomly. The bull is generally much darker. The coat is usually finely mottled, lacking large patches of varying colour, and may appear as a uniform black when wet. The bull has a much broader face, and the bridge of the nose is slightly convex in profile. The bull also has much heavier shoulders and foreflippers, and the skin around the neck and shoulders is often rough and scarred as a result of conflicts with other seals.

A pup will be fed by the cow for the first two to three weeks of its life. A newborn pup has silky golden fur and is very thin, with the skin appearing loose. Over the next few days the golden colour will fade to white, and the pup will put on weight rapidly filling out the ill-fitting skin. A pup is capable of swimming from the day of its birth, and if the beach where it lives is inundated by the tide it may well be forced to do so, but in its early days its swimming is weak and its movements poorly co-ordinated.

Sea shells – home for what?

At first glance there might not appear to be much wildlife on the beach but closer observation will pay off. What lives where depends on a number of factors – the type of shore (whether salt marsh, mud, sand, shingle or rock), the tides, how exposed the shore is and how far up it creatures need to live.

You may think that life on a beach is fairly easy. In fact it can be to experience nothing less than marine terrorism.

Seashells are the hard outside skeleton of a group of animals called molluscs. Molluscs may be swallowed alive by waders, flatfish or starfish, killed with their digestive juices and the inedible shell unceremoniously ejected. They may be dropped from a great height by herring gulls or forced open by oyster-catchers whose long red beak has been recorded as 'the next best thing to a burglar's jemmy'. There are an astonishing number of molluscs (1.5 million in an acre [0.4 ha] of cockle flats, for example) and they use a variety of methods to make the most of different habitats.

The limpet feeds on the fine vegetation which covers the rocks, its favourite food being newly-settled seaweed spores. Its feeding trail of over a metre can be seen on the rock it uses as a base, always returning to the same place, clasping the rock tightly to avoid drying out unless conditions are very humid. However, you may find an empty limpet shell with the tell-tale jemmy marks of an oyster catcher around the margin or a hole drilled by a dog whelk.

The flat winkle browses on seaweed. With its bladder-like appearance it can hide easily in amongst bladder wrack.

Whelks are carnivorous. The widely-distributed common dog whelk is the chief predator of barnacles, especially the acorn barnacle. The dog whelk exudes purpurin, a poisonous secretion which relaxes the barnacle's muscles. This yellow dye turns purple in the sun and was used to dye the purple edge of Roman emperors' togas and to illuminate mediaeval manuscripts. The dog whelk may also spend two days boring a hole in the shell of the limpet, using the rasping surface of its belt-like tongue and then sucking out the flesh.

The common whelk or buckie is widely distributed in the muddy gravel or sand of the lower shore and below. You may find their shells with large holes in them on a road or promenade, having been dropped by a herring gull. And all whelks can have the top part of their shell removed by the shore crab or have it smashed entirely open by the claws of an edible crab or lobster.

Mussels, doing no more harm than to feed by filtering food and oxygen through enlarged gills, may have their shells pulled open by the five arms or rays of the

Edible winkle Netted dog whelk Barnacles Dog whelk Limpet

Common whelk Tube worm Cockle Horse mussel Blunt gaper Grooved razor

Oyster Thin tellin Flat winkle

Scallop

beautiful orange common starfish. Like cockles and limpets, mussels may be hunted by the oyster catcher.

Cockles are typical of sand, gravelly mud and extensive sand flats. Buried just below the surface, they extend two siphons when the tide comes in. Water enters through one, is sieved through the gills for suspended food particles and then ejected through the other. Cockles are hunted by starfish, flatfish and people.

The razorshells are easily recognised as they look like old-fashioned cut-throat razors. Their well-designed shape offers the least resistance to the sand when the animal decides to pull itself deeper, and under attack it can disappear extremely fast.

Scallops live on the seabed and have the useful capacity, by closing their valves together very quickly, to leap for a considerable distance, enough to get away from a hungry starfish.

Although acorn barnacles look like molluscs, they are related to crabs and shrimps and can be found fixed head-downwards on rocks or wood. Their bodies are protected by a series of plates but when immersed by the sea this trapdoor opens and six pairs of feathery legs protrude and retract, kicking food particles inside.

You may find the empty tubes that were the home of sand mason worms after a storm. Using a sticky mucus to bind sand and shell particles together, they build a tube out of which they reach up when the tide is in, extending their tentacles and gills to collect food particles. When the tide is out only the top end is visible and the worm is fairly safe from the elements and predators. Mermaid's purses are the horny eggcase of the dogfish (if white) and of the skate or ray (if black). White papery egg-cases are those of whelks. The sea potato, a white skull-like fragile capsule is the test or internal skeleton of the heart urchin, related to the sea urchin and starfish. When alive its hydraulic tube-like feet emerged from the five rows of holes.

Some beaches are particularly good for finding shells. Mochras (Shell Island) has even given its name to it. If you would like to find out more about marine life there are aquaria at Maes Artro near Harlech and at Aberaeron.

The teredo worm and its attack on Barmouth viaduct

The teredo worm (also known as the shipworm) is not really a worm but a mollusc. Its shell is reduced to a small highly-specialised boring instrument at the end of a long naked body like that of a worm. It lives exclusively within timber in sea water, and in large numbers can completely destroy wood. This is what was happening, progressively, to the Barmouth viaduct, the largest timber estuarine bridge in Britain – 800 ft / 244 m long with 113 spans of 500 piles – carrying the Cambrian Coast railway line over the Mawddach estuary. The viaduct was in good company, however, as shipworms have been known and dreaded since classical times. They riddled the planking of Greek triremes and Roman galleys, destroyed Sir Francis Drake's Golden Hind and in 1730 weakened the dyke timbers in Holland so much that they threatened to burst.

The teredo's plankton settles on a piece of wood and bores a hole in which to hide. It grows and continues to bore, cutting with a twisting movement of its shell, the original entry hole remaining the same size. Amazingly, although the borings may appear to be random, none of them impinges on the burrowings of a neighbour.

The shipworm is equipped with a rare enzyme to digest cellulose which enables it to obtain some food from the wood. It also has siphons which extend out through the entry hole to filter food. A pair of special hard pallets close off the hole when the siphons have been withdrawn.

It is difficult to protect timber against the depredation of *Teredo*. In the case of the Barmouth viaduct, British Rail have replaced much of its timber with a tropical hardwood called greenheart, the most resistant to the sea and the attack of boring creatures.

Barmouth Viaduct over the Mawddach

Using the coastline

Sea resorts

In the Georgian period unsupported medicinal claims were made concerning the benefits of seawater. These claims resembled those made about spa water, and so the seaside resort was added to places to be visited. This medical slant however made the life of the seaside resort very different from that of today. The main advantages to invalids probably came from the fresh air and exercise; ladies spent a good deal of their time collecting seaweed and shells. Nevertheless the seaside cure must have been preferable to the normal eighteenth century remedies of repeated bleedings and purgatives or for the richer and more 'fortunate' invalids, galvanism or violent electrical shocks.

Whilst only the unfortunate few were required to drink seawater, most made use of the bathing machine. At Aberystwyth they 'were of the usual form, constructed of wood, topped in a pavilion shape, and running on four wheels. Three or four (were) allotted in one quarter to the ladies: and as many in another to the gentlemen'. When the people were aboard changing, the machines were rolled out into the sea so that they could get into the water without being seen. At Aberystwyth this was without the indecorous mingling of the sexes such as happened at the spa of Bath.

The whole attitude of the tourists was very different from that of the locals – fresh air, salt water and exercise were considered safe only if taken in very small doses. It was a long time before the idea of bathing for pleasure was generally accepted.

In the early part of the nineteenth century the traveller Mavor wrote on the habits of local people:

'The natives of both sexes among the mountains on the sea coast of Cardiganshire and probably in other places, are much addicted to sea-bathing, during the light summer nights. The manner of their collecting together, is by blowing horns the

A Bathing Place, Aberystwyth

whole way as they advance towards the deep. When arrived on the beach, they strip, and take a promiscuous plunge without any ceremony. This kind of ablution is generally performed on Saturdays, in order that they may enjoy rest the next day. It is generally daylight before they return to their houses, and the noise they make is sure to disturb those who are not engaged in these aquatic orgies.'

William Green, a staunch Methodist and native of Aberystwyth who built much of early Aberaeron, protested to the Court Leet. This led to a fine of 2 shillings (10p) being imposed on anyone taking part in such an activity and the practice ceased.

As the railways reached some parts of the coast from the 1860s other towns developed as resorts. At Borth the Cambrian Terrace of boarding houses was built to accommodate visitors. The early neo-Gothic hotel venture at Aberystwyth to offer 'package holidays' by the sea was a little too early, however, and failed.

The cult of sea-bathing spread gradually into remoter parts such as Barmouth, and building began on the flat land behind the shoreline. The arrival of the railway in 1866 speeded up the process of development and separate three-storey blocks of boarding houses were built very close to the shore. Unlike Llandudno they were never completed to form a continuous parade. The railway opened up the area to both the ardent Victorian hillwalker and day excursionist who explored the hills in the company of local guides.

Aberporth also, towards the end of the nineteenth century, began to accommodate holidaymakers who came to relax by the sea. The first regatta was held in August 1909 to provide an added attraction for visitors. There were swimming and boating races, diving for plates from the smack 'Charming Nancy' in the bay and, as a finale, a fireworks display after dark.

The gradual decline of fishing and boat-building industries has seen the development of places such as New Quay into 'resorts' and all have become 'traditional' places to holiday with donkey and pony rides, fairgrounds and playgrounds,

Aberdyfi

putting, fishing, beach-huts and deckchairs, swimming and paddling pools, tennis, sailing and caravan sites.

Fishing

Cardigan Bay used to be one of Britain's most productive fisheries. There is a wide variety of freshwater and sea fish and many different shellfish. Fishing was originally a supplementary activity to farming, helping coastal communities with another source of food if the harvest failed, but later many craftsmen and traders became part-time fishermen for extra income and cheap food. In the autumn many part-time fishermen would fish herring up until Christmas.

Herring used to shoal in huge numbers off the Cardigan Bay coast in the late summer. In the Middle Ages Aberystwyth (mentioned as early as 1206) and Tenby, and later Aberporth and Nefyn in Gwynedd were the principal herring ports in Wales. The size of the Aberporth herring is recorded in this rhyme:

'Sgadan Aberporth
Dau fola ac un corff.

The herring of Aberporth
Two bellies and one body.

In order to preserve the fish quickly they were salted in layers, head to tail in barrels or smoked (kippers) or a combination of both. There was a special room in many houses for storing the salt fish. These were important domestic crafts and from the sixteenth to the late-eighteenth centuries herring were one of Dyfed's major exports to markets throughout Britain and the Mediterranean. The trade began to go down in the 1830s and in the past fifty years there has been a sharp decline in herring.

The requirements of the fishing industry (especially salt and nets) were brought from Ireland. As the herring began to dwindle the fishermen turned to mackerel, another migratory fish shoaling along Cardigan Bay throughout the summer. New Quay trawlers further out would land mackerel and a number are still landed and processed.

Other fish (such as salmon, sprats and grey mullet) were caught by fish traps (goredau) at Aberaeron and Llanddewi Aberarth. These large semi-circular walls of stone were covered with water at high tide. As the tide ebbed it left the stranded fish. The traps can be seen on the Aberarth shore at low tide, now fallen into disrepair and last used about 1930. You can also see them at the mouth of the River Cledan at Llansantffraed and Llanon. In 1184, soon after the inception of Strata Florida, the Lord Rhys (of Deheubarth – the leading Welsh magnate of the period) granted the fishing rights to the Abbey.

There is a tradition that in the fifth century Gwyddno Garahir of the legendary Cantre'r Gwaelod owned a fish trap near Aberarth which had such amazing fish-catching properties that it was included in the 'thirteen precious things of the Isle of Britain'.

Queen scallops are dredged off Aberporth and along with other shellfish such as crabs and lobsters are often exported to Europe. They grow slowly and the stocks are gradually being depleted. The University College of Wales is working on an experimental project to restock Cardigan Bay with lobster raised in a laboratory in Menai Bridge, Anglesey.

For the amateur or holiday fisherman mackerel can be caught from boats and the shore, and pollack particularly from the rocks at New Quay.

Smuggling

The coast of Cardigan Bay, far from the centre of government with plenty of secluded inlets, was and is one of the ideal places to bring contraband goods ashore safely and without detection. During the late seventeenth and eighteenth centuries Continental wars made it difficult to get certain items. High rates of duty on luxury goods such as French brandy, tobacco and lace (the most profitable items) as well as tea, wines and salt (which came from Ireland and was vital for preserving the herring catch) also encouraged the growth of the smuggling trade. In those days it was 'the Excise' or 'the Revenue' smugglers had to avoid. Today drugs and armaments are the main contraband which smugglers try to land on secluded beaches, sought by the Customs and Excise service as well as the police.

The quiet six miles and secluded coves between New Quay and Llangrannog provided an ideal environment for hiding illegal landings of contraband until it could be carried safely inland on horseback and disposed of inland at Tregaron and Lampeter at greatly reduced rices. Receivers of smuggled goods advertised their wares by putting up particular signs, especially on doorways. In 1704 customs officers apprehended three vessels laden with salt off New Quay, while 200 packhorses and 150 men waited on shore. In the skirmish which followed one smuggler was shot and critically wounded. Ninety years later New Quay was described as a place of 'infamous notoriety' providing shelter for several vessels involved in the smuggling trade. The headland was reputedly riddled with a network of caves used for the storage of contraband goods. In 1765 a Revenue officer was found dead at the foot of Craig Ddu, near Aberarth, a favourite place to unload wine before carrying it inland to store in a cellar on Brynwithell Bog.

One notorious smuggler using Cwmtudu cove was Sion Cwilt, called after his patchwork coat. He travelled by night, managing to avoid the Excise men on several occasions. Mystery still surrounds his true identity.

Boat building

Boats for coasting traffic from the eighteenth to the early twentieth century had to be flat-bottomed to stand upright on open beaches for the unloading of their cargo. Even where there were quays the harbours were generally dry at low tide when the carts came alongside. The boats which fitted the bill, having also to sail in creeks and channels with very little draught, were simple, single-masted smacks (or sloops). They were of limited size and tonnage and the older ones had quite bluff bows which made jibbing difficult.

Smacks were usually built locally, sometimes in places quite unconnected with maritime activity today, let alone ship-building. Boats were built on the foreshore at

Borth and the grassy banks on the south side of Aberaeron were once shipyard sites. All that was needed was some level ground, room to dig a sawpit, and a secure supply of timber (mostly from inland estates as oak does not grow very well in salty breezes). Models were used rather than detailed drawings and plans as most of the workforce were unable to read and write. With simple tools and years of experience very many sloops were put to sea, with all the workmen and village coming out to celebrate. The 40-ton sloop the *Blessing* was built in a field half a mile from the beach at Penbryn near Llangrannog in 1777 and then hauled along difficult tracks to the beach.

Boats were usually owned by a consortium of farmers, merchants, industrialists and some seamen in holdings of 1/64. The most common share was 4/64 (or 1/16, known as an ounce).

The mid-nineteenth century ketch rig with a shortened mainsail boom and a shorter mizzen mast aft of the main mast was an improvement on the sloop. Although many sloops were improved to this design not many ketches were built in Wales. Many came from the West Country, such as the *Garlandstone*, built on the Tamar in 1909 and now to be seen at Porthmadog at the Maritime Museum.

Larger long-distance vessels were built at some of the more important yards. New Quay (and the nearby yards at Cei Bach and Traethgwyn) developed as a shipbuilding and trading centre in the early nineteenth century. As well as becoming one of the main suppliers of coastal vessels, it built schooners and larger vessels bound for North and South America, China and Australasia. At the height of the boom in the 1840s there were over 300 skilled workers employed, six blacksmiths' shops, three sail-lofts, three rope walks and a foundry. There were also private schools where navigation was taught until the end of the nineteenth century.

Sailmaking was generally carried on in large light lofts (such as the top floor of the present building on the pier at New Quay). Many sails were needed. The brig (many of which were built in the first half of the nineteenth century) carried 15 and a full spare set. There were enough apprentices employed by one New Quay sailmaker to form a brass band.

The seafaring boom of the nineteenth century was founded on the need for culm (anthracite dust), coal and limestone as well as salt and some general household goods brought from South Wales to the coastal settlements. There were few exports apart from a little surplus bacon and herring and boats were often ballasted with sand. The coastal trade flourished until the roads improved and the railways came in the nineteenth century, when trade declined and many shipyards closed down. There is little need for them today as most pleasure craft have mass-produced reinforced fibreglass hulls.

The complete crew of a sailing vessel often came from the same village, were of much the same social background and sometimes were all members of the same non-conformist chapel. They made a key contribution to the development of maritime trrade in the nineteenth century.

Mining and smelting

Mining and smelting was important for centuries in the hinterland of Aberystwyth and Montgomeryshire. Recent discoveries in mid-Wales (at Cwmystwyth and Nantyreira, three-quarters of the way up Plynlimon) as well as in North Wales indicate that the earliest-known mining activity in Britain was probably here. Copper was probably mined around 1,800–1,000BC and used to make the many bronze items which gave the Bronze Age its name.

During the Roman occupation the rich deposits of lead and silver lodes in this area's badly-faulted sedimentary shales and grits were exploited.

Demand for lead was rekindled with the use of gunpowder and lead shot in Britain in the sixteenth century. During the Civil War Thomas Bushell, a Royalist, smelted lead at Aberystwyth to produce shot and also produced enough silver to be granted royal permission for a Mint at Aberystwyth in 1637.

In the late eighteenth century lead ore from the Rheidol and Ystwyth valleys was the most important commodity leaving the improved and convenient Aberystwyth harbour. Despite Aberystwyth's relative convenience for exporting ore it was too expensive to import coal to the remote lead mine sites of mid-Wales. Instead water power was generally used, although peat was tried for a time at one site.

Systems of leats or water channels provided the water to the great waterwheels in their pits supplying the energy for pumping, hauling, crushing and operating other machinery. The machinery caused severe vibration and shocks, so heavy timbers were employed to distribute loading and reinforce the masonry.

Waste material was dug out with the lead and zinc ores and now forms a scree, often too poisonous for natural vegetation to colonise. There may be some stunted oaks growing but, in general, the screes do not merit planting with trees. The eastern part of the Vale of Rheidol is studded with many old mine entrances and their associated spoil heaps.

The lead which now prevents vegetation from growing caused the early death of many miners, although they drank the dust away in such pubs as the Miners' Arms at Pontrhydygroes. Their graves can be seen at the Calvinist Methodist chapel at Aberffrwd.

Profits from the lead mines were shared by a few powerful families: the Prices, Vaughans and the Powells who built the mansion of Nanteos.

All mine sites are potentially dangerous due to unstable buildings and unpro-tected open shafts. The element of risk is always present and it is unwise to visit them alone. Luckily it is possible to find out more in safety by visiting the open-air Llywernog silver-lead mine at Ponterwyd near Aberystwyth. The mine operated from 1740 to 1910 and has now been restored to its Victorian splendour, showing all the constituent parts of a typical mid-Wales lead mine. You can go underground into the dripping depths of Balcombe's Level, see the working waterwheels which once powered the mineral extraction and follow the Miners' Trail.

The Dyfi furnace on the A487 near Eglwysfach used the power from the River Einon which plunges down a beautiful waterfall. This drove the bellows of the charcoal-fired furnace to smelt iron-ore. The waterfall has such force that it must have been used from the earliest times. Thomas Bushell certainly operated a silver mill here during the Civil War in the seventeenth century. The waterwheel is 30 ft / 9 m in diameter and is operated during the summer months. The charcoal store is behind the wheel.

At Cwmystwyth there are possibly the oldest, richest and most extensive lead mines in the area; they did not close until this century. The mines date from at least Roman times and were later owned by Strata Florida. The results of mining activity dominate the landscape. All that was necessary to strike lead was to drive levels into the mountain side; it was not even necessary to sink shafts.

Other extensive mining remains can be seen just over the border into Montgomeryshire at Dylife, for example, or the Bryntail lead mine, near the great Clywedog dam.

ABOVE
Diagram of Dyfi Furnace near Eglwysfach

RIGHT
Waterwheel at Dyfi Furnace

Myths and legends

Cantre'r Gwaelod

Cantre'r Gwaelod (the cantref or 'hundred', a mediaeval administrative unit, of the bottom) is the name of the lost land of 16 noble and rich cities on the fertile plain now under the sea. The land extended from the River Teifi to Bardsey Island, a distance of 40 miles by 20 miles, and was defended by an embankment and sluices. When Gwyddno Garahir was Lord of the Cantref, Seithennin, a drunkard, was keeper of the embankment. One evening Seithennin had drunk too much after a great banquet and left open the sluices. The sea broke through and only a few inhabitants escaped from drowning.

Five stone causeways which extend straight out for miles into Cardigan Bay are thought to lead to the land. Sarn Badrig (St Patrick's Causeway) is near Shell Island, south of Harlech, Sarn y Bwlch lies off Tonfanau, north of Tywyn and Sarn Gynfelyn extends out from Wallog, north of Aberystwyth. The other two, Sarn Ddewi, near Aberarth and Sarn Gadwgan a little further south are not as long.

When the sea is very still and the water very clear the great walls and the buildings of the cities can be seen. The faint music of the church bells can also be heard as the water moves them to and fro. The bells are also reputed to be heard ringing in times of trouble, as recorded in the song 'The Bells of Aberdyfi' from Dibden's eighteenth-century opera, 'Liberty Hall'.

For realists, it is now thought that the boulder ridges are side moraines, thrown up where parallel glaciers met as they pushed into Cardigan Bay. The legend probably refers back in folk history to the time many years ago when the sea-level rose submerging forests.

Branwen, daughter of Llŷr

One of the stories told in the Mabinogion, 11 mediaeval Welsh prose tales, the result of centuries of oral storytelling, is that of Branwen, daughter of Llŷr who lived at Harlech. The Mabinogion stories preserve much of the colour and energy of the early Celtic world.

Matholwch, King of Ireland, visited Branwen's home at Harlech in Ardudwy and eventually she married him. When the newly-married couple arrived in Ireland they were greeted with great rejoicing. 'No gentleman or lady of Ireland who came to visit Branwen left without being given a brooch or ring or treasured royal jewel and it was a marvellous sight to watch these being carried off.' She gained a good reputation in Ireland but then her husband began to treat her cruelly. In desperation she sent a pet starling with a message for help to Wales. Her brother, the giant Brân the Blessed, came in response to her call and some extremely exciting and unpleasant killing took place before Branwen and Brân sailed back to Wales.

A sculpture portraying the legend is to be seen outside Harlech Castle, overlooking Cardigan Bay.

Plant de Bat and Devil's Bridge
The River Rheidol is joined at Devil's Bridge by the River Mynach plunging 400 ft / 122 m down the Mynach Falls from the plateau above.

There are three bridges at Devil's Bridge, the first one over the tributary reputedly giving the bridge its name.

There is a story that the first bridge was built by the Devil for an old woman so that she could rescue her cow, stuck on the other side. He did this on condition that he should get the first living thing to cross over the bridge. Wise woman that she was, she fooled him by tossing a crust across for a small dog.

In reality the Abbot at Strata Florida Abbey probably had the first bridge built, a masonry arch with a 16 ft / 4.9 m span, so that the monks could reach the sheep pastures on the other side. Interestingly the churchyard enclosure at Ysbyty Cynfyn on the other side has been adapted from an ancient pagan stone circle.

In Tudor times the Devil's Bridge area was the haunt of a gang of robbers and murderers, the most notorious of whom, two brothers and a sister, were called the *plant de bat* (bat children) who may have been so-called as they lived in a cave below the gorge. Eventually they were smoked out and hanged at Rhayader.

The second bridge with a span of 32 ft / 9.75 m was built in 1708 to ease the journey for travellers. It is slightly wider in order to take horse-drawn vehicles and in 1814 additional masonry and a pretty cast-iron balustrade was added. Finally a steel lattice girder 60 ft / 18.3 m long was put in place 7 ft / 2.1 m above to cope with motor traffic.

The bridges and the Mynach Falls can be seen from the Jacob's Ladder walk which goes right down into the gorge, to the bottom of the Falls. The Robber's Cave and the Devil's Punchbowl are also to be seen.

Saints of the Western Shore
The 'Dark Ages' of the fifth century after the Romans left Britain were an important period in the life of Wales. Some knowledge of this remote time adds to an appreciation of cultural features in today's landscape such as the names of the saints, the sites they established and the settlements which grew up around their churches.

Although these people are talked of as saints they were probably more like monks who were popularly credited with magical powers enabling them to perform miracles and fight pagan gods or devils. At that time there was a strong monastic movement in the Celtic Church which came from the early Christian hermits of the Egyptian desert. The monks wanted a spartan, ascetic hermit's existence in desolate places such as mountain tops, stormy headlands, offshore islands and the deep and dark recesses of the forested valleys. Even today many Celtic churches are still in isolated positions.

As the barbarian raids of the Angles, Saxons and Jutes grew in intensity large numbers of wandering saints left Wales for other lands or arrived on her shores. They came by sea, either singly or in groups from the Celtic north, from Ireland, Cornwall and Brittany.

For these monks the sea was often an easier highway for communication and

The Two Kings, *a bronze sculpture by Ivor Roberts-Jones,*
outside Harlech Castle

travel than overland and the western sea routes were safer from the barbarians than the English Channel and the North Sea. In West Wales they seemed to favour closeness to tidal water and sandy beaches on which it was easy to land. In the old area of Ardudwy around Harlech, before Madocks built the cob at Porthmadog, all churches (except Trawsfynydd) were within sight of the sea.

One way of telling whether a settlement was that of an early Celtic saint is by its name. Christian Romans dedicated their churches to a Biblical saint, often a member of the Holy Family. Early Celtic churches or monasteries on the Atlantic fringe of Europe, however, were generally called by the names of their original founders or their monastic patrons. Llangrannog, for example, was founded by St Carannog (or Carantoc), who arrived some time after AD500. In legend he is the uncle of Dewi (St David), the patron saint of Wales.

The word 'llan' indicated land consecrated to or by the saint whose name followed. Today, it is used in its secondary meaning of church. Even in Wales, though, place names with the prefix 'llan' do not always contain the name of a Celtic saint. Llanfair (St Mary's church) may indicate rededication to the Virgin Mary which was common after the Norman penetration of Wales in the eleventh century. Llanfihangel (St Michael's church) reflects the popularity of the cult of the Archangel Michael in the tenth and eleventh centuries. St Michael's church, Penbryn is thought to be one of the oldest churches in Wales and is situated on the old circular enclosure.

Not all churches dedicated to Celtic saints and their settlements in Wales have the prefix 'llan-'. They may have other prefixes (such as bod-, tre-, llech-, maen- or tŷ-) or may just have the name of the saint. Gwbert is one such place which takes its name from a wandering saint thought to have landed on the east side of the Teifi estuary.

Scholars have unravelled where the saints originally came from. The Cornish saints are common in the hinterland of the Teifi estuary – at, for example, Llandyfriog, Llangrannog and Gwbert. Cadfan, a well-known Breton saint, may have had his first settlement at Tywyn. Pen Trwyn Cynwyl, the spur near Aberporth takes its name from St Cynwyl, a saint from northern Britain thought to have visited in the sixth century and to whom the church is dedicated. Llanrhystud commemorates a sixth-century Breton missionary, Rhystud.

There are fewer dedications to Irish saints than one might think. Caron may have been Irish (commemorated in Tregaron and the bog Cors Caron). St Ffraed (Bride or Brigid) of Kildare, who founded a monastery where she died in AD523 was the most popular, especially in the eleventh century. The patron saint of dairy maids, she is reputed to have sailed from Ireland to Wales on a piece of turf. She is commemorated at Llansantffraed. It has been suggested that her popularity can be traced to her replacing a Celtic fire goddess of earlier times.

Other places associated with Celtic saints include Mwnt, a strategic point on the pilgrim route to Bardsey Island, the traditional saints' burial place, and to St David's in the south. Seafaring coracles of wickerwork covered in hide probably landed here in the seventh century bringing a community of saints. The church of the Holy Cross (dating from about 1400) is built on the earlier Celtic site and the walls of the enclosure are built in a common Cornish herring-bone pattern thought to originate from the Mediterranean. The sixth-century St David's, originally hidden from view of the sea, is at Aberarth. Llannon records Non, a woman of Welsh origin and probably a nun in the local Celtic monastery. At this time nuns and monks might be married and Non is reputed to have been the mother of St David, probably born around AD500. The Non Stone, which originally had a carving of a woman with a child in her arms, traditionally commemorates this and can be seen in Ceredigion Museum. Llandanwg, now on the sandy foreshore of Cardigan Bay but originally lying further inland, is dedicated to St Tanwg.

Welsh a living language

Welsh, one of the oldest languages in the British Isles, is related most closely to Cornish and Breton and then to Scots Gaelic, Irish and Manx. A form of Welsh was the language spoken in ancient Britain when the Romans invaded and it is still very much a living language used at home and work by tens of thousands of people.

You may find the following points useful as you start making out Welsh words.

• There are some differences between the language spoken in the north and south. In the south milk is *llaeth*, in the north, *llefrith*.

• Welsh has a device called 'mutations', which means that words sometimes change their initial letters.

• There are two 'you' forms: one for speaking to elders and betters, the other for children, animals and close friends.

One of the easiest ways to pick up Welsh words and phrases is to listen to parents and children talking.

paid! – don't!
brysia! – hurry up!
tyd! (in the north) or *dere!* (in the south) – come here!
da iawn – very good, well done

Many official signs in Wales are bi-lingual which offers a ready-made translation of sorts for the beginner.
Cymru – Wales
Maes parcio – car park
Canolfan Croeso – Tourist Information Centre
Toiledau or *Cyfleusterau* – Toilets or Conveniences
Dynion – Men
Merched – Women
Gwesty – Hotel
Tŷ bwyta – Restaurant
Gwely a brecwast – Bed and breakfast
Llwybr cyhoeddus – Public footpath
Dim cŵn No dogs

Some places have both Welsh and English names.
Newtown – *Y Drenewydd*
Welshpool – *Y Trallwng*
Abergavenny – *Y Fenni*
Brecon – *Aberhonddu*
New Quay – *Cei Newydd*
Builth Wells – *Llanfair ym Muallt*
Rhayader – *Rhaeadr*
Montgomery – *Trefaldwyn*
Strata Florida – *Ystrad Fflur*
Snowdonia – *Eryri*

Plynlimon – *Pumlumon*
Lake Bala – *Llyn Tegid*
River Severn – *Afon Hafren*

As in any country or language Welsh placenames are not always what they seem, but here are a few of the main elements and their mutations.

aber – the mouth of a river or its confluence with another (for example, Aberystwyth)

afon – river (for example, *Afon Hafren* – River Severn)

bach/fach – small or little

bryn/fryn – hill (for example, Bryneglwys)

cae/gae – field

caer/gaer – fort (for example, Caersws)

capel/gapel – chapel (for example, Capel Bangor)

castell – castle (for example, Castell Harlech)

coch/goch – red

coed – trees/wood

cors/gors – bog (for example, *Cors Caron* – Tregaron Bog)

craig/graig – rock

cwm/gwm – valley or coombe (for example, *Cwm Elan* – Elan Valley)

du/ddu – black

eglwys – church

glan – bank, shore (for example, Glansevern)

gwyn/wyn – white

hafod – summer dwelling place

hen – old

hendre – winter dwelling place

llan – village or parish. Often followed by a saint's name (for example, *Llanfair* – Mary's parish)

llyn – lake (for example, *Llyn Tegid* – Lake Bala)

maes – field

morfa – bog, fen, sea marsh (for example, Morfa Harlech)

mynydd – mountain (for example, Mynydd Du)

nant – stream or valley

pentre – village

plas – mansion (for example, Plas Tan-y-Bwlch)

rhaeadr – waterfall (for example, *Rhaeadr* – Rhayader)

tref/tre/dref/dre – town (for example, Trefaldwyn)

tŷ – house

ynys – island (for example, Ynyshir)

There is a variety of events and courses available for the Welsh language learner. The Brecon Beacons National Park have summer guided walks where the language used is Welsh and the Snowdonia National Park run very popular singalongs. A number of educational establishments (such as Coleg Harlech) have Welsh language courses for adults.

Birds and wildlife

bird – *aderyn*
birds – *adar*
buzzard – *boncath*
jay – *sgrech y coed* (screech of the wood)
kingfisher – *glas y dorlan* (blue of the undercut bank)
red kite – *barcud*
swallow – *gwennol*
columbine – *troed y barcud* (kite's foot)
cowslip – *dagrau Mair* (tears of Mary)
flowers – *blodau*
ox-eye daisy – *esgob gwyn* (white bishop)
trees (or wood) *coed*
Welsh poppy – *pabi Cymraeg*
badger – *mochyn daear*
butterfly – *iâr bach yr haf* (little hen of summer) or *pili pala*
dragon fly – *gwas y neidr* (the snake's servant)
red dragon – *draig goch*

Farm animals

bull – *tarw*
cat – *cath*
cow – *buwch*
cattle – *gwartheg*
dog – *ci*
dogs – *cŵn*
duck – *hwyaden*
goat – *gafr*
goose – *gŵydd*
pig – *mochyn*
pony – *merlyn*
pony trekking – *merlota*
rabbit – *cwningen*
one sheep – *dafad*
more than one sheep – *defaid*

POB LWC! – GOOD LUCK!

The Editor

Moira Kathleen Stone was born in 1955 in Dorchester, Dorset. Her interest in natural history, rural affairs, culture and language continued to develop during her education in North Berkshire and at Newnham College, Cambridge. She worked in adult continuing education (including adult literacy) and community development before becoming a freelance writer and researcher. Since 1977 she has lived in Wales for periods of time, currently in Snowdonia. Welsh is now her second language.

Contributors

This book would not have been written or produced without the encouragement, support and contributions of a number of individuals and organisations. Notable amongst these are Matthew Davies, Gareth Evans, Michael D Smith and Arwel Jones. The latter's hard work ensured that the idea came to fruition.

CYNEFIN, A Welsh Conservation Foundation, would like to place on record its sincere thanks to the following people for their contributions.

Ros Alexander: *The grey seals of Cardigan Bay*
David Bellamy: *Foreword*
Mark Chapman (Montgomeryshire Wildlife Trust): *The Upper Severn and Roundton Hill*
Matthew Davies (Festival of the Countryside): *Badgers, The drovers' roads and Sacred enclosures and yew trees*
Lorna Froud: *Artists' inspiration*
Rod Gritten (Snowdonia National Park Authority): *Rhododendron, scourge of the Park*
Malcolm F Howells (British Geological Survey): *Rocks of Southern Snowdonia*
Arwel Jones (Festival of the Countryside): *The Welsh Poppy, The Dynamic Coastline, Otters, Geology and ecology of the Brecon Beacons*
Dai Jones: *The drovers' roads*
Peter Hope Jones (Nature Conservancy Council): *Moorlands and the black grouse*
Ella Lloyd (Antur Efyrnwy): *Llanwyddyn (Lake Vyrnwy)*
Allen Meredith: *Sacred enclosures and yew trees*
Gareth Morgan: *Badgers*
Alun Price (formerly National Trust, now Snowdonia National Park Authority): *There's gold in those hills*
Dafydd Roberts (Museum of the North): *Quarries and caverns*
David Saunders (Dyfed Wildlife Trust): *The Lower Teifi*
Jim Saunders (Powys County Council and Countryside Commission): *Offa's Dyke*
Fred Slater (University College, Cardiff): *Wildlife of the River Wye*
Stephanie Tyler (Royal Society for the Protection of Birds): *The red kite and The buzzard*
Merfyn Williams (Snowdonia National Park Authority): *Plas Tan y Bwlch.*

Illustrations and maps (page numbers in brackets);
Antur Tanat Cain (9, 91, 92 top)
Neil Badger (123)

Colin Baglow (95, 128, 129, 130 right, 148)
M E Baines (163)
Alan Bartram (23 bottom, 50)
R J C Blewitt (125)
Brecon Beacons National Park Authority (139 right, 142)
British Rail Publications/Avon & Anglia Publications (188)
Centre for Alternative Technology (37)
Coed Cymru (54)
Crown Copyright (CADW: Welsh Historic Monuments) (45)
Matthew Davies (21, 99, 103, 105, 112 right, 127, 130 left, 131, 154 bottom, 158, 159, 160, 183, 185, 208 right)
Olwen Caradoc Evans (17, 24, 29, 38, 202)
John Flower (10–13)
Glynvivian Art Gallery, Leisure Services Department, Swansea City Council (34)
Arwel Jones (18, 19, 47, 139 left, 151, 193 top)
Brian Jones (201)
Keith Jones
Terence Lambert (53, 199)
Jeremy Moore (196)
Montgomeryshire District Council (59, 61, 65, 66, 67, 73, 76 right, 90 bottom)
John Morgan & Son (174)
Nature Conservancy Council (30, 36, 136, 193 bottom, 195, 203)
Portmeirion (49)
Martin W Roberts (211)
David Rowe (116)
Jim Saunders (96, 109)
Michael D Smith (51, 70, 71, 76 left, 79, 86, 88, 90 top, 119, 134, 147, 170 right)
Snowdonia National Park Authority (41, 56)
Meg Stevens (39)
Moira K Stone (165, 167, 171)
Tate Gallery, London (33)
Wales Tourist Board (23 top, 25, 63, 64, 93, 95, 112 left, 120, 154 top, 157, 170 left, 177, 186, 189, 190, 208 left)
Western Mail & Echo (152)
Alex Williams (135, 147)

We would also like to thank the Countryside Commission, Mid Wales Development, the Nature Conservancy Council and the Wales Tourist Board for their support.

Selected bibliography

Borrow, George. *Wild Wales – its people, language and scenery* (Collins, 1862. Fontana, 1977)

Colyer, Richard. *Roads and Trackways of Wales* (Moorland Publishing, 1984)

Colyer, Richard J. *The Teifi – Scenery and Antiquities of a Welsh River* (Gomer, 1987)

Condry, William M. *The Natural History of Wales* (Collins, 1981)

Haslam, Richard. *The Buildings of Wales – Powys* (Penguin, 1979)

Hilling, John B. *The Historic Architecture of Wales* (University of Wales Press, 1976)

Houlder, Christopher. *Wales – An Archaeological Guide* (Faber, 1978)

Jenkins, David. *The Maritime History of Dyfed* (National Museum of Wales, 1982)

Jenkins, J Geraint. *The Flannel Makers – a brief history of the Welsh woollen industry* (Gomer, 1985)

Jones, Anthony. *Welsh Chapels* (National Museum of Wales, 1984)

Millward, Roy, and Robinson, Adrian. *Landscapes of North Wales* (David and Charles, 1978)

Phillips, Pauline. *A View of Old Montgomeryshire* (Christopher Davies, 1977)

Rowan, Eric. *Art in Wales – an Illustrated History 1850–1980* (Welsh Arts Council, 1985)

Sale, Richard. *Owain Glyndŵr's Way – through the heartland of mediaeval Wales* (Hutchinson, 1985)

Saunders, David (ed.). *The Nature of West Wales* (Barracuda Books, 1986)

Slater, Fred (ed.). *The Nature of Central Wales* (Barracuda Books, 1988)

Soden, R W. *A Guide to Welsh Parish Churches* (Gomer, 1984)

Styles, Showell. *Snowdonia National Park Countryside Commission Official Guide* (Webb and Bower/Michael Joseph, 1987)

Thomas, Roger. *The Brecon Beacons National Park Countryside Commission Official Guide* (Webb and Bower/Michael Joseph, 1987)

Index